The
Reference Shelf®

Internet Abuses
and Privacy Rights

The Reference Shelf
Volume 89 • Number 2
H.W. Wilson
A Division of EBSCO Information Services, Inc.

Published by
GREY HOUSE PUBLISHING
Amenia, New York
2017

The Reference Shelf

The books in this series contain reprints of articles, excerpts from books, addresses on current issues, and studies of social trends in the United States and other countries. There are six separately bound numbers in each volume, all of which are usually published in the same calendar year. Numbers one through five are each devoted to a single subject, providing background information and discussion from various points of view and concluding with an index and comprehensive bibliography that lists books, pamphlets, and articles on the subject. The final number of each volume is a collection of recent speeches. Books in the series may be purchased individually or on subscription.

Publisher's Cataloging-In-Publication Data
(Prepared by The Donohue Group, Inc.)

Names: H.W. Wilson Company.
Title: Internet abuses and privacy rights / [compiled by] H. W. Wilson, a division of EBSCO Information Services.
Other Titles: Reference shelf ; v. 89, no. 2.
Description: [First edition]. | Amenia, New York : Grey House Publishing, 2017. | Includes bibliographical references and index.
Identifiers: ISBN 978-1-68217-452-4 (v. 89, no. 2) | ISBN 978-1-68217-450-0 (volume set)
Subjects: LCSH: Computer crimes--United States--Sources. | Internet--United States--Sources. | Privacy, Right of--United States--Sources. | Network neutrality--United States--Sources. | Electronic surveillance--United States--Sources. | Computer security--United States--Sources.
Classification: LCC HV6773.2 .I58 2017 | DDC 364.1680973--dc23

Contents

3

New Challenges to Privacy

4

Internet News and Accountability

5

The Power and Influence of Technology

Preface

Dangers of the Digital Age: Cyberthreats and Privacy

The Digital Age is the period in human history defined by the advent of personal computing and its integration into society. The era has also been called the Information Age, as one of the fundamental features of the era involves dramatic changes in the way that individuals create, manage, access, and share information. English statesman and scientist Sir Francis Bacon is credited with writing "scientia potentia est," which translates as "knowledge is power," and the substrate of the Internet is exactly that: data, the raw material that is used to create knowledge and thus power. While digital technology and the Web have empowered the populace with information, the Digital Age has also seen the rise of a new class of criminals and political agents who steal data from individuals, corporations, and governments, and use it for financial or political gain. The exploitation and misuse of personal data, both by criminals and by corporations and governments, also comprises a fundamental challenge to personal and intellectual privacy and has led to a global debate over the right to privacy and the ownership of data.

Ownership of Digital Data

If the Web is seen as a virtual community made up of individuals around the world participating in a massive global *agora* (in Greek, "a public open space"), then the individuals who participate can be seen as creating and presenting a virtual version of themselves through their communication and commercial transactions. In the 2010s, there is an emerging concept of digital citizenship, meaning the practices, standards, and norms needed to navigate the Web and participate in the digital economy. Digital citizenship is the principle that individuals who want to participate in the Web must learn how to use digital tools safely and responsibly and to behavior according to certain ethical rules that will prevent them from harming others with their digital activities.[1]

Properly defined, which consists of thousands of servers and hubs connected by more than 113,000 miles of cable, is the physical system that produces the Web[2] The Internet has been created through the combined effort of individuals, corporations, researchers, and government agencies. Internet Service Providers (ISPs), companies like Verizon and AT&T, create much of the infrastructure that makes the Internet and the Web work and then sell access to their infrastructure to individuals and other companies. The Web, by contrast, is made up of thousands of websites and services that individuals see when they use a computer or another digital device to access the Internet.

Data is the raw material of the Web and most data is created by digital citizens who use the Web for commerce and communication. The central question is: Who owns this data? The ISPs that transmit data over the Web claim partial ownership in return for access to their infrastructure. On top of this is another layer of companies, like Facebook, Google, and Amazon, who provide Web services. These companies also claim partial ownership of user data in return for their services, a fact that is stated in the corporate "terms of service" for companies like Facebook, Twitter, and Google. Companies collect and evaluate data from users and then use this data to market products and additional services to their customers/subscribers. In addition, because of laws established under the Patriot Act, the government has the right to collect and evaluate data transmitted through cellular or Web-based communication channels, which the government proposes is needed to help protect citizens from terrorism and other national security risks.[3] The digital citizens who provide most of the data traveling through the Internet therefore have the least control over what happens to that data because they only indirectly contribute to Internet infrastructure and cannot directly control the development of legislation that governs whether companies and government agencies are permitted to collect and use data voluntarily transmitted through corporate websites and digital equipment.

In the United States, there is no specific right to privacy explicitly guaranteed by the Constitution, though sections of the Constitution, such as First Amendment guarantee of free speech and Fourth Amendment protections against unreasonable government search and seizure can be used together to establish legal precedent for a general right to privacy in one's communications and beliefs. However, living in a society necessarily means surrendering some degree of privacy. Most Internet users may never feel personally affected by the fact that government agencies could potentially be reading their e-mails and text messages or that companies like Facebook and Google routinely monitor their Web-behavior in an effort to determine their likes and dislikes. Nevertheless, many are concerned about the erosion of privacy in the Digital Age and the US government and legal system has been slow to adopt measures to protect digital privacy.

Law Professor Julie E. Cohen argues that, at present, privacy is treated as an instrument used to protect other principles, like liberty or control of one's life, and that this view of privacy is part of the reason that governments and corporations have been able to ignore privacy concerns in favor of other goals such as protecting national security, preventing crime, or creating convenient new Web tools. Cohen proposes that the general concept of privacy should be redefined as fundamental freedom to engage in a process of self-development and to develop values that may-be distinct or separate from broader societal values and culture. In a 2013 article in the *Atlantic*, journalist Jathan Sadowski argued, "…we must decide if we really want to live in a society that treats every action as a data point to be analyzed and traded like currency."[4]

The Criminal Element

Another danger to digital privacy comes from cybercriminals who participate in an underground, illegal economy of data, stealing and selling information from digital citizens through hidden websites and servers comprising what is now called the Dark Web. Hackers have created a growing list of devious programs that help them steal data and wreak havoc on digital technology, including viruses, malware, adware, spyware, ransomware, and a host of other applications. A 2014 report indicated that cybercrime, including the theft of credit and debit card numbers, medical information, and personal data used to commit identity theft, costs the global economy more than $445 billion each year.[5]

Combating the criminal dangers of cyberspace requires digital citizens to stay on top of an ever-changing list of threats, and to learn about the behavioral changes and technological tools that can help keep their data safe and their Web-based communications private. There is also a continuing debate over the role of corporations in combating data theft. In numerous cases, cybercriminals have obtained consumer data by infiltrating the records of corporations like Target, Sony, and Home Depot, which collect and store e-mail addresses and credit/debit card numbers. Even with corporate data theft becoming more common, most corporations spend relatively little to prevent it because the costs of cybercrime are minimal compared to the costs of building better information technology (IT) security systems. For instance, when Home Depot was invaded by cybercriminals stealing 56 million credit and debit card numbers and 53 million e-mail addresses, the company lost $28 million, essentially amounting to less than 0.01 percent of the company's 2014 revenues.[6] This situation is fluid however, as consumer preference often dictates corporate policy. If consumers decide that cybersecurity is a priority and seek out companies that offer data-theft guarantees, corporations will likely adopt more aggressive security policies.

Politics in the Digital Realm

Cybercrime and cybersecurity aren't just a concern for consumers, but also for governments. The United States has been a leader in cyberwarfare, using hackers and digital tools to combat foreign threats, while the United States has also been the target of foreign cyberweapons. Increasingly, foreign governments have been linked to invasions of US corporations, stealing intellectual data that can be used to give other societies an economic advantage. With economic and political rivals like China, Russia, and North Korea working to develop cyberweapons and terrorist organizations like the Islamic State likewise using the Web and social media to spread their agendas, cyberwarfare is one of the biggest national security concerns of the twenty-first century.

In 2016, the United States was the victim of an entirely new type of cyberattack, when it was revealed that Russian hackers, operating under the direction of the Russian government, had stolen sensitive data from both the Republican and Democratic National Conventions and used the data they acquired to support Donald Trump's presidential campaign. While the revelation was shocking to many, and has been criticized by Trump as an overt conspiracy to delegitimize his leadership, the National Security Agency (NSA), Central Intelligence Agency (CIA), and Federal Bureau of Investigation (FBI) have all verified that the hack occurred. Investigators aren't certain why the Russian government was willing to risk an international incident to help President Trump win the election, but Trump and allies' considerable economic ties to Russia and the fact that Trump, unlike past presidents, has not expressed any interest in pressuring Russia to improve its human rights record through sanctions, are believed to be aspects of why Russian President Vladimir Putin favored Trump as the next American president. There has also been speculation that Trump supporters and advisers such as Secretary of State Rex Tillerson, for instance, have close ties to the Russian oil industry.[7]

The Russian hack may be an example of the first known effort of a foreign government to use cyberwarfare to sway an American election and can be regarded as an act of political warfare directed against the United States. This event alone demonstrates the increasing importance of cyberwarfare and indicates some of the more subtle ways that political information can be weaponized.

No less dramatic in 2016-2017 has been the controversy over "fake news;" defined generally as any factually false news item created for profit or as propaganda to promote one's political/social views. Fake news is an old feature of US politics, but one with greater and greater influence as the share of digital citizens who get all or most of their news online has increased. The fake news environment of the 2016 election polarized the populace, obfuscating important issues in favor of sensationalized or patently false news items published through social media and unscrupulous websites. As thousands of Americans were deceived into believing that Hillary Clinton was involved in a child sex ring in Washington D.C., for instance, the legitimate media felt compelled to cover the controversy rather than focusing on more important issues, such as how Trump and Clinton, as candidates, were prepared to cope with income inequality, the decline of the US working class, racism, and inequality, or even, fittingly, national cybersecurity. The mainstream media spent so much of its time during the 2016 campaign fact checking outrageous claims by candidates and correcting rumors spread by fake news items that policy issues took a backseat for much of the year.

The perils of the Digital Age are numerous and complex, leaving many digital citizens confused about how to protect themselves from threats like surveillance, data theft, or the manipulation of fake news. Digital citizens are responsible for learning about cyberthreats and for taking the steps needed to mitigate the danger posed to themselves and others, but also must hold companies and their governments responsible for enacting legislation and policies to protect the digital privacy and intellectual property of their customers/constituents. When it comes to misinformation, the problem is more complex, but the solution is largely the same. Digital citizens cannot depend on politicians or media marketers to tell them where and how to get information, but must endeavor to develop a more informed critical approach to news and data, essentially becoming an *investigative news reader* to protect themselves from manipulation. If knowledge is power, then knowing where and how to get reliable data about the world is the key that allows a person to transform that data into knowledge, and so into personal, economic, and political power.

Micah L. Issitt

Works Used

"Cyber Crime Costs Global Economy $445 Billion a Year: Report." *Reuters*, Reuters. Jun 9 2014. Web. 3 Mar 2017.

"Nine Elements." *Digital Citizenship,* Mike Ribble. 2017. Web. 3 Mar 2017.

Powers, Shawn M. and Michael Jablonski. *The Real Cyber War: The Political Economy of Internet Freedom.* Chicago: University of Chicago Press, 2015.

Rubin, Jennifer. "Commentary: Why Did Russia Want Trump to Win?" *Chicago Tribune*, Tribune Media. Dec 12 2016. Web. 3 Mar 2017.

Sadowski, Jathan. "Why Does Privacy Matter? One Scholar's Answer." *The Atlantic*, Atlantic Monthly Group. Feb 26 2013. Web. 3 Mar 2017.

Sherman, Erik. "The Reason Companies Don't Fix Cybersecurity." *CBS News*, CBS. Mar 12 2015. Web. 3 Mar 2017.

Simonite, Tom. "First Detailed Public Map of U.S. Internet Backbone Could Make It Stronger." *MIT Technology Review*, MIT Press. Sep 15 2015. Web. 25 Feb 2017.

Notes

1. "Nine Elements," *Digital Citizenship.*
2. Simonite, "First Detailed Public Map of U.S. Internet Backbone Could Make It Stronger."
3. Powers and Jablonski, "The Real Cyber War," 150-65.
4. Sadowski, "Why Does Privacy Matter?"
5. "Cyber Crime Costs Global Economy $445 Billion a Year: Report," *Reuters.*
6. Sherman, "The Reason Companies Don't Fix Cybersecurity."
7. Rubin, "Commentary: Why Did Russia Want Trump to Win?"

1

Personal Cybersecurity

Credit: temniy

Digital lock sign on binaric background.

The Personal Data Dimension

Cybersecurity, or information technology security, is the effort to protect computers, networks, programs, and the data created and transmitted through these systems, from being intercepted, changed, or destroyed by others. Cybersecurity is an issue with personal, professional, and governmental implications and the very nature of the Internet, being a nebulously owned physical/virtual network involving millions of users, computers, corporations, and other entities, makes the process of protecting data both complex and *essential* for the evolution of society in the Digital Age. While the average computer user may feel he or she has little data worth protecting, every computer compromised by viruses, hackers, or other cyberthreats, is potentially a gateway through which the infection can spread.[1] A virus infecting a computer in suburban Iowa could potentially pose a threat to national networks or even federal government data.

In 2015, the cybersecurity industry, made up of companies providing software and other equipment to protect user and corporate data, was estimated to have a value of $75 billion, with expected growth to $170 billion by 2020.[2] Protecting data is not *only* a corporate concern that can be fixed with a technological bandage, however, as the effort to make the Internet safe is also a matter of public education and helping users to understand why protecting data is important and how behavioral and technological tools can help to protect them, and others, from cyberthreats.

The Illusion of Privacy

Who owns data? In the Digital Age, this is not a trivial or purely philosophical question. Data is the raw material used to create economic, social, and political power, and the ownership of digital data—even personal data—once it has been shared or transmitted through the vast nebula of the Internet, has NOT been determined.

Personal computing tools have made using the Internet *feel* like a private activity, but the sense of privacy is an illusion. Corporations routinely analyze and use data submitted by users to determine what kind of products a user might buy or to create pinpoint marketing campaigns. Governments have nearly unfettered access to private communications, including e-mails, text messages, social media posts, and even photos and audio picked up by built-in microphones and cameras, which they use at their discretion in the effort to identify threats to national security. The biggest risk to user privacy is the user her- or himself as ANY data shared through the Web, even privately between friends, can all too easily become public. News stories over the past decade document the increasingly common phenomenon in which individuals whose photos and posts have gone viral after unintentionally or intentionally being made public. In numerous widely publicized instances, Individuals have lost their jobs, been removed from office, or suffered public shame, ridicule, and even threats to their safety. The fact that the phrase "Internet shaming," is now well known in the popular lexicon, reflects how often this occurs and how disastrous the consequences can be.[3]

Understanding Cyberthreats

Cyberthreats—defined as any individual, program, or entity with the potential to intercept, alter, or destroy data—come in many forms. Hackers are individuals skilled in programming or cybersecurity who are adept at entering secure computer systems or networks. The hackers known in the community as "black hats" who may also be called cybercriminals, penetrate security systems for personal gain, stealing personal information, credit card numbers, and a variety of other data that can be sold for profit.[4] One study described in a 2016 *Slate* magazine article found traced 320 different transactions involving cybercriminals selling data stolen from computer users, which resulted in between $1 and $2 million in profit. The criminals sold their stolen credit card numbers and other data through a series of clandestine websites known as the "Dark Web."[5]

Hackers have created a variety of tools to help them infiltrate computers and networks. Among the best known and most widely studied are viruses, which are programs that can replicate themselves (like their molecular namesakes) and can then spread from one computer on a network to others. Hackers can also use programs called "bots," that perform automatic functions once installed on a system, such as accessing or corrupting files or allowing a user in another area to gain access to a person's data, to watch them browse the Internet, to take complete control of their computer, or even to access built-in cameras and microphones to watch or listen to a computer owner.

In most cases, infiltrating a computer requires the computer owner or user to make some mistake that gives the hacker access. Cybercriminals may try to trick users to click on images or links or to visit certain websites by sending fake e-mails or instant messages. The message may appear to come from a friend or the criminal may try to entice the user with a financial reward or threaten the user by pretending to be from a known authority, such as the Internal Revenue Service (IRS) or the police. Once the user clicks on a link, message, or other active object, a program is installed on his or her computer. These programs, whether bots, malware, or viruses, cause the computer to perform various functions, such as sending out spam messages to individuals in the user's contact list, or giving the criminal who sent the bug access to the user's documents, photos, or other data. Hackers often use "phishing," which is a method of data theft that uses deceptive messages, links, websites, or other means to trick users into volunteering sensitive information, such as their social security number, account numbers, or other data typically used in security questions such as the person's grade school friends, first pets, mother's maiden name, etc.

Personal Cybersecurity Tools

For those who think the risk to their data is minimal, visiting the website www. haveibeenpwned.com can be illuminating. The website provides a list of e-mail addresses found in various "data dumps," which are collections of data publically posted after cybercriminals hacked into companies like Yahoo!, Target, Google, and LinkedIn. Many of the largest, most widely used companies have been hacked, and the data provided by users to these sites has therefore been compromised as well.

So, how does one protect his or her personal data? The process involves both behavioral changes and technological tools. A short guide to some of the basic steps might be as follows:

Behavioral:

1) Use caution when posting on social media and communicating on the Web. Consider that all social media or Web-based communications could become public.

2) Do not open e-mails or messages from unknown senders or that appear unusual.

3) Clean up one's social media presence.

Technological:

1) Use stronger passwords, at least 10-characters, but preferably 30-characters.

2) Use a password manager.

3) Do not use the same password on multiple sites/programs.

4) Use two-factor or multifactor authentication when available.

5) Use a Tor Browser to keep Web activity private.

6) Use a Virtual Private Network (VPN) to enhance privacy on the Web.

To start with, Internet users should NOT consider the Web a safe place to share sensitive or potentially damaging information and this is *especially* true for social media. Users should think critically about *what* they share online and *how* information is being shared. Posting on social media is essentially like speaking aloud in a crowded room, surrounded by mixed company. The message may be meant for friends, but can easily be overheard by the strangers on all sides. Most of those strangers probably don't care, but some might, and they might share that information with others.

It is important for Web users to understand that their cyberidentity, the information and personality that they present to other social media users and companies through their presence on the Web, shopping habits, and other virtual activities, is the same as crafting a public persona. Others are watching, so every user must be aware and take steps to ensure that he or she is presenting a version of themselves fit for the public. In addition, experts recommend cleaning up one's social media presence regularly, going through sites and networks to remove data that might be compromising.[6]

In terms of technological tools, there are many choices for personal cybersecurity. Antivirus and antimalware software can help to protect personal computers from malicious programs, while other tools help protect a user's privacy when browsing the Web or help to keep their personal data secure when visiting their favorite sites or Web services.

Password strength is a major area of concern for Web security, as it takes only minutes for a hacker using sophisticated programs to hack into a system protected by a typical 8-character password. Longer passwords, with combinations of letters, numbers, and special characters, are typically recommended. It is also important NOT to use a password that could be easily guessed by someone with knowledge of the individual's family, life, or history. Security specialists recommend using 10-character passwords for sites or programs that contain little sensitive data, and 30-character passwords for especially sensitive sites or programs such as banks, medical insurance sites, etc.

Alternatively, users are increasingly choosing to use password managers, which are software systems that generate complicated passwords for all the sites and programs that a user accesses and only require the user to remember a single password, which is used to access the password manager program.[7] In some cases, users may have the option of using multifactor authentication systems, which are security programs that require the user to provide more than one method of authenticating their identity before they can gain access. For instance, 2-factor authentication (2FA), used on many secure sites, typically requires the user to first enter their password and user name, and then complete a second step, such as using a fingerprint or voice print to authenticate their identification.[8]

More advanced tools may be of interest to those who are more concerned about Web privacy. For instance, VPN- service, which creates a secure, encrypted connection between the Web and the user's computer, essentially scrambles a computer's unique identification address, thus making it difficult to gain information about the user's identity and location. Virtual private network services do not protect against all forms of data intrusion, but are sufficient to protect user data against most casual data leaks, including the processes used by companies for corporate data mining and some levels of digital surveillance.[9] Another step for those concerned about Web privacy is to use a Tor browser when browsing the Web. TOR was developed by researchers looking to create a browser that was more difficult to hack and resistant to surveillance and shifts data back and forth between multiple points, making it more difficult for any individual intercepting data to determine where the data came from or where it is ultimately going.

The Internet is a fantastic tool that has ushered in a new era in information and collaboration that continues to shape the world in myriad ways, but the public consciousness has not caught up with the technological revolution. Data is power and power needs to be handled with respect, protected from foreign and domestic threats, and made safe from accidental damage or distribution. Personal cybersecurity *is* public security and, in some ways, is *also* national security and learning about the behavioral and technological tools needed to keep data safe can be considered, in the changing postdigital revolution world, akin to learning new rules of citizenship.

Micah L. Issitt

Works Used

Eddy, Max. "The Best VPN Services of 2017." *PC Mag,* Ziff Davis, LLC. Jan 31, 2017.

Gordon, Whitson. "Here's Everywhere You Should Enable Two-Factor Authentication Right Now." *Lifehacker*, Gizmodo Media Group. Dec 10, 2013.

Holt, Thomas. "Here's How Hackers Make Millions Selling Your Stolen Passwords." *Slate*. Slate Group. Jun 29, 2016.

Magid, Larry. "Why Cyber Security Matters to Everyone." *Forbes*. Forbes Inc. Oct 1, 2014.

Morgan, Steve. "Cybersecurity Market Reaches $75 Billion in 2015; Expected to Reach $170 Billion by 2020." *Forbes*. Forbes, Inc. Dec 20, 2015.

Pogue, David. "The Bright Side of Internet Shaming." *Scientific American*. Oct 1 2016. Web. 25 Feb 2017.

Rubenking, Neil J. "The Best Password Managers of 2017." *PC Mag*, Ziff Davis LLC. Feb 15 2017. Web. 26 Feb 2017.

Sammons, John and Michael Cross. *The Basics of Cyber Safety: Computer and Mobile Device Safety Made Easy*. New York: Syngress, 2017.

Wang, Jie and Zachary A. Kissel. *Introduction to Network Security: Theory and Practice*. Hoboken, NJ: Wiley Press, 2015.

Zimmerman, Carlota. "6 Ways to Spring Clean Your Social Media Presence." *The Huffington Post*, Huffington Post Co. Apr 8 2015. Web. 25 Feb 2017.

Notes

1. Magid, "Why Cyber Security Matters to Everyone."
2. Morgan, "Cybersecurity Market Reaches $75 Billion in 2015."
3. Pogue, "The Bright Side of Internet Shaming."
4. Wang and Kissel, *Introduction to Network Security*, 25-30.
5. Holt, "Here's How Hackers Make Millions Selling Your Stolen Passwords."
6. Zimmerman, "6 Ways to Spring Clean Your Social Media Presence."
7. Rubenking, "The Best Password Managers of 2017."
8. Gordon, "Here's Everywhere You Should Enable Two Factor Authentication Right Now."
9. Eddy, "The Best VPN Services of 2017."

How to Protect Your Digital Privacy in the Era of Public Shaming

By Julia Angwin
ProPublica, January 26, 2017

Every January, I do a digital tuneup, cleaning up my privacy settings, updating my software and generally trying to upgrade my security. This year, the task feels particularly urgent as we face a world with unprecedented threats to our digital safety.

We are living in an era of widespread hacking and public shaming. Don't like your political rivals? Beg Russia to hack them, and their emails mysteriously show up on Wikileaks. Don't like your exspouse? Post a revenge porn video. Don't like your video game opponents? Find their address online and send a SWAT team to their door.

And, of course, the US government has the capability to do even more. It can spy on much of the globe's Internet traffic and has in the past kept tabs on nearly every American's phone calls. Like it or not, we are all combatants in an information war, with our data under constant siege.

So how can ordinary people defend themselves? The truth is you can't defend everything. But you can mitigate threats by reducing how much data you leave exposed for an intruder to grab. Hackers call this minimizing your "attack surface."

The good news is that there are some easy steps you can take to reduce the threat. Here is what I am doing this year:

Updating Software

Every year, I ditch old buggy software that I don't use and update all the software that I do use to its most current version. Exploiting software with known holes is one of the ways that criminals install ransomware—which holds your data hostage until you pay for it to be released.

Making Passwords Longer

This year, I'm working to lengthen my passwords to at least 10 characters for accounts that I don't care about and to 30 characters for accounts I do care about (email and banking). After all, in 2017, automated software can guess an eightdigit password in less than a day.

Most importantly, don't reuse passwords. You don't have to think of unique passwords yourself—password management software such as 1Password, LastPass will do it for you. EFF technologist Jacob HoffmanAndrews makes a very good case for password management software being the best defense against a phishing attack. (Phishing is how the email of John Podesta, Hillary Clinton's campaign chairman, got hacked).

Securing Communications

The good news is that it's never been easier to send encrypted text messages and make encrypted phone calls on the phone apps Signal and WhatsApp. However, please note that WhatsApp has said it will share users' address books with its parent company, Facebook, unless they opted out of the latest privacy update.

Of course, people who receive your messages can still screenshot and share them without your permission. On Signal you can make it slightly harder for them by setting your messages to disappear after a certain amount of time. In WhatsApp, you can turn off cloud backups of your chats, but you can't be sure if others have done the same.

Protecting Mobile Web Browsing

The websites that you browse are among the most revealing details about you. Until recently, it was hard to protect mobile web surfing, but this year there are a lot of good options for iPhones. You can use privacy protecting standalone web browsers such as Brave or Firefox Focus, or install an addon such as Purify that will let you browse safely on Safari. In an excess of excitement, I'm currently using all three!

Of course, blocking online tracking also means blocking ads. I hate to deny worthy websites their advertising dollars, but I also think it's unfair for them to sell my data to hundreds of ad tracking companies. Brave is building a controversial system that pays publishers for users' visits, but it remains to be seen if it will work. In the meantime, I try to subscribe or donate to news outlets whose work I admire.

Dropping DropBox

You wouldn't leave your most sensitive documents in an unlocked filing cabinet, so why do you keep them in cloud services such as Google Drive and DropBox? Those companies have the keys to unlock your files. One option is to password protect your files before uploading them. But I prefer a cloud service that encrypts for me. In my usual overkill approach, I'm using Sync.com to synchronize files and SpiderOak for backup.

Deleting Some Data

Consider whether you really need to store all your old emails and documents. I recently deleted a ton of emails dating back to 2008. I had been hanging onto them thinking that I might want them in the future. But I realized that if I hadn't looked at them until now, I probably wasn't going to. And they were just sitting there wait-ing to be hacked.

Reconsidering Installing Cameras and Microphones at Home

As Internetenabled devices—ranging from smart hairbrushes to voiceactivated speakers—invade the home, criminals are finding new ways to penetrate their de-fenses.

Hackers have spied on women through the womens' webcams and used net-works of online cameras and other devices to bring down the Internet in Liberia. Like many people including the Pope and Facebook CEO Mark Zuckerberg, I have covered the cameras on my computers with stickers and magnetic screens to avoid peeping Toms. But until device makers heed the Federal Trade Commission's secu-rity recommendations for internetenabled devices, I won't introduce new cameras and microphones into my home.

Opting Out of Data Brokers

Fears that President Donald Trump might build a Muslim registry prompted thou-sands of Silicon Valley tech workers to sign a pledge stating that they wouldn't par-ticipate in building any databases that profile people by race, religion or national origin. But only three of the hundreds of data brokers that sell lists of people have affirmed that they would not par-ticipate in a registry. Two

> Of course, blocking online tracking also means blocking ads. I hate to deny worthy websites their advertising dollars, but I also think it's unfair for them to sell my data to hundreds of ad tracking companies.

other data brokers told a reporter that the price for such a list would range from about $14,000 to $17,000.

It's not easy to remove personal data from the hundreds of data brokers that are out there. Many of them require you to submit a picture of your photo ID, or write a letter. But if you do it—as I did two years ago—it is worth it. Most of the time when a new data broker emerges, I find that my data is already removed because I opted out from the broker's supplier. I compiled a list of data broker optouts that you can use as a starting point.

Taking a Deep Breath

The size of the problem and the difficulty of the solutions can be overwhelming. Just remember that whatever you do—even if it's just upgrading one password or opting out of one data broker—will improve your situation. And if you are the sub-ject of a hateful, vitriolic internet attack, read Anita Sarkeesian's guide to surviving online harassment.

Correction, Jan. 31, 2017: This article incorrectly said that Google and DropBox files are unencrypted. The post has been updated to clarify that those services are encrypted, but that those companies have the ability to unlock users' files.

Print Citations

CMS: Angwin, Julia. "How to Protect Your Digital Privacy in the Era of Public Shaming." In *The Reference Shelf: Internet Abuses and Privacy Rights*, edited by Betsy Maury, 9-12. Ipswich, MA: H.W. Wilson, 2017.

MLA: Angwin, Julia. "How to Protect Your Digital Privacy in the Era of Public Shaming." *The Reference Shelf: Internet Abuses and Privacy Rights*. Ed. Betsy Maury. Ipswich: H.W. Wilson, 2017. 9-12. Print.

APA: Angwin, J. (2017). How to protect your digital privacy in the era of public shaming. In Betsy Maury (Ed.), *The Reference Shelf: Internet Abuses and Privacy Rights* (pp. 9-12). Ipswich, MA: H.W. Wilson. (Original work published 2017)

Passing the Email Privacy Act Has Never Been More Urgent

By Andy Greenberg
Wired, **February 6, 2017**

It's safe to say that any digital privacy bill written more than three years before the invention of the World Wide Web is probably due for an overhaul. But the Electronic Communications Privacy Act has persisted intact for more than three decades, including its anachronistic loophole that allows the warrantless collection of emails from US citizens. Now, in its second attempt in two years, Congress is poised to reform the most outdated elements of ECPA. With Trump's incoming Justice Department, that reform seems more urgent than ever.

On Monday evening, the House of Representatives unanimously passed the Email Privacy Act, a bill that would reform ECPA were it to become law. In particular, it would newly require government agencies to obtain a warrant before seizing a criminal suspect's online communications that are more than 180 days old. Under the ECPA's existing logic, those older communications are considered abandoned, and thus not subject to a reasonable expectation of privacy.

Think, though, of how many emails currently in your inbox are from six months ago or more. The ECPA applies to cloud technologies as well, making Dropbox files from as recently as last summer easily accessible to the feds. In an era where companies like Gmail and Yahoo! store our emails for years, that law is long past due for an update. It's so patently archaic, in fact, that Obama's Justice Department had committed to avoiding the law's loophole, seeking warrants before accessing those older emails anyway.

But now that President Trump has appointed surveillance hawk Senator Jeff Sessions to lead the Justice Department, privacy advocates are arguing that finally passing ECPA reform has taken on new importance.

"Given Trump's nominees…the stakes for privacy have never been higher," says Robyn Greene, policy counsel at the New America Foundation's Open Technology Institute. "It's crucial Congress act on ECPA reform so that Americans can feel safe in their 4th amendment rights."

ECPA reform passed the House unanimously last year as well. But when the bill came to the Senate, Sessions and fellow Republican Senator John Cornyn added controversial surveillance-friendly amendments to the bill that caused it to falter and expire. Sessions wanted to grant law enforcement the ability to demand data

---

> **"Given Trump's nominees... the stakes for privacy have never been higher,"** says Robyn Greene, policy counsel at the New America Foundation's Open Technology Institute.

from internet firms without a warrant in ill-defined "emergency" cases, despite the fact that many companies already do voluntarily hand over personal data in emergency situations. Even a retired Washington, DC, homicide detective of 27 years called that amendment "unwise and unsafe."

Cornyn, meanwhile, attempted to expand the power of the FBI's national security letters, which can be secretly used to demand private information from internet firms. That expansion would have allowed national security letters to be used without warrants to grab metadata, like a target's browsing history and IP addresses. Dozens of civil liberties groups and tech firms including Google and Yahoo! signed a letter opposing the amendment, but it ultimately delayed the bill too long to reach a vote before the end of the Congressional session.

With the bill's reintroduction, Sessions' eventual move to the Justice Department might help clear the way for the bill to pass the Senate without those poison-pill additions. Considering that same move puts a vocal surveillance advocate in charge of the ECPA's implementation, activists argue that updated safeguards are also more needed than ever.

"We shouldn't be reliant on a particular administration policy to ensure that Americans' fourth amendment rights are protected," says Neema Singh-Giuliani, an attorney with the ACLU. "The public wants to know that their information is protected whether the president is Donald Trump or anyone else."

In fact, the question of the privacy of stored communications has already been decided in the courts: In the 2008 case of *Warshak v. USA*, a Sixth District Appellate Court found that seizing the older stored emails of a criminal suspect without a warrant violated his fourth amendment right to protection from unconstitutional searches. But that case hasn't been tested nationwide, and the passage of the Email Privacy Act would seal its result in law rather than depend on Trump's Justice Department not to fight it in court.

Despite flying through the House tonight, with Sessions not yet confirmed as Attorney General and Cornyn still in office, the Senate prognosis remains less certain. "I hope they've abandoned their tactics of trying to create a surveillance bill out of a privacy bill," says OTI's Greene. "It's critically important to recognize this is something both members of Congress and the American public are demanding."

This story has been updated to reflect the passage of the Email Privacy Act in the House.

Print Citations

CMS: Greenberg, Andy. "Passing the Email Privacy Act Has Never Been More Urgent." In *The Reference Shelf: Internet Abuses and Privacy Rights*, edited by Betsy Maury, 13-15. Ipswich, MA: H.W. Wilson, 2017.

MLA: Greenberg, Andy. "Passing the Email Privacy Act Has Never Been More Urgent." *The Reference Shelf: Internet Abuses and Privacy Rights*. Ed. Betsy Maury. Ipswich: H.W. Wilson, 2017. 13-15. Print.

APA: Greenberg, A. (2017). Passing the email privacy act has never been more urgent. In Betsy Maury (Ed.), *The Reference Shelf: Internet Abuses and Privacy Rights* (pp. 13-15). Ipswich, MA: H.W. Wilson. (Original work published 2017)

Practicing Good Personal Cybersecurity Isn't Just about Protecting Yourself

By Josephine Wolff
Slate, February 7, 2017

Last Thanksgiving, while other people's families were arguing about politics, my family and I managed to get into a fight over whether they should be paying more attention to the security of their computers and data. One insisted she doesn't do any online banking; another pointed out that his email is incredibly boring; and, anyway, they pretty much all assume anyone who wanted to would be able to access everything anyway.

Computer security tools and tactics are a tough sell for many people: They're not interested in learning about it, they don't feel they have any particularly important data to protect, they can't imagine that they would ever be interesting targets, or they don't really believe they'll be able to stop determined adversaries. I imagine those people (including my mother) feel about articles on how to configure a virtual private network or set up two-factor authentication roughly the way I feel about articles on how to turn old plastic bottles into sumo wrestler bowling pins.

I get it: You're not an investigative journalist protecting sources, you're not a criminal hiding illegal plots, and your work email consists mostly of passive-aggressive queries about moldy leftovers in the office refrigerator. But the security of your devices and your data does matter—for you, individually, and also for society.

You may not need to use a VPN constantly or activate two-factor authentication for every account or encrypt all your communications. But you should probably be doing all of these things at least some of the time. So even if you've convinced yourself that you have absolutely nothing to hide—that no one could conceivably be interested in the contents of your digital life—it's worth taking 15 minutes to understand a few of the security options available to you and when and why you might want to be using them.

Rest assured, you have something to lose. You have money that can be stolen if criminals manage to find your financial information or account numbers tucked among your files and emails. You have work that can be lost if those same adversaries compromise your devices and delete the contents—or hold them for ransom. You've sent snarky text messages and emails, and you've searched Google for information about an embarrassing rash.

Protecting yourself online is about dealing with a lot of different threats all at once: your most hated colleagues, organized crime rings, and surveillance powers of both foreign nations and your own government. Many of the same technical tools that protect against one also protect against the others. So give up the idea that you, yourself, have nothing to defend and no one you need to defend it from.

Beyond just protecting your own self-interest, improving your computer security also benefits society at large. Even if your devices and communications contain absolutely nothing of any value to you or anyone else, they can still be used as weapons against others if compromised. For instance, your devices can be infected to become part of a bot and used to launch large-scale distributed denial of service attacks. Or your email account can be compromised and used to send emails to your contacts to breach their accounts. Or your computer can be used as an intermediary staging ground for routing an attack to its ultimate target, making it more difficult to identify the real perpetrator and easier to trick the target into accepting malicious traffic that appears to originate from an innocent or trusted network. Or the ransomware you accidentally downloaded could demand that you infect your friends in order to free your files.

> **Protecting yourself online is about dealing with a lot of different threats all at once: your most hated colleagues, organized crime rings, and surveillance powers of both foreign nations and your own government.**

Your online security has broader implications when it comes to government surveillance as well. You may feel you have absolutely nothing to hide from national governments, but there are probably some people whose work you think is important: political activists and journalists, for instance. Using tools such as DuckDuckGo, Tor, and Signal provides support for services that many people really do need, both by driving revenue or donations and by making these tools more ubiquitous and therefore better maintained. It also makes it harder to single out the people using these services and treat them as criminals.

If you've never gotten very worked up about digital surveillance because you've always basically trusted the U.S. government until now, this is a good moment to make it a little bit more difficult for it to collect and monitor all of your data. The U.S. government has vast surveillance powers, of course, and if it really wants to figure out what you're doing, odds are good that it will find a way. But there's value in making that process a little harder, a little slower, and a little more difficult to scale up and apply indiscriminately to the entire country.

Protecting computers and communications is ultimately about protecting people. And while the phrase "cybersecurity self-defense" suggests this is mostly about protecting yourself, that's only one reason to finally learn about all the technologies you've been conscientiously avoiding for years. Ramping up your cybersecurity practices is as much—if not more—about protecting other people as it is about protecting yourself.

Print Citations

CMS: Wolff, Josephine. "Practicing Good Personal Cybersecurity Isn't Just about Protecting Yourself." In *The Reference Shelf: Internet Abuses and Privacy Rights*, edited by Betsy Maury, 16-18. Ipswich, MA: H.W. Wilson, 2017.

MLA: Wolff, Josephine. "Practicing Good Personal Cybersecurity Isn't Just about Protecting Yourself." *The Reference Shelf: Internet Abuses and Privacy Rights*. Ed. Betsy Maury. Ipswich: H.W. Wilson, 2017. 16-18. Print.

APA: Wolff, J. (2017). Practicing good personal cybersecurity isn't just about protecting yourself. In Betsy Maury (Ed.), *The Reference Shelf: Internet Abuses and Privacy Rights* (pp. 16-18). Ipswich, MA: H.W. Wilson. (Original work published 2017)

The Watchers: Assaults on Privacy in America

By Jonathan Shaw

Harvard Magazine, January-February 2017

Do people behave differently when they think they are being watched? Security Agency contractor Edward Snowden revealed the mass surveillance of American citizens in June 2013, the question suddenly grew in importance. Can the behavior of an entire population, even in a modern democracy, be changed by awareness of surveillance? And what are the effects of other kinds of privacy invasions?

Jon Penney was nearing the end of a fellowship at Harvard Law School's Berkman Klein Center for Internet & Society in 2013, and he realized that Snowden's disclosures presented an opportunity to study their effect on Americans' online behavior. During research at Oxford the following year, Penney documented a sudden decline in Wikipedia searches for certain terrorism-related keywords: Al Qaeda, Hezbollah, dirty bomb, chemical weapon, and jihad, for example. More than a year later, when the study ended, such searches were still declining. "Given the lack of evidence of people being prosecuted or punished" for accessing such information, Penney wrote in the *Berkeley Technology Law Review* (which published his research last June), he judged it unlikely that "actual fear of prosecution can fully explain the chilling effects suggested by the findings of this study." The better explanation, he wrote, is self-censorship.

Penney's work is the sort of evidence for negative social effects that scholars (and courts of law) demand. If democratic self-governance relies on an informed citizenry, Penney wrote, then "surveillance-related chilling effects," by "deterring people from exercising their rights," including "...the freedom to read, think, and communicate privately," are "corrosive to political discourse."

"The fact that you won't do things, that you will self-censor, are the worst effects of pervasive surveillance," reiterates security expert Bruce Schneier, a fellow at the Berkman and in the cybersecurity program of the Kennedy School's Belfer Center for Government and International Affairs. "Governments, of course, know this. China bases its surveillance on this fact. It wants people to self-censor, because it knows it can't stop everybody. The idea is that if you don't know where the line is, and the penalty for crossing it is severe, you will stay far away from it. Basic human conditioning." The effectiveness of surveillance at preventing crime or terrorism can be debated, but "if your goal is to control a population," Schneier says, "mass surveillance is awesome."

That's a problem, he continues, because "privacy is necessary for human progress. A few years ago we approved gay marriage in all 50 states. That went from 'It'll never happen' to inevitable, with almost no intervening middle ground." But to get from immoral and illegal to both moral and legal, he explains, intervening steps are needed: "It's done by a few; it's a counterculture; it's mainstream in cities; young people don't care anymore; it's legal. And this is a long process that needs privacy to happen."

As a growing share of human interactions—social, political, and economic—are committed to the digital realm, privacy and security as values and as rights have risen in importance. When someone says, "My life is on my phone," it's meant almost literally: photos, passwords, texts, emails, music, address books, documents. It is not hard to imagine that the Declaration of Independence, redrafted for an information society, might well include "security and privacy," in addition to the familiar "life, liberty, and the pursuit of happiness," among its examples of "unalienable rights."

Although Snowden highlighted government surveillance, it may not be the worst problem. Corporations hold vast and growing troves of personal information that is often inadequately protected, its use largely unregulated. Since 2005, hackers have stolen hundreds of millions of credit-card numbers from major retailers such as Target, Home Depot, TJX, and eBay. In 2014, someone stole the keys to half a billion Yahoo! accounts without being detected. And everyday threats to privacy are so commonplace that most people are numb to them. In exchange for free email, consumers allow companies such as Google to scan the content of their digital messages in order to deliver targeted ads. Users of social media, eager to keep in touch with a circle of friends, rarely read the standard agreement that governs the rights and use of what they post online. Smartphones know their owners' habits better than they themselves do: where and with whom they sleep, what time they wake up, whom they meet, and where they have been. People accept such tradeoffs in exchange for convenience. They don't really have a choice.

> Smartphones know their owners' habits better than they themselves do: where and with whom they sleep, what time they wake up, whom they meet, and where they have been. People accept such tradeoffs in exchange for convenience. They don't really have a choice.

Bemis professor of international law and of computer science Jonathan Zittrain, faculty chair of the Berkman Klein Center, worries that the ubiquity of privacy threats has led to apathy. When a hacker released former Secretary of State Colin Powell's private assessments of the two leading presidential candidates prior to the recent election, "I was surprised at how little sympathy there was for his situation, how it was treated as any other document dump," Zittrain explains. "People have a hard time distinguishing, for instance, between government documents and private documents authored by people who were once government officials, [between] documents released under the Freedom of Information Act, and documents leaked by a whistleblower. It's all just seen as…'stuff is porous, and we can get it.'" As "the ability to hack is democratized," Zittrain worries that people have lost sight of the original value behind whistleblowing, which is to make powerful institutions publicly accountable. Now everyone is vulnerable. "Over time," he wrote recently, "continued leaks will lead people to keep their thoughts to themselves, or to furtively communicate unpopular views only in person." "That does not seem sustainable to me," he said in an interview, "and it doesn't seem healthy for a free society."

The perception that the Information Age has put privacy and security at risk is widespread. Necessarily, the search for solutions is equally broad-based. In Washington, D.C., Marc Rotenberg '82, president and director of the Electronic Privacy and Information Center (EPIC), seeks legal solutions to privacy problems). At Harvard, research into privacy and security is focused at the Berkman Klein Center; at the Paulson School of Engineering and Applied Sciences' Center for Research on Computation and Society; at the Kennedy School's cybersecurity program; at the Institute for Quantitative Social Science's (IQSS) Data Privacy Lab; and also within the schools of medicine and public health (and at the affiliated hospitals), where researchers seek to protect patient data so that it can be shared appropriately, particularly in the case of rare conditions. Solutions to privacy and security problems thus involve computer scientists and legal scholars, as well as experts in healthcare, government, and business.

Security: "We Have Lost Control"

Assuring the privacy of information means making it secure. "I actually can't give you privacy unless you have security," Bruce Schneier points out: that involves protecting data through technological or legal means. Door locks, tall fences, and burglar alarms work well in the physical world. The problem, he explains, is that "in security, technology scales badly." If a burglar gets past a lock to rob a single house in a community of 100,000 people, that may be a tolerable risk. But anyone who finds a flaw in all digital locks could break into every home. "What happens," Schneier asks, "when systems become connected such that our risks are connected?"

Ordinary individuals, he points out, can do very little to mitigate this kind of systemic risk. Advice like don't have an email address, don't use your credit card, is "moronic. You can't be a fully functioning human being in the twenty-first century [like that.] So in a lot of ways, we have lost control."

In the past 15 years, entire corporations, even nations, have found their data and systems vulnerable to attack. The intrusion at the U.S. Office of Personnel and Management, disclosed in April 2015, was reportedly the most significant breach of federal networks to date: hackers, thought to be state-sponsored, took personal data for four million employees and political appointees, leading to the recall of American intelligence agents posted abroad. The 2016 digital break-in at the Democratic

National Committee's headquarters was like a modern iteration of Watergate, but initiated by a foreign power seeking to interfere in the presidential election.

The stakes can become very high indeed. "Someone is learning to take down the Internet," wrote Schneier in September. He described how an unidentified entity had been probing the defenses of companies that provide critical Internet infrastructure, slowly ramping up repeated, carefully metered attacks, as if seeking to quantify precise points of failure.

Although his best-selling book, Data and Goliath: The Hidden Battles to Collect Your Data and Control Your World, has led to his reputation as a consumer-privacy-rights advocate, Schneier is also chief technology officer for Resilient, an IBM company that handles online incident response. He brings that security background to a new fellowship at the Kennedy School's Cyber Security Project. The project focuses on policy research into the U.S. military's operations in cyberspace; it puts "people with a technical background together with people with policy experience," in order to help inform debates in Washington, says project director Michael Sulmeyer, former director for plans and operations for cyber policy at the Department of Defense. "One of the biggest debates going forward will be the roles and missions for the military's 6,000-person force for cyberspace operations."

That Cyber Command is charged with protecting the Defense Department's weapons systems, millions of computing devices, and more than 15,000 data networks (say, in support of network operations for a battalion in Afghanistan fighting the Taliban). It also provides offensive cyber capabilities to commanders around the world in the event that hostilities break out (analogous to the access they have to air and sea power capabilities). And it is responsible for defending the nation—including aviation, financial, and power-transmission systems—against a significant cyberattack.

The structure of the Internet itself makes that defensive mission difficult. Eviatar Matania, the head of Israel's National Cyber Bureau, discussed that challenge last September at the Kennedy School. He noted that unlike the agricultural and industrial revolutions, the cyber revolution has both restructured society and created a space, "a new artificial domain." Israel's bureau was founded five years ago as a way to allow that small country to be "much bigger and stronger than in a physical domain," Matania continued. But defending cyberspace is extremely difficult because it lacks both borders and distance. There are no clear boundaries between countries, and no clear divisions between corporate and government networks: "Everyone is connected to everyone."

That implies that the defense mission is expansive. Admiral Michael Rogers, director of the NSA and head of U.S. Cyber Command, said during an October visit to the Kennedy School that the unit increasingly finds itself "helping defend systems across the broader U.S. government" and even "being called upon to…help within the private sector. These are big growth areas for us."

But as the mission grows, vulnerabilities are becoming more complex, not less. The Internet of Things—chip-equipped, network-connected household items such as living-room televisions that can respond to commands to change the channel—present huge security (not to mention privacy) concerns. "The increased interconnectivity of the world we are living in," explained Rogers, has led to "a level of vulnerability that we don't truly understand." The automobile, for example, used to be "a mechanical system with a one-way radio"; today it's "a series of interconnected software applications and capabilities," involving a host of remote connections that the driver doesn't understand or even know about. "That offers both amazing capability, insight, and knowledge—data that could make the car safer, make decisions faster, and eventually lead to remotely piloted autonomous vehicles." But "that car now has a whole lot of vulnerabilities that it never had before."

Openness: "We Have to be Extremely Skeptical"

It may seem logical for a centralized military organization to provide national cybersecurity and defend against cyber war. But Yochai Benkler points out how 9/11 led to war and "unjustified claims for extending surveillance powers, or extending detention and kidnapping powers, let alone torture." The Berkman professor for entrepreneurial legal studies argues that "We have to be extremely skeptical of claims made in the name of national security in general, not because the people making them are bad people, but because the people making them... operate in a world where the only downside to failing to extend their power is that one day somebody will look at them and say, 'Where were you when the world came down?'

"We should take with many grains of salt the claims of national security experts who see cyber war as the next domain," he continues, "and operate in an environment where they want to control everything as much as possible in order to minimize risks, but come to their conclusions from a framework that...is relatively insulated from potential alternative viewpoints."

Accordingly, Benkler advocates systems that allow personal data to remain in the hands of consumers—minimizing the privacy risks posed by governments, corporations, and hackers because personal information is not concentrated in a single place. (The technical term is "distributed network ecosystems based on open-source software.") "Relying on a small number of high-end companies to provide security creates a single point of failure for hundreds of millions," he says, referring to the 2014 theft of Yahoo! user accounts. "If all those...people had decentralized email storage at home, and sign-on credentials that were not valid for diverse critical sites, collecting [that information] would be much harder."

"It's a challenge to get people to adopt safe habits," he admits, "but it's not impossible. You have to change users' culture, and you have to design secure systems that are under the control of end users, not single companies." The iPhone, secured with a PIN or a fingerprint, is an example of such encrypted, secure-by-default systems. Such devices aren't hard to build—but, he says pointedly, "It's hard to do so [within] a business model that depends on spying on your customers so you can sell them to advertisers."

Furthermore, says Benkler, systems built in part with "free software developed by communities that don't have the imperatives either of profit-making companies, or of dealing with the tensions between rights and the state of emergency, get better as their vulnerabilities are constantly probed, exposed, and then corrected in a constant, evolutionary, back and forth." Such robustness is obviously desirable.

But it may not be as practicable as he hopes. Although the idea that users can enjoy more privacy and better security in a distributed computing environment is becoming more tangible as smartphones' computing power rivals that of desktops, executing it consistently poses significant challenges. Ben Adida, a software engineer and architect and former fellow of Harvard's Center for Research on Computation and Society, acknowledges this is "the vision that many security advocates, myself included, pushed for for a very long time."

But now he thinks "we are far less secure" adopting that technological approach. Adida developed Helios, one of the first encrypted yet verifiable online voting systems; he's now head of engineering at Clever, a startup that manages private student data for schools. Providing security to a range of companies has led him to discover how easy it is for small companies to err when implementing and defending the security of their systems, whether in cryptography, access control, network-level security, or in the internal audit processes used to ensure data is compartmentalized. A large company like Google, on the other hand, "does a really good job of making sure that only I can log in," he explains. "They've added two-factor authentication, they have all sorts of heuristics to check whether a person is logging in from a different location than usual. There's all sorts of work that they do to make sure that only the right people are accessing the right data."

Like Benkler, Adida agrees that centralized data is too easily accessed by law enforcement, but says that for now, "We need to rethink how to defend that data through a combination of legal and technical means." Technically, that might mean discarding chats more than few months old, for example; and legally, resisting official requests for user data in court. He advocates "evolution in the law, too." The Fourth Amendment guarantees the "right of the people to be secure in their persons, houses, papers, and effects, against unreasonable searches and seizures...," but historically, that has been interpreted to mean that obtaining data held by a third party doesn't require a search warrant. That means personal documents stored in Google's cloud, for example, are exposed. Adida says he nevertheless keeps "extremely private data hosted by a third party because that is the right operational thing to do. Everybody hosting their own stuff just doesn't make any sense" —but he hopes that someday, if the government wants access to that information, it "would require a warrant, just as if they were knocking down someone's door."

Confidentiality: "Privacy Is about Accountability"

In the here and now, using encryption, firewalls, and passwords is one way to keep information secret. But secrecy is just "a very small slice" of what privacy is about, says Marc Rotenberg of EPIC. Through "creative advocacy, litigation, and public engagement," the Washington, D.C.-based nonprofit aims to shape policy and advance the legal framework for safeguarding personal liberty. Rotenberg, an attorney and adjunct professor at Georgetown University Law Center, has won cases before the Supreme Court, filed numerous amicus briefs, testified before Congress, and given awards to leading privacy advocates across the political spectrum.

"Privacy is about accountability," he says. "It's about the fairness of decisionmaking. It's about holding large government actors and private companies accountable for their decisionmaking. It turns out to be an extraordinarily powerful and comprehensive human-rights claim, particularly in the digital age, because so much about us is based on our data."

"Privacy turns out to be an extraordinarily powerful and comprehensive human-rights claim, particularly in the digital age, because so much about us is based on our data."

Getting a loan or health insurance, or gaining admission to a certain school, are all data-driven determinations, Rotenberg points out. He asks how those data are being used. What personal information does an organization consider relevant? Are people pulled out of line at an airport because of their nationality, their religion, or because of a book purchased on Amazon? Given all the ways in which personal information drives decisions, Rotenberg says, secrecy "almost isn't even relevant to the discussion. Because paradoxically, what we keep secret is almost certainly what we don't need privacy law for. We need privacy law for everything else: for the things that we don't have the physical ability to control. When you give sensitive test information to your doctor, for example, it's no longer in your control. The credit card company has all your transactional records. What are you going to do? Nothing. That's when we start to ask questions about what type of safeguards are in place to protect our personal information held by others."

"I see privacy as closely tied to the strength of democratic governance," he continues. Recalling the first time he read the NSA's foreign intelligence surveillance court order demanding that Verizon turn over all customer telephone-call records (perhaps the most significant of Snowden's revelations), Rotenberg says, "I looked at that order, 'Provide all records, because all records are relevant,' and actually thought it was satirical, a joke from The Onion, or an exercise attached to a privacy-law exam asking students to draft an unlawful court order....And then I realized it was a real order—that the NSA thought it had the authority to collect all domestic telephone records on all U.S. telephone customers."

> **It is not hard to imagine that the Declaration of Independence, redrafted for an information society, might well include "security and privacy," in addition to the familiar "life, liberty, and the pursuit of happiness," among its examples of "unalienable rights."**

EPIC brought a petition to the Supreme Court arguing that the Foreign Intelligence Surveillance Court had exceeded its legal authority, and a broad coalition of legal experts and former members of Congress joined the campaign. But the Court did not rule on the merits of the petition. "That was after the Solicitor General twice sought extensions," Rotenberg explains, "which gave the foreign intelligence surveillance court enough time to issue an opinion justifying the program. We call that just-in-time lawmaking." The EPIC petition nevertheless marked the beginning of a broad bipartisan coalition to pass legislation, the USA Freedom Act of 2015, ending the NSA's bulk collection of such information.

Such battles almost never stay won, says Rotenberg. "The Europeans were very upset, obviously, about the U.S. surveillance activities that Snowden had documented, but then you had the terrible tragedy of Charlie Hebdo, and suddenly the French government created new surveillance authorities that go beyond what the U.S. does."

"When governments make these decisions," he reflects, "it is almost as if they're saying, 'We can't afford as much democracy, we can't afford as much openness, we can't afford to trust our citizens as much, we need to engage in more surveillance, we need less judicial review and less accountability.'" But privacy, he says, is not a trade-off: "I've been in Washington long enough to know that when someone says, 'We need to strike the right balance,' it means they probably don't know what they're talking about. A sacrifice of privacy is also a sacrifice of democracy."

In the mid 1990s, the *New York Times* quoted Rotenberg saying that the protection of privacy in the Information Age would be like the protection of the environment in the Industrial Age— "which is to say it's so much a part of the nature of economic production today, you don't solve it, you have to manage it." Many people predicted the end of privacy. But Rotenberg believes people don't understand the full consequences: "Among other things, you would lose your democratic state if everyone said, 'Why do we care if the government knows everything about us? Who needs a private phone call? Who needs a building with walls? Why should data be accurate?' Everything collapses. And we know what that world looks like: that's what [Jeremy] Bentham described as the Panopticon" —designed so an observer can watch everything, but without being seen. "When you're under constant surveillance," says Rotenberg, "you're in a prison."

On the corporate front, EPIC brought the complaint that forced Snapchat, the photo-sharing service, to fulfill its promise to delete images. When Google tried to move all Gmail users onto Buzz, its social-media platform, EPIC complained to the Federal Trade Commission (FTC), and established a significant precedent for Internet privacy. When WhatsApp announced that it would share users' secure-message data with Facebook (which had recently acquired the company), EPIC intervened. Likewise, when Facebook started changing user privacy settings after consumers had set them, EPIC brought the matter to the FTC, which stopped the practice. Most recently, EPIC has been active in the discussion over how student data are collected and used.

EPIC may seem the proverbial finger in the dike, barely holding back the flood. But Rotenberg says he is "actually a bit of an optimist about all of this," citing the Supreme Court's "remarkable 9-0 opinion, written by Chief Justice Roberts, that says the search of a cell phone following an arrest requires a warrant" —a case in which EPIC's extensive brief was cited. Rotenberg calls the 2014 decision "a strong statement about privacy in the modern age. And the fact that it was a unanimous court, I think, was remarkable."

EPIC also studies diverse privacy laws to advance legal protections. A project begun in 2015 to identify states with the best privacy laws examines data security and breaches, drone surveillance, police body cameras, and student privacy, to name a few. EPIC considers Massachusetts's 2007 data-protection law one of the best in the country; California has crafted very good data-breach-notification regulations. Farther afield, Rotenberg admires the European Court of Justice's decision on the "right to be forgotten," which involved personal bankruptcy records that had been published in a newspaper 10 years earlier. The Spanish plaintiff asked both the newspaper and Google to remove the records. Spain's privacy agency decided not to touch the newspaper, but ordered Google to remove the record from search results—drawing "a very thoughtful line" between the protected free expression of news organizations and the commercial operations of data brokers, who commodify personal information.

Discrimination:"Algorithmic Accountability"

Rotenberg has recently begun advocating for laws that would require companies to disclose how algorithms use personal data—for hiring, credit determinations, or online advertising. As businesses demand more information from people, he thinks companies should reveal how they make decisions. Businesses regard their algorithms as intellectual property, but Rotenberg argues that their rights "extend as far as my personal data....And if that creates a problem for them, don't collect my data." The algorithms act invisibly and without accountability. Rotenberg says the solution is straightforward: "There should be algorithmic accountability. We should be able to open the code."

One computer scientist, famous for her work on privacy technology and re-identification of anonymous subjects in large data sets, approaches this problem as a technologist, seeking to expose the inner workings of algorithms in ways that make them susceptible to existing laws.

Google seemed to think professor of government and technology in residence Latanya Sweeney might have an arrest record. A simple search for the name of this African-American computer scientist, now faculty dean of Currier House, yielded ads implying that she had a criminal past. When former Reuters reporter Adam Tanner, now an Institute for Quantitative Social Science (IQSS) fellow, suggested that resulted from her "black-sounding name," Sweeney at first resisted his explanation. Then she discovered that a search for "Latanya" turned up images of black women, and a search for "Tanya" turned up images of whites. She decided to dig deeper.

Because she runs Harvard's Data Privacy Lab, based in IQSS, Sweeney has resources to find out what makes an algorithm tick. Using lists of first names given more often to black babies than to white ones, she Googled the names of real people from Internet addresses around the country, capturing 100,000 ad impressions. For some names, ads implied the existence of an arrest record as much as 80 percent of the time, even when there was none. "Blacks are a protected group. Employment is a protected setting," she notes. If an employer Googles an applicant's name and ads pop up implying that there is an arrest record, she says, that is enough to trigger a federal discrimination investigation.

Her work showed, Sweeney says, that these unforeseen consequences can be studied and the results used "to empower the government structures we already have for oversight." Rather than demanding new laws that focus on new technologies, she used science to expose the workings of technology, so existing law could be applied.

Armed with this tool for "algorithmic accountability," Sweeney took a year's sabbatical in 2014 to work as chief technology officer at the FTC. The commission had lacked pertinent technological expertise to investigate the issue; Sweeney's presence persuaded the chairwoman to hire additional technologists.

While at the commission, Sweeney studied the practices of advertisers targeting the sites of sororities, fraternities, and other student groups, including Omega Psi Phi, a black fraternity celebrating its centennial. Ads routed to its website included options for graduate education and for travel—and one that implied the need for a criminal lawyer. Credit-card ads included only the lowest-ranked cards, whereas Sweeney found that the sites of similar fraternal student organizations turned up ads for American Express Blue. How, she wondered, did that decisionmaking occur in a supposedly neutral algorithm? "If, through their practices, technology companies are dominating the online experience" and shaping people's experiences of the Internet, she says, "then it's those practices that have to be addressed, or at least connected to…societal norms. Just because Google or Facebook implement business practices and technology together in a package in a certain way doesn't mean that's the only way. The technology…and the business practices didn't have to be that way. And that has to be unpacked."

Commerce: "Surveillance Capitalism"

Shoshanna Zuboff, the Wilson professor of business administration emerita, would agree. She thinks about the information landscape in economic terms and says that there is even more at stake than privacy. Zuboff says that corporate use of personal data has set society on a path to a new form of capitalism that departs from earlier norms of market democracy.

She draws an analogy from the perfection of the assembly line: Ford engineers' discovery a century ago, after years of trial and error, that they had created "a logic of high-volume, low- unit cost, which really had never existed before with all the pieces aligned." Today, many corporations follow a similar trajectory by packaging personal data and behavioral information and selling it to advertisers: what she calls "surveillance capitalism."

"Google was ground zero," Zuboff begins. At first, information was used to benefit end users, to improve searches, just as Apple and Amazon use their customers' data largely to customize those individuals' online experiences. Google's founders once said they weren't interested in advertising. But Google "didn't have a product to sell," she explains, and as the 2001 dot.com bubble fell into crisis, the company was under pressure to transform investment into earnings. "They didn't start by saying, 'Well, we can make a lot of money assaulting privacy,'" she continues. Instead, "trial and error and experimentation and adapting their capabilities in new directions" led them to sell ads based on personal information about users. Like the tinkerers at Ford, Google engineers discovered "a way of using their capabilities in the context of search to do something utterly different from anything they had imagined when they started out." Instead of using the personal data to benefit the sources of that information, they commodified it, using what they knew about people to match them with paying advertisers. As the advertising money flowed into Google, it became a "powerful feedback loop of almost instantaneous success in these new markets."

"Those feedback loops become drivers themselves," Zuboff explains. "This is how the logic of accumulation develops…and ultimately flourishes and becomes institutionalized. That it has costs, and that the costs fall on society, on individuals, on the values and principles of the liberal order for which human beings have struggled and sacrificed much over millennia—that," she says pointedly, "is off the balance sheet."

Privacy values in this context become externalities, like pollution or climate change, "for which surveillance capitalists are not accountable." In fact, Zuboff believes, "Principles of individual self-determination are impediments to this economic juggernaut; they have to be vanquished.

They are friction." The resulting battles will be political. They will be fought in legislatures and in the courts, she says. (See EPIC's cases, above.) Meanwhile, surveillance capitalists have learned to use all necessary means to defend their claims, she says: "through rhetoric, persuasion, threat, seduction, deceit, fraud, and outright theft. They will fight in whatever way they must for this economic machine to keep growing." Consumer-citizens feel the assault, but for the surveillance capitalists, their creation is like "a living organism now, that has to grow."

"In surveillance capitalism, rights are taken from us without our knowledge, understanding, or consent, and used to create products designed to predict our behavior."

"Privacy," according to Zuboff, "is having the right to decide how you want to live, what you want to share, and what you choose to expose to the risks of transparency. In surveillance capitalism, those rights are taken from us without our knowledge, understanding, or consent, and used to create products designed to predict our behavior." These products are then sold into new markets that she calls "behavioral futures markets." At each stage, "our lives are further exposed to others without our consent." In losing decision rights, we lose privacy, as well as autonomy and self-determination. Such rights don't vanish, she points out. "We lose them to someone else. Google is an example of a company that amasses 'decision rights' that once belonged to us. Decision rights are fundamentally political. So these are concentrations of political power, in institutions that we have not authorized. We didn't elect them, we didn't vote for them, we didn't sanction this transfer of rights and power."

Targeted ads—about which consumers already express concern—are the beginning of a much more ambitious program of modifying and influencing behavior toward profitable ends, Zuboff argues. "No one ever said mass production was only for automobiles, and surveillance capitalism isn't only for advertisers." There are many other companies and industries, she says, that want to participate in the new behavioral futures markets. Early examples include sectors such as insurance, retail, and health.

Behavioral futures markets develop in stages, she explains. Predictive analytics is a familiar use of data in which patterns are identified in order to predict whether somebody might be pregnant, or getting married, or has just lost a loved one. (The technique is already being used to place police officers in locations where crime is more likely to occur.) Zuboff notes that Google Maps, to take another example, recently introduced a feature that suggests a destination based on what it knows about users before they've even

> **Technology is never a thing in itself. It is always designed and deployed to reflect the aims and needs of a particular economic order.**

indicated where they're going. "Maybe it picked up from an email that you've recently moved and need to get tools for the workshop," Zuboff explains, "so it suggests a hardware store that you can go to. Would you think that hardware store is an innocent recipient of Google's largess?"

The stakes are getting higher. She points to the wildly popular game Pokémon Go, which rewards players with virtual experiences. "I can send you to the dry cleaner, I can send you to the car mechanic, I can send you to the restaurant—anywhere I want to with this reward system. All these entities pay to play in the new marketplace for behavior." Even before the game launched in Japan, McDonald's had paid to designate its 3,000 restaurants as destinations (called "gyms") within the game. The game's developer is Niantic, formerly a lab within Google run by John Hanke, who also led Google's geolocation services. (The core mapping technology was funded by the CIA's venture-capital arm.) Having mapped a virtual world onto the physical one with Google Maps and Google Earth, use of smartphone location services closes the loop, populating that cyber domain with people in the physical world.

At the moment, the project is "allowing the public to get exposed to this kind of interaction, and become habituated to it," says Zuboff. Pokémon players have fun, without realizing that it is also another form of social and economic control.

"I think it's very important to connect the dots," she explains, "and see that all of this makes sense when we frame it as a new form of capitalism that has particular requirements in order to be successful. Technology is never a thing in itself. It is always designed and deployed to reflect the aims and needs of a particular economic order. Suddenly, we can see that these ventures are part of a cohesive, internally consistent, and coherent economic logic. And when we can do that, then I think as a society we are far better positioned to increase and expand our advocacy and re-form efforts, [to figure out how] to successfully tether information-based capitalism to pro-social and pro-democratic values and principles," rather than solely serving third-party economic interests. "The challenge of surveillance capitalism becomes part of the larger historical project of harnessing capitalism to society."

Surveillance capitalism, driven by the profit motive, "has been able to gather to itself concentrations of knowledge and power that exceed anything imaginable even a few years ago," she says. "One of its consequences is the deletion of privacy. But if we fight this only on the grounds of privacy, we're bound to meet with constant frustration and limited success. This is an economic logic that must delete privacy in order to be successful." This is why, despite the "brilliant and heroic scholarship" that has come out of Berkman, and despite the "brilliant and heroic advocacy that has come from many quarters in the United States, including Marc Rotenberg and his amazing team at EPIC,…this thing keeps growing."

History may suggest better ways to respond, she says. "We have experience in taming capitalism, and binding it to pro-social and pro-democratic principles. In the late nineteenth century, the Gilded Age, there was no protection for labor, and capital had complete freedom to do whatever it wanted to do with resources, with people, with communities, producing extreme economic and social inequality along the way." The twentieth century "was a long journey to correct that imbalance." The social challenge now, she says, is to insist on a new social contract, with its own twenty-first century legislative and regulatory innovations, that harnesses information capitalism to democratic values and norms. This begins, she believes, with deepening social understanding and awareness. "We have to create the political context in which privacy can be successfully defended, protected, and affirmed as a human right. Then we'd have a context in which the privacy battles can be won."

Print Citations

CMS: Shaw, Jonathan. "The Watchers: Assaults on Privacy in America." In *The Reference Shelf: Internet Abuses and Privacy Rights*, edited by Betsy Maury, 19-31. Ipswich, MA: H.W. Wilson, 2017.

MLA: Shaw, Jonathan. "The Watchers: Assaults on Privacy in America." *The Reference Shelf: Internet Abuses and Privacy Rights*. Ed. Betsy Maury. Ipswich: H.W. Wilson, 2017. 19-31. Print.

APA: Shaw, J. (2017). *The watchers: Assaults on privacy in America*. In Betsy Maury (Ed.), *The Reference Shelf: Internet Abuses and Privacy Rights* (pp. 19-31). Ipswich, MA: H.W. Wilson. (Original work published 2017)

Open Technology: Values, Compromises, and Ownership

By Brynne Morris, Georgia Bullen, Steph Alarcon,
Fernanda Lavalle, Nat Meysenburg, and Chris Ritzo
New America Weekly, October 27, 2016

Technology has impacted everything from how we understand and interact with the world around us to how we manage our own personal data. For years, we stored our family photos in shoeboxes. We kept our phone numbers in black books and rolodexes. Then as technology advanced, we stored these important items on computers, then floppy disks, then CDs. Finally, we just put it in "the cloud."

When the "cloud" was introduced to store that data, it seemed to solve a multitude of problems—it took up less space, could be accessed anywhere, and would be safe from unforeseen disasters like fire, flooding, or robberies. This ease and seeming security of centralized solutions are often too good to resist, but we very rarely stop to ask if it was the best solution. Maybe we should.

Frequently, we focus on the "open source" side of "open technology," meaning the software from which the technology is made is licensed openly. But open technology is not limited to software. It applies to where emails live; who owns your personal data; where that data is hosted; how it's secured; how much control and authority you have over managing your data; and your relationship with the technology. All of these raise questions, and if we don't even consider what we should be asking, we will never get the answers we need.

We asked our technologists—Chris Ritzo, Steph Alarcon, Georgia Bullen, Fernanda Lavalle, and Nat Meysenburg—at the Open Technology Institute to take a step back and ask the questions for us:

What are the benefits to using open technology versus using a centralized or owned service?

Chris: *Deciding to go with a form of open technology allows you to create a system that addresses your needs exactly without having to pick and choose from software or services that fill general needs. You could also save money that would otherwise be spent on software, hosting and support, if you have the people and resources to configure and use open technology.*

Here's a scenario: you volunteer at a local community radio station, and they want to record live broadcasts and make them available on their website afterward, or stream live shows on the internet. You could purchase the software, hosting, and support from a company to do this. There is also open source software to meet this need. You could download, install, and run the open technology yourself; you could get help from someone else to do that work; and, in some cases, you could purchase support and hosting for the open source products that do this over the closed source/proprietary options. Depending on your needs and the expertise you have to "do it yourself," you can support open tech options and get a solution that you could continue to use, customize, and improve. Given enough skill, time and expertise, you could contribute your customizations and improvements back to the open source project.

Steph: *[Open technology] ensures that in the end, you own and control your data, memories, and more. Why would this level of control even be an issue when I have easy access to my stuff online? Well, one reason is that you can't always trust that your photos, data, and other files will be kept safe, secure, and truly private. There are lots of examples in recent news where a company providing a free service like email, photo sharing, etc., has had a data breach, and emails all of their users about changing passwords, going through a security check up, etc. What happens when you lose access to your email account or your online photos because of an event like that? Will the company care that you're now missing all the pictures you had stored on their service?*

> **It's the classic issue where you have to ask—if this service is free, what is the actual cost? Frequently, the service is selling is your data to third parties, e.g., your photos, information about you, etc.**

Probably not. You likely won't have much recourse. If you're hosting these services yourself using open source software, you at least have the data on your own server, and you can take all the steps you need to assure it's backed up, secure, and only available to those who you want to have access to it.

Nat: *In addition to the points Chris and Steph make, I also see an inherent value in not having software monocultures. By using centralized services, we are entrusting those providers to also be the only innovators in that space. If no one but a few large companies, like Apple or Google, run email servers, by default, no one but those companies will figure out how to make email better. If no one but Slack does chat, we will entrust innovation of that to them, by default.*

Additionally, that kind of monoculture leads us to thinking of an internet service (and computers in general) as an appliance with a single purpose, rather than a toolbox with which you can build many things.

I'm not saying that everyone should write their own mail server software. However, I worry about the fact that large, well-resourced institutions like universities are losing institutional knowledge about things like email.

Doesn't choosing something that does not have the resources of a company mean there is more upkeep and possibly more bugs? Why would someone choose to self-host services?

Georgia: *Yes and no—like many things in life, it's more complicated than that!*

When you host things, like email, yourself, you control everything about it, and you decide when to accept updates to the tools that you are using. "Bugs" aren't going to happen as a result of just choosing to self-host, but rather by automatically accepting updates or changes that haven't been reviewed. It's just like the "early adoption" problem on any new technology: sometimes there hasn't been enough testing in the real world. If you run your own services, you can decide when something is ready for primetime and upgrade.

Steph: *For the independence from a company's interests—you don't have to worry about what the terms of service say or how they change, because you own your data. For example, if you want to use encryption, you can use encryption.*

Georgia: *But you are responsible for keeping the services up and secure. You can use open cloud services to help here, such as MayFirst and Linode, but ultimately it's still you who are responsible for keeping those servers secure and working.*

Nat: *[Not every self- hosted solution means that it is buggy or requires more upkeep than a centralized solution.] It is complicated in that it varies by service. There are dozens of implementations of email servers, some better than others. However, there are several that are mature, and, while there is no such thing as bug free software, the number of critical bugs may actually be quite low.*

Company interest? Own your data? What do you mean?

Georgia: *Take a look at most of the terms of service for photo sharing platforms like Facebook or Instagram. Most of them actually say that, by uploading your photos to them, the company is allowed to use them, unless you have your settings in a specific configuration that keeps your ownership of the photos. It's the classic issue where you have to ask—if this service is free, what is the actual cost? Frequently, the service is selling is your data to third parties, e.g., your photos, information about you, etc.*

Nat: *As Al Jazeera pointed out, there are today questions, as in "what is happening with my data now?" And tomorrow questions, as in "what will happen with my data 10 years from now?" This is a really important distinction to me. I may be okay with the way services are using my data now. However, as market forces and tastes change, what happens when a large company that has been gathering data for years goes under? If you* *had asked someone 15 years ago if Yahoo! would go belly up, it may have seemed ridiculous. My worry is that, on the way down, some of these companies will do anything they can to extract resources from the data mine, and some have even been forced to do so.*

Knowing the security concerns or ownership concerns you've stated, why would you choose to go with a centralized or owned service?

Chris: *Many people choose to use free, centralized cloud services provided by large companies for the simple ease of use and convenience they provide. Broad adoption of services like Gmail or Google Drive are also a factor—if I can easily connect and share with friends and family using the same services, that convenience and broad adoption by others can outweigh the tradeoffs of potential security and ownership concerns. I could host a mail or file server on my own, and be the person responsible for maintaining and securing those services, or I could use a major company's free (or paid) services.*

Additionally, many would argue that, the larger a company, the more likely they are to provide a more secure service than I could provide running my own server.

Fernanda: *Typically, there is an ease of use and lower labor cost that make centralized solutions attractive. There's also a perceived infinite labor cost to the alternative because many people don't feel knowledgeable enough to use an open source solution.*

There are counterexamples, like Firefox, which is developed through an open source community, including Mozilla as a company. It is equally easy to use and requires no more labor or cost, but offers fewer services and tools than the range of integrated services that "centralized" providers offer.

Nat: *Running my own server instead of using cloud-provided services means I'm also responsible for maintaining and supporting the server, keeping it updated with security patches, monitoring it for potential attack, and also supporting anyone who might be using the services running on it.*

Since there is a significant amount of time that I, or anyone, might need to spend staying on top of this stuff, as well as the time it takes to support other folks, it can be worth it to make the decision to use a cloud service. If I'm using a cloud service from a large company, I have access to all their documentation for supporting people using the service, and someone else is responsible for maintaining the servers and services.

Sometimes that is simply a better use of my time, despite the fact that I would generally prefer to have control over the services I depend on.

But not if you haven't first asked yourself whether it's better and why.

Print Citations

CMS: Morris, Brynne, Georgia Bullen, Steph Alarcon, Fernanda Lavalle, Nat Meysenburg, and Chris Ritzo. "Open Technology: Values, Compromises, and Ownership." In *The Reference Shelf: Internet Abuses and Privacy Rights*, edited by Betsy Maury, 32-36. Ipswich, MA: H.W. Wilson, 2017.

MLA: Morris, Brynne, Georgia Bullen, Steph Alarcon, Fernanda Lavalle, Nat Meysenburg, and Chris Ritzo. "Open Technology: Values, Compromises, and Ownership." *The Reference Shelf: Internet Abuses and Privacy Rights*. Ed. Betsy Maury. Ipswich: H.W. Wilson, 2017. 32-36. Print.

APA: Morris, B., G. Bullen, S. Alarcon, F. Lavalle, N. Meysenburg, & C. Ritzo. (2017). Open technology: Values, compromises, and ownership. In Betsy Maury (Ed.), *The Reference Shelf: Internet Abuses and Privacy Rights* (pp. 32-36). Ipswich, MA: H.W. Wilson. (Original work published 2016)

2
Net Neutrality and Government Surveillance

Credit: Andrew Harrer/Bloomberg via Getty Images

Ajit Pai, chairman of the Federal Communications Commission (FCC), speaks during a Senate hearing in Washington, D.C. on Wednesday, March 8, 2017. Pai is a Republican lawyer who was nominated yesterday by U.S. President Donald Trump to serve a second term at the FCC.

Cyberpolitics: Neutrality, Privacy, and Security

One of the most important topics emerging in digital technology is government reg-ulation, meaning the degree to which governments should be allowed to regulate the Internet and digital technology to protect citizens and foster innovative growth in American industry. Among the most pressing issues in this field are the debates over net neutrality, controversial warrantless surveillance of citizens, and concerns over the Trump administration's role in crafting security policy in coming years.

The Promise and Pitfalls of the Open Web

In 2002, Columbia University law professor Tim Wu coined the term "net neutral-ity," an idea that all traffic on the Web, wherever it originates, should be treated equally. This essentially means that corporations should not be allowed to favor data from one source over data from another. Wu, and supporters of net neutrality, be-lieve that the equal treatment of all Web traffic is essential to encourage small-scale innovation, in which individuals or start-up companies producing new products or services are able to reach consumers because their sites and services receive equal priority from ISPs (Internet Service Providers) like Sprint, Verizon, and AT&T. Ad-ditionally, supporters of neutrality argue that equal treatment of data protects free speech and the freedom of the press.

For those wondering what effect this might actually have, consider that an ISP like Verizon could slow down Web traffic for any customers using Verizon Internet attempting to access services, websites, or other products produced by companies that might compete with the ISP or any of their corporate partners. The ISP could also create "Internet fastlanes" that provide faster service to products or services supporting the company or its corporate. Internet service providers could then charge websites higher rates to access higher speeds for customers, thus creating a situation in which start-up Web businesses would be unable to compete with larger, established companies. Companies like Comcast also provide entertainment con-tent to subscribers, in the form of cable and streaming services, and so would have incentive to slow down traffic to competing providers, like PBS, Netflix, or Hulu.[1] In addition, some are concerned that companies aligned with political allies might restrict or promote traffic to favor certain political or ideological views, thus limiting the democratic nature of the Web and its utility in promoting free speech, expres-sion, and potential for open educational research.

Opposition to net neutrality comes primarily from the corporations who invest in Internet infrastructure, spending millions to run lines of cable and to produce devices, services, and websites for users to shop, browse, or communicate across the Web.[2] In 2005, Ed Whitacre, then CEO of AT&T, summarized the corporate position with the argument that AT&T built the Internet "pipes" and that the other companies wanted to use their pipes for free. Whitacre believed that his company should have the right to manage Web traffic in a way that benefitted his company financially. Opponents of net neutrality also argue that forcing companies to treat all traffic equally discourages corporations from investing in infrastructure and therefore reduces the likelihood of innovative new products and services.[3]

It is important to note that companies involved in providing utility services, like electricity, gas, water, and telephone services, are required to adhere to federal regulations put in place to protect consumers. This is because utilities are considered to be so essential to society that the regulation is needed to protect consumers from price gauging and other forms of corporate manipulation. The debate over net neutrality is essentially a debate about whether or not Internet access is important enough to daily life to be treated like a public utility and regulated in the public trust. The Federal Communications Commission (FCC) is the organization that regulates telephone communication and is responsible for enacting laws regarding the regulation of the Internet. When Internet was delivered through the telephone system, it was protected as a public utility under existing laws regarding telephone lines. In the 1990s, as consumers switched from telephone to cable internet, laws pertaining to telephones no longer applied. In 2005 after months of debate, the FCC adopted four net neutrality principles, elucidating the rights of Internet customers to access any lawful content, to run any lawful applications or services, to connect any device that does not harm the network, and the right to choose between competitive offers by other ISPs and services.[4]

In 2007, it was discovered that Comcast was restricting traffic to BitTorrent, a file-sharing site that offered access to music and movies and so competed with Comcast's media offerings. The FCC condemned the action, but did not penalize the company. Comedian John Oliver brought the issue to fans of his television program and told them to write to the FCC. The FCC then invited commentary from consumers, and received over 3.7 million comments, with an estimated 98-99 percent favoring regulations to preserve neutrality.[5] Surveys and studies found similar findings, such as a University of Delaware Center for Political Communication study in November 2014 that indicated more than 81 percent of people opposed allowing ISPs to charge websites to access faster speeds.[6] On February 26, 2015, the FCC approved an open Internet rule, under Title II of the Communications Act, essentially reclassifying broadband Internet as a telecom service and thus giving the organization greater power to regulate corporate behavior. Some of the most powerful ISP's filed suit against the FCC, but the US Court of Appeals for the DC Circuit rejected the challenge and upheld the FCC's Open Internet Order in 2016.

Concern about net neutrality has grown since the election of Donald Trump as Trump appointed Ajit Pai, an outspoken opponent of neutrality and advocate for corporate rights, to lead the FCC. In February 2017, the three-member panel voted 2-1 in favor of dismantling rules that forced large ISPs to disclose information about their fees, rates, and speeds to the FCC. This change essentially makes it impossible for the FCC to monitor the behavior of ISPs in regards to maintaining neutrality. Pai, who formerly worked as a lawyer for Verizon, believes that government regulation stifles innovation and violates the rights of companies and his appointment has been seen by some as evidence that the Trump administration will prioritize corporate profits ahead of consumer protections.[7] Net neutrality continues to enjoy majority support among the public and it therefore remains to be seen whether Pai and Trump's efforts to dismantle neutrality and consumer protections will result in a significant response from consumers.

Big Brother Is Watching

In 2013, former CIA agent Edward Snowden, working with investigative journalists, revealed that the National Security Agency (NSA) had been gathering tremendous amounts of data on American citizens taken from ISPs and cell phone companies. The documents revealed that the NSA is able to gain nearly unfettered access to e-mails, text messages, telephone calls, and a variety of other data from programs like Facebook, Gmail, and Outlook. The controversial program was made possible by changes to national security laws under the Patriot Act, and specifically alterations to Section 702 of the Foreign Intelligence Surveillance Act (FISA), which was amended to allow intelligence agencies to collect bulk data with the approval of a secret FISA court and therefore without any level of public transparency until the program was illegally revealed by Snowden's leaks.[8]

The "right to privacy" is one of the so-called "unenumerated" rights, defined as rights that are not explicitly guaranteed in the Constitution, but are derived from other rights that are specifically listed. Key court cases, beginning with *Meyer v. Nebraska* in 1923 have established legal precedent for a right to privacy under certain circumstances based on aspects of the First Amendment, guaranteeing privacy and freedom of beliefs, and the Fourth Amendment, which is particularly relevant for discussions of government surveillance as it guarantees freedom form unreasonable searches. Opponents of NSA/CIA surveillance argue that collecting bulk data from citizens, without sufficient judicial oversight and public transparency, constitutes an unreasonable search, which is prohibited by the Fourth Amendment. For a search to be reasonable, the agency must first prove, to an independent judiciary, that the agency has sufficient *reason* to warrant violating the individual's right to privacy.[9]

In March of 2017, the website WikiLeaks revealed a series of documents, called the "Vault 7" documents, allegedly detailing the Central Intelligence Agency (CIA)'s covert hacking programs that enabled the organization to hack into smartphones running iOS and Google's Android operating system. Allegedly, the CIA could use its programs to bypass encryption on Internet capable televisions as well as phones. The WikiLeaks data dump had been screened by the organization to remove names and identifying information contained within the documents and the organization refrained from releasing computer code for cyberweapons allegedly used in the program. One of the controversial tools revealed, code named "Weeping Angel" and developed in conjunction with British Intelligence, allegedly allows intelligence agents to use Samsung smart televisions to listen to conversations, even when the television is turned off.[10]

A 2015 study by Pew Research found that a majority (54 percent) of Americans disapproved of warrantless surveillance and a full 74 percent believed it was not necessary for Americans to sacrifice their privacy to enhance national security.[11] Since 2013, court cases have placed limits on the warrantless interception of use of digital data, including e-mails from confiscated cell phones, without first obtaining specific permission from the courts and demonstrating probable cause for searching the suspect's digital device(s). There have been no significant developments between 2013 and 2017 to limit NSA surveillance and the revelation, in early 2017, that AT&T was selling data from its users to police and the Federal Bureau of Investigation (FBI) reignited concerns about transparency and privacy. The surveillance issue is especially pressing in 2017, because Section 702 of FISA expires on December 31, 2017, and Congress will thereafter need to determine whether or not to renew or change the provision. Despite a majority (56-57 percent) of Republican voters disapproving of NSA surveillance, Trump supported the NSA program during his campaign and it is widely believed that his administration will favor national security over privacy rights.

The Age of the "Cyber" and the Human Factor

In a September 2016 presidential debate, Donald Trump said, "The security aspect of cyber is very, very tough. And maybe, it's hardly doable." Trump was ridiculed and mocked mercilessly for his use of the term "cyber," apparently a shorthand way of referring to "cybersecurity," which is generally defined as the various measures used to protect computers, data, and networks from infiltration or attack. The abbreviation "cyber" is not used in the tech community, or among the general public, and, to some, Trump's remarks seemed to indicate that the 69-year-old has little substantive understanding or familiarity with the world of the "cyber" and what it entailed.[12] These fears seemed to be affirmed during the first month of Trump's presidency as dozens of separate leaks emerged from the White House.

One widely reported leak described a telephone call that Trump reportedly placed at 3 a.m. to Lt. General Mike Flynn, a friend and former nominee for national security advisor, asking whether a strong US dollar (one with a high value relative to global currency) is actually good or bad for the US economy. It is a reasonable and complex question as a strong dollar benefits some facets of the population (buyers, primarily) while a weak dollar benefits others (exporters, primarily),[13] but the fact that Trump called Flynn, who has no economic expertise and reportedly told the president to consult an "economist," portrayed Trump as impulsive and ill-informed regarding how to understand complex issues. Another series of leaks led to General Mike Flynn's resignation after it was revealed that Flynn had engaged in inappropriate contact with the Russian government and failed to disclose details of his conversation with the president and vice president.[14] Coming at the heels of another Russian scandal—in which intelligence experts revealed that state-sponsored Russian hackers obtained confidential documents from the Democratic and Republican National Conventions and used their data to support Trump's campaign—Flynn's resignation raised serious concerns about the government's ability to securely handle data.

Trump announced an executive order on cybersecurity that was later postponed, though he criticized the media for reporting on the leaks, which he called "fake news," and promised that he would take steps to enhance security. Trump's plans for cybersecurity remain largely unknown and the leaks that plagued the administration during its debut were more suggestive of transitional chaos and internal mistrust than of the administration's inability to protect sensitive data.[15] In each instance so far noted, an individual has decided to make inside information from the White House public and this is not a technological problem, but a human one.

Micah L. Issitt

Works Used

Chavez, Danette. "New FCC Chairman Is Making Good on Threats to Dismantle Net Neutrality." *A.V. Club*, Onion Inc. Feb 24, 2017. Web. 25 Feb 2017.

Ehrenfreund, Max. "New Poll: Republicans and Democrats Both Overwhelmingly Support Net Neutrality." *The Washington Post*, Nash Holdings. Nov 12 2014. Web. 25 Feb 2017.

Gao, George. "What Americans Think about NSA Surveillance, National Security and Privacy." *Pew Research*, Pew Research Center. May 29 2015. Web. 25 Feb 2017.

Gross, Grant. "What to Expect from the Trump Administration on Cybersecurity." *CSO*, IDG News Service. Feb 22, 2017. Web. 25 Feb 2017.

Hu, Elise. "3.7 Million Comments Later, Here's Where Net Neutrality Stands." *NPR*, National Public Radio. Sep 17 2014. Web. 25 Feb 2017.

Lafrance, Adrienne. "Trump's Incoherent Ideas about 'the Cyber.'" *The Atlantic*, Atlantic Monthly Group. Sep 27, 2016. Web. 25 Feb 2017.

Madrigal, Alexis C. and Adrienne Lafrance. "Net Neutrality: A Guide to (and History of) a Contested Idea." *The Atlantic*, Atlantic Monthly Group. Apr 25, 2014. Web. 25 Feb 2017.

"Net Neutrality." *EFF*, Electronic Frontier Foundation. 2015. Web. 25 Feb 2017.

"Network Neutrality, Explained." *Vox*, Vox Media. May 21 2015. Web. 25 Feb 2017.

Reardon, Marguerite. "Net Neutrality: How We Got from There to Here." *CNET*, CBS Interactive, Inc. Feb 24, 2015. Web. 25 Feb 2017.

Sagar, Rahul. "Trump Says That Classified Leaks Are Devastating America: Here's the Real Issue with Secrets and Leaks." *The Washington Post*. Feb 27 2017. Web. 27 Feb 2017.

Shane, Scott, Mazzetti, Mark, and Matthew Rosenberg. "WikiLeaks Releases Trove of Alleged C.I.A. Hacking Documents." *The New York Times*, The New York Times Co. Mar 7 2017. Web. 7 Mar 2017.

Sottek, T.C. and Joshua Kopstein. "Everything You Need to Know about PRISM." *The Verge*, VOX Media. Jul 17, 2013. Web. 25 Feb 2017.

Stelter, Brian. "How Leaks and Investigative Journalists Led to Flynn's Resignation." *CNN*, Cable News Network. Feb 14 2017. Web. 26 Feb 2017.

"The Right to Privacy." *UMKC*, University of Missouri Kansas City. 2015. Web. 25 Feb 2017.

Thompson, Derek. "Trump's 3 a.m. Phone Call." *The Atlantic*, Atlantic Monthly Group. Feb 8 2017. Web. 25 Feb 2017.

Notes

1. Madrigal and Lafrance, "Net Neutrality: A Guide to (and History of) a Contested Idea."
2. "Net Neutrality," *EFF*.
3. "Network Neutrality, Explained," *Vox*.
4. Reardon, "Net Neutrality: How We Got from There to Here."
5. Hu, "3.7 Million Comments Later, Here's Where Net Neutrality Stands."
6. Ehenfreund, "New Poll: Republicans and Democrats both Overwhelmingly Support Net Neutrality."
7. Chavez, "New FCC Chairman Is Making Good on Threats to Dismantle Net Neutrality."
8. Sottek and Kopstein, "Everything You Need to Know about PRISM."
9. "The Right to Privacy," *UMKC*.
10. Shane, Mazetti, and Rosenberg, "WikiLeaks Releases Trove of Alleged C.I.A. Hacking Documents."
11. Gao, "What Americans Think about NSA Surveillance, National Security, and Privacy."
12. Lafrance, "Trump's Incoherent Ideas about 'the Cyber.'"
13. Thompson, "Trump's 3 a.m. Phone Call."
14. Stelter, "How Leaks and Investigative Journalists Led to Flynn's Resignation."
15. Sagar, "Trump Says That Classified Leaks Are Devastating America: Here's the Real Issue with Secrets and Leaks."

Follow Obama's Lead on Cybersecurity

By Robert Knake

The Cipher Brief, **January 22, 2017**

In the fall of 2008, a bipartisan group of cybersecurity experts delivered some sage advice to Barack Obama, set to become president in January: "Don't start over." That group, organized by the Center for Strategic and International Studies, made a strong and persuasive case that the Obama Administration needed to build from the progress that the Bush Administration had made. Specifically, the new team needed to follow through with the Comprehensive National Cyber Initiative (CNCI), which began the previous winter.

It was good advice. The tendency to discount the value of anything done in the previous administration runs high in Washington, particularly after a contentious election. Yet on cybersecurity, a rough bipartisan consensus has developed in the two decades since President Bill Clinton signed Presidential Decision Directive-63. That document outlined the public-private partnership that has been the bedrock of U.S. cyber policy for 20 years.

Over time, that approach has been tested and challenged, and no alternative has been found. Solutions that would take responsibility away from the private sector and make cybersecurity a government mission alone have been found wanting. Any effort to interpose government between the private sector and the network they rely on to reach customers and conduct business will be a cure worse than the disease. After a failed attempt at expanding regulation threatened to split apart that partnership, the Obama administration focused on finding ways to work with the private sector that were less adversarial.

President Donald Trump's new cyber team would be wise to pick up where the Obama team left off. Many who served in the Bush administration will see elements of programs they started alive and well today. Trump, a master at branding, can chalk up big wins on cybersecurity by simply rebranding many of the initiatives that the Obama administration began. If he can also convince Congress to start spending, he will be able to make progress in a host of areas where Obama could not.

The Trump team should start with a federal agency for cybersecurity. Taking a "not on my watch" attitude to the kind of breaches that occurred in the Obama administration, Trump should move quickly to finish implementation of the programs kicked off under the Cyber National Action Plan.

From *The Cipher Brief* January 22 © 2017

Getting Congress to sign off on the IT Modernization Fund to speed the replacement of antiquated and vulnerable federal computing systems should be an easy sell in a friendly Congress. The Trump team should also build out the vision for shared services and networks for small agencies, something that will take an infusion of cash up front but will reduce costs over the long term.

To better defend federal civilian agencies and assist with the private sector, Trump should work with his allies in Congress to create a civilian cybersecurity agency within the Department of Homeland Security as proposed by Chairman of the House Homeland Security Committee Mike McCaul (R-TX) earlier this month.

To better defend federal civilian agencies and assist with the private sector, Trump should work with his allies in Congress to create a civilian cybersecurity agency within the Department of Homeland Security as proposed by Chairman of the House Homeland Security Committee Mike McCaul (R-TX) earlier this month.

If the Trump team really wanted to stick its thumb in the eye of the outgoing administration it could say nasty things about how the Obama administration did not do enough for the 22 million Americans who had their personnel records stolen from the Office of Personnel Management. It could then launch a free program to provide the victims a trusted identity solution based on one of the many successful pilots to come out of the National Strategy for Trusted Identities in Cyberspace.

Working with the private sector, Trump needs to ensure that his cybersecurity team completes the work of enhancing the mechanisms for sharing cybersecurity information. Programs such as Enhanced Cybersecurity Services and Automated Indicator Sharing as well as the network of Information Sharing and Analysis Organizations require a real boost in time, attention and resources.

Internationally, the Trump team needs to keep the pressure on China to maintain its commitments to stop stealing intellectual property from U.S. companies. That task may be made more difficult if disputes over trade lead to a deteriorating relationship more generally. However, the playbook left by Obama's team for how to handle China—by threatening its great-power status and market access—will continue to work if applied judiciously.

The harder challenge will be how to handle Russia. The current honeymoon with Putin is unlikely to last as U.S. and Russian interests will inevitably clash. Anyone who thinks otherwise should recall that it was none other than Hillary Clinton who tried to orchestrate a "reset" with Russia in 2009.

No matter what his hopes are for better relations with the Kremlin, Trump needs to demonstrate that the United States will not tolerate interference in our election process. Even if there is no truth to the dossier released by *Buzzfeed*, Trump should fear that Russia or other countries might try and do to him what was done to Clinton in 2016. The Obama Administration has begun to implement a response to Russia's meddling in U.S. elections that Trump would be wise to continue and build on it.

The Trump team should no doubt develop their own strategy for securing the nation in cyberspace but, in doing so, they should build off of the many successes and lessons learned from Obama's eight years in grappling with these issues.

Print Citations

CMS: Knake, Robert. "Follow Obama's Lead on Cybersecurity." In *The Reference Shelf: Internet Abuses and Privacy Rights*, edited by Betsy Maury, 45-47. Ipswich, MA: H.W. Wilson, 2017.

MLA: Knake, Robert. "Follow Obama's Lead on Cybersecurity." *The Reference Shelf: Internet Abuses and Privacy Rights*. Ed. Betsy Maury. Ipswich: H.W. Wilson, 2017. 45-47. Print.

APA: Knake, R. (2017). Follow Obama's lead on cybersecurity. In Betsy Maury (Ed.), *The Reference Shelf: Internet Abuses and Privacy Rights* (pp. 45-47). Ipswich, MA: H.W. Wilson. (Original work published 2017)

Consumers Are Going to Love the End of Net Neutrality—at First

By Christopher Mims

The Wall Street Journal, **February 12, 2017**

One of the most basic principles of the internet is, depending on whom you ask, either in mortal peril or undergoing a rapid evolution.

Advocates for "net neutrality"—the principle that all data transmitted through the internet should be treated equally—argue it is needed for America to cultivate innovative web-focused startups. Critics say that alternatives to net neutrality could lead to innovation and competition in the country's communications infrastructure, where they are badly needed.

This is a battle of titans. Major internet companies—if not the hardware manufacturers that enable them—have vocally supported the prerogative of the Federal Communications Commission to enforce strict net neutrality, while most telecommunications companies have opposed regulation that preserves it. As President Donald Trump's FCC appointees appear set to target current net neutrality rules, companies on both sides may be taking a wait-and-see approach.

Microsoft Corp., Alphabet Inc.'s Google, Netflix Inc., Verizon Communications Inc. and Amazon.com Inc. declined to comment. AT&T Inc. didn't respond.

This debate is likely to persist, but in the near term it looks like advocates of net neutrality will be dealt a major blow. That's because consumers are going to love the Trump administration's potential first steps at dismantling net neutrality. It starts with an ever-widening array of services that are "zero-rated."

Zero-rating involves internet service providers giving customers free data services, such as unlimited video streaming. Big carriers including AT&T, Verizon, T-Mobile, Comcast and Sprint already offer some forms of zero-rated services. T-Mobile's Binge On program allows customers to stream Netflix, for instance, and AT&T lets subscribers stream its own DirecTV Now service, each without eating into their monthly data allowances.

The FCC appeared to be in the process of banning the practice in some instances, on the grounds that it could unfairly privilege carriers' own services. The agency had flagged the zero-rated services from both AT&T and Verizon for further review, says Commissioner Mignon Clyburn. Then on Feb. 3, Trump-appointed FCC Chairman Ajit Pai closed the agency's investigation of all zero-rating practices.

Critics of zero-rating say it presents consumers with a choice they can't refuse. Who would say no to video they can stream free or for a flat fee when the alternative is video

The Trump administration looks likely to change a foundational principle of America's tech ecosystem.

from competing services that may eat up all their expensive data? This is the reason zero-rating was banned in India, a country that viewed Facebook's attempts to give free data to its users as tantamount to colonialism.

Zero-rating resembles "paid prioritization," in which companies pay to have their data delivered first, a practice that is prohibited under the FCC's current rules. Net-neutrality proponents also argue that carriers shouldn't block any content or throttle its delivery speed. Whether they're promoting one service or blocking another, all these moves potentially hurt competition by favoring services in which the carrier has an interest.

The real risk isn't that deep-pocketed internet giants would be unable to pay for telecom play. Rather, it's that any would-be next big thing will instead be smothered in the cradle.

In Snapchat creator Snap Inc.'s IPO filing, the company listed the end of net neutrality as a potential threat to its long term prospects. If a company potentially valued at $25 billion is worried about having to pay carriers to be competitive with other zero-rated peers, imagine what these changes might mean to a startup at the seed stage, with only a few million in investment.

Headlines and news conferences aside, even most opponents of net neutrality don't believe we should do away with it completely.

Based on Mr. Pai's public statements and recent actions, the FCC chairman appears to oppose the Obama-era FCC judgment that the commission has the power to regulate internet service providers the way it regulates telecoms more broadly. Mr. Pai's office declined to make him available for comment.

Roslyn Layton, a visiting fellow at the American Enterprise Institute who studied net-neutrality practices in other countries, was part of Mr. Trump's transition team. She believes we need what she calls "soft net neutrality," where multiple stakeholders, including both big internet companies and carriers come together and make the rules together. (Our current reality actually represents some of this compromise already.)

In Ms. Layton's view, the rules should be set by Congress, not the FCC. This is a likely scenario. There are bills in the works from members of both the House and the Senate that would restore to the FCC some limited authority to regulate net neutrality, but would limit its powers.

Investors are proceeding with caution. "We're assuming that net neutrality in its wired and wireless fashion is gone," says Andy Weissman, a venture capitalist at Union Square Ventures who has been an outspoken defender of net neutrality. He's investing in Tucows, an internet service provider that is beginning to roll out fiber in some areas. Tucows will be "pure pipes" he says, which means in the future, it could differentiate from incumbent carriers by committing to equal treatment for all data.

The consumer impact is much more difficult to predict. The pace at which the U.S. turns out new internet startups could slow. With new cash flow opportunities, competition among internet service providers could increase, lowering prices.

What makes it so hard to calculate is that we've never really lived in a world without net neutrality. Even before the FCC's 2015 rules on net neutrality, fear of those regulations kept internet service providers in check, says Michael Cheah, general counsel at video streaming company VHX and its parent company Vimeo. Video-intense businesses such as his are most threatened, since they tend to require more bandwidth than other kinds of internet-dependent firms.

Doing away with the FCC's current power to enforce net neutrality is, he says, like lawmakers tossing away an umbrella just because it's not raining outside, forgetting that big carriers have every incentive to make it rain—for themselves.

Print Citations

CMS: Mims, Christopher. "Consumers Are Going to Love the End of Net Neutrality—at First." In *The Reference Shelf: Internet Abuses and Privacy Rights*, edited by Betsy Maury, 48-50. Ipswich, MA: H.W. Wilson, 2017.

MLA: Mims, Christopher. "Consumers Are Going to Love the End of Net Neutrality—at First." *The Reference Shelf: Internet Abuses and Privacy Rights*. Ed. Betsy Maury. Ipswich: H.W. Wilson, 2017. 48-50. Print.

APA: Mims, C. (2017). Consumers are going to love the end of net neutrality—at first. In Betsy Maury (Ed.), *The Reference Shelf: Internet Abuses and Privacy Rights* (pp. 48-50). Ipswich, MA: H.W. Wilson. (Original work published 2017)

Government's Privacy Rights Don't Exceed the Public's

By Noah Feldman
Bloomberg, July 25, 2016

When it comes to metadata, is turnabout fair play? The New Jersey Supreme Court will decide that question in a fiendishly clever case brought by a libertarian who is demanding the e-mail logs of town officials under the state's Open Public Records Act.

What makes the case so piquant is that, as Edward Snowden's leaks revealed, the federal government engaged in bulk metadata collection under a questionable interpretation of the Foreign Intelligence Surveillance Act. The authorization relied on for the data collection has since expired, but the legal principle remains. The New Jersey lawsuit in effect asks: if metadata isn't that private, why not give the public access to the government's records of who contacted whom, and when?

As if on cue, lawyers representing local New Jersey officials gave an answer that echoes the concerns that privacy advocates have been raising for years about metadata: they said you could figure out so much information from metadata that it would compromise confidentiality. "There is a great deal of concern about citizens finding out who the chiefs of police are communicating with, and with what frequency," the lawyers told reporters. "A list of all the people a chief of police is communicating with could compromise investigations and reveal the identities of victims of crimes and witnesses while an investigation is unfolding."

That's correct, of course—and it's also the point of the lawsuit. The case was brought by John Paff, chairman of the Open Government Advocacy Project of the New Jersey Libertarian Party. His position is being supported by the New Jersey American Civil Liberties Union as well as the Electronic Frontier Foundation, an important privacy watchdog.

In 2013, Paff requested a log of e-mails—sender, recipient, date and subject—made by the chief of police and town clerk of Galloway Township for a two-week period in June of that year. Paff says he doesn't remember exactly why he chose that period, but the information-technology specialist in charge of the records testified that the period corresponded to an internal investigation by the police chief.

A local trial court ordered the town to release the records after the IT person testified that he could generate the record in two or three minutes. The judge not only reasoned that the material was covered by the state's open records law, he

> **Properly analyzed, metadata reveals a network or web of relationships. Frequency and duration of messages deepen the picture. The actual content of what people have to say becomes almost unimportant, because it can be inferred from the circumstances and the information.**

also gave short shrift to concerns about compromising the confidentiality of investigations, noting that the request would provide "access to no more than the sender/receiver/date/time of emails" on the dates requested.

A state appellate court reversed. Its reasoning was highly formalistic. It held that because the public records act only requires disclosure of existing records, and there was no existing metadata list, there was no obligation to disclose it. Given that the e-mails exist and are preserved, and that the metadata can be generated electronically in seconds, the argument was pretty clearly intended to solve the confidentiality problem.

The court admitted that public officials could redact the metadata to avoid disclosing any confidential information. But it said that the redaction process would be too burdensome.

The reality in the information age is that disclosing metadata can give a smart interpreter almost all the information needed to figure out what's being said. That's exactly why the National Security Agency was so eager to gather metadata in the first place. Properly analyzed, metadata reveals a network or web of relationships.

Frequency and duration of messages deepen the picture. The actual content of what people have to say becomes almost unimportant, because it can be inferred from the circumstances and the information.

For these reasons, the public almost certainly shouldn't be able to get access to the metadata of police communications. The patterns and networks of police communication would be of tremendous use to enterprising criminals. Redaction might appear to solve the problem of a particular individual's privacy interests. But that's not the real problem with mass disclosure of police metadata. The true danger lies in compromising the effectiveness of law enforcement.

In other words, the police have something like the same privacy interests in their communications metadata that you and I should have in ours.

Although the U.S. Court of Appeals for the Second Circuit vindicated Snowden in 2015 by holding that the metadata collection program was unlawful in going beyond statutory authorization, courts have been slow to recognize a fundamental privacy interest in metadata. The New Jersey case gives the state Supreme Court a chance to send the message that metadata deserves to be private.

What would be perverse would be to give government communications greater protection than those we should rightfully enjoy as individuals. The constitutional right to privacy under the Fourth Amendment applies to "the people," not the government.

Print Citations

CMS: Feldman, Noah. "Government's Privacy Rights Don't Exceed the Public's." In *The Reference Shelf: Internet Abuses and Privacy Rights*, edited by Betsy Maury, 51-53. Ipswich, MA: H.W. Wilson, 2017.

MLA: Feldman, Noah. "Government's Privacy Rights Don't Exceed the Public's." *The Reference Shelf: Internet Abuses and Privacy Rights*. Ed. Betsy Maury. Ipswich: H.W. Wilson, 2017. 51-53. Print.

APA: Feldman, N. (2017). Government's privacy rights don't exceed the public's. In Betsy Maury (Ed.), *The Reference Shelf: Internet Abuses and Privacy Rights* (pp. 51-53). Ipswich, MA: H.W. Wilson. (Original work published 2016)

Documents Show AT&T Secretly Sells Customer Data to Law Enforcement

By Nicky Woolf
The Guardian, October 25, 2016

Telecommunications giant AT&T is selling access to customer data to local law enforcement in secret, new documents released on Monday reveal.

The program, called Hemisphere, was previously known only as a "partnership" between the company and the US Drug Enforcement Agency (DEA) for the purposes of counter-narcotics operations.

It accesses the trove of telephone metadata available to AT&T, who controls a large proportion of America's landline and cellphone infrastructure. Unlike other providers, who delete their stored metadata after a certain time, AT&T keeps information like call time, duration, and even location data on file for years, with records dating back to 2008.

But according to internal company documents revealed Monday by the *Daily Beast*, Hemisphere is being sold to local police departments and used to investigate everything from murder to Medicaid fraud, costing US taxpayers millions of dollars every year even while riding roughshod over privacy concerns.

Access to Hemisphere costs local police between $100,000 and more than $1m a year, the documents reveal, and its use requires just an administrative subpoena—a much lower judicial bar than a search warrant because it does not need to be issued by a judge.

Until Monday, Hemisphere's use was kept secret from the public—and even from judges, defense attorneys and lawmakers—by an agreement between law enforcement and AT&T which means police must not risk disclosing its use in public or even in court.

This means that police take leads from Hemisphere, but then construct cases around that lead so that the program can be protected from scrutiny, a practice known as "parallel construction," according to the Beast.

The revelations come as AT&T prepares for its controversial $85bn acquisition of Time Warner, a deal which has been widely attacked as being bad for consumers, with both presidential candidates speaking out against the merger.

Contacted for comment, Fletcher Cook, a spokesperson for AT&T, sent the Guardian the same statement they provided the Beast: Like other communications companies, if a government agency seeks customer call records through a subpoena, court order or other mandatory legal process, we are required by law to provide this non- content information, such as the phone numbers and the date and time of calls. Asked for further details, Cook did not respond.

The secrecy of Hemisphere echoes that which surrounds the use of the sophisticated surveillance devices known as Stingrays, or cell-site simulators, which are suitcase-sized devices which work by pretending to be cellphone towers in order to strip metadata and content from phones which connect to them.

> **The secrecy of Hemisphere echoes that which surrounds the use of the sophisticated surveillance devices known as Stingrays, or cell-site simulators, which are suitcase-sized devices which work by pretending to be cellphone towers in order to strip metadata and content from phones which connect to them.**

In 2015, a *Guardian* investigation revealed that police departments had to sign a non-disclosure agreement with the FBI in order to use Stingray devices which said that police must hide the program's use from defense lawyers and the public, even mandating that they abandon a case if they fear the program's use might be revealed in court.

Nate Wessler, a staff attorney with the American Civil Liberties Union's speech, privacy and technology project, said that, as with the Stingray agreement, "what is so disturbing about these documents is the lengths to which the company and law enforcement have gone to keep this secret."

"The longer these kind of surveillance programs are kept from the public, the harder it is to ensure there are appropriate checks and balances in place," Wessler said.

For Wessler, an instructive part of what the documents reveal is that while the program was apparently instigated as part of the war on drugs, "this data is being used for run-of-the-mill criminal investigation at a local level."

"Once law enforcement has access to this kind of data it becomes a tremendously attractive tool for everything they do."

Print Citations

CMS: Woolf, Nicky. "Documents Show AT&T Secretly Sells Customer Data to Law Enforcement." In *The Reference Shelf: Internet Abuses and Privacy Rights*, edited by Betsy Maury, 54-56. Ipswich, MA: H.W. Wilson, 2017.

MLA: Woolf, Nicky. "Documents Show AT&T Secretly Sells Customer Data to Law Enforcement." *The Reference Shelf: Internet Abuses and Privacy Rights*. Ed. Betsy Maury. Ipswich: H.W. Wilson, 2017. 54-56. Print.

APA: Woolf, N. (2017). Documents show AT&T secretly sells customer data to law enforcement. In Betsy Maury (Ed.), *The Reference Shelf: Internet Abuses and Privacy Rights* (pp. 54-56). Ipswich, MA: H.W. Wilson. (Original work published 2016)

Concerns Loom Over a Data-Sharing Pact to Protect Privacy of Europeans

By Natalia Drozdiak and Sam Schechner

The Wall Street Journal, **February 8, 2017**

The ability of companies to transfer everything from payroll files to social media posts to the U.S. from Europe could be in jeopardy, tech executives and European officials worry, should the Trump administration consider removing existing privacy protections for Europeans.

Strict privacy laws in the European Union allow companies to store personal information about Europeans on American soil only if the companies commit to guaranteeing European levels of privacy protection.

But one of the main legal mechanisms to do so, agreed between the U.S. and EU last year and used by almost 2,000 firms, is underpinned legally by written assurances and a presidential directive enacted under former President Barack Obama's administration—much of which could be undone with the stroke of a pen by President Donald Trump.

"We are watching with some measure of anxiety," said a senior staffer at one U.S. tech firm that uses the mechanism, called Privacy Shield.

So far, the Trump administration has given no indication that it aims to exit from the Privacy Shield agreement. But some worry that Mr. Trump's pledges to toughen the country's approach to national security, specifically in contrast with Europe, could conflict with the framework's assurances to protect Europeans against indiscriminate mass surveillance.

The White House didn't respond to a request for comment.

In the absence of clear guidance from the White House, the fragile foundation of the agreement is creating new uncertainty for businesses, some executives say. Any interruption to EU-U.S. data flows would upend billions of dollars of business that traffics personal information, from online advertising to cloud computing, executives say.

More than 1,700 firms use Privacy Shield, including Alphabet Inc.'s Google, Microsoft Corp. and many other smaller companies. All types of companies transfer personal information to the U.S. for business reasons, but free data flows are particularly important for tech companies, which typically handle large sets of data.

Some tech executives say they think the Trump administration's pro-business tilt will lead it to support Privacy Shield, because it helps American firms do business in the EU. "If there is a political will to allow businesses on both sides of the Atlantic to exchange data, then they will figure out a way to do that," a U.S. tech executive said.

Tech firms, officials say, don't know how President Trump will deal with the Privacy Shield agreement.

But concerns rose among tech executives and European officials in late January after Mr. Trump signed an executive order that excludes individuals who are not U.S. citizens or lawful permanent residents from the protections of the U.S.'s Privacy Act. EU officials and tech lawyers quickly said the order wouldn't affect Privacy Shield because the agreement is based on other assurances made by the Obama administration, not the Privacy Act.

Mr. Trump's order nevertheless raised concerns because of its explicit reduction of some privacy protections for Europeans and other foreigners. Jennifer Granick, director of civil liberties at the Stanford Center for Internet and Society, at a Brussels conference last month called the executive order "a statement of intention that's at odds with what's necessary for data flows to take place."

Privacy Shield went into effect last year, after the EU's top court overturned a previous framework in 2015 because of concerns over mass surveillance by U.S. intelligence agencies. At least two lawsuits have already been filed against the new deal on similar grounds.

A crucial piece of Privacy Shield depends on Mr. Obama's presidential policy directive 28, which mandates that U.S. intelligence agencies, when they collect personal information, must recognize that all individuals have a right to privacy, regardless of their nationality or where they reside.

While there is no indication Mr. Trump intends to change that directive, some tech executives and lawyers said they were worried the administration's "America First" approach to security could lead in that direction. Overturning directive 28 "would be a disaster," said one EU official. "There would be no other solution than to suspend the Privacy Shield."

EU Justice Commissioner Vera Jourova said at a recent press conference that the EU is "carefully estimating and assessing whether we can be absolutely sure whether the U.S. [under the Trump administration] will continue what we started." Ms. Jourova plans to visit the U.S. in the spring to discuss the data-transfer agreement.

Companies have other legal mechanisms apart from Privacy Shield that they can use to avoid legal problems when sending data to U.S. data centers. Those methods, such as using model contractual language that is preapproved by the EU, are more cumbersome.

And beginning Tuesday, that preapproved language is the subject of a challenge in an Irish court, which is deciding whether to ask the EU's top court to rule on their legality. That mechanism is likely to face a stiffer challenge if there are policy shifts to reduce the protection of Europeans from surveillance in the U.S., lawyers say.

—John D. McKinnon in Washington, D.C., contributed to this article.

Print Citations

CMS: Drozdiak, Natalia, and Sam Schechner. "Concerns Loom Over a Data-Sharing Pact to Protect Privacy of Europeans." In *The Reference Shelf: Internet Abuses and Privacy Rights*, edited by Betsy Maury, 57-59. Ipswich, MA: H.W. Wilson, 2017.

MLA: Drozdiak, Natalia, and Sam Schechner. "Concerns Loom Over a Data-Sharing Pact to Protect Privacy of Europeans." *The Reference Shelf: Internet Abuses and Privacy Rights*. Ed. Betsy Maury. Ipswich: H.W. Wilson, 2017 57-59. Print.

APA: Drozdiak, N., & S. Schechner. (2017). Concerns loom over a data-sharing pact to protect privacy of Europeans. In Betsy Maury (Ed.), *The Reference Shelf: Internet Abuses and Privacy Rights* (pp. 57-59). Ipswich, MA: H.W. Wilson. (Original work published 2017)

Trump's FCC Pick Quickly Targets Net Neutrality Rules

By Cecelia Kang
The New York Times, February 5, 2017

In his first days as President Trump's pick to lead the Federal Communications Commission, Ajit Pai has aggressively moved to roll back consumer protection regulations created during the Obama presidency.

Mr. Pai took a first swipe at net neutrality rules designed to ensure equal access to content on the internet. He stopped nine companies from providing discounted high-speed internet service to low-income individuals. He withdrew an effort to keep prison phone rates down, and he scrapped a proposal to break open the cable box market.

In total, as the chairman of the F.C.C., Mr. Pai released about a dozen actions in the last week, many buried in the agency's website and not publicly announced, stunning consumer advocacy groups and telecom analysts. They said Mr. Pai's message was clear: The F.C.C., an independent agency, will mirror the Trump administration's rapid unwinding of government regulations that businesses fought against during the Obama administration.

"With these strong-arm tactics, Chairman Pai is showing his true stripes," said Matt Wood, the policy director at the consumer group Free Press. "The public wants an F.C.C. that helps people," he added. "Instead, it got one that does favors for the powerful corporations that its chairman used to work for."

Mr. Pai, a former lawyer for Verizon, was elevated by Mr. Trump to the position of chairman after serving as a minority Republican member for the past three years. Known for being a stickler on conservative interpretations of telecommunications law and the limits of the F.C.C.'s authority, Mr. Pai said he was trying to wipe the slate clean.

He noted that his predecessor, Tom Wheeler, had rammed through a series of actions right after the presidential election. Many of those efforts, Mr. Pai argued, went beyond the agency's legal authority.

"These last-minute actions, which did not enjoy the support of the majority of commissioners at the time they were taken, should not bind us going forward," Mr. Pai said in a statement released Friday. "Accordingly, they are being revoked."

The efforts portend great changes at the federal agency at the center of the convergence of media, telecommunications and the internet. The biggest target will be net neutrality, a rule created in 2015 that prevents internet service providers from blocking or discriminating against internet traffic. The rule, which was created alongside a decision to categorize broadband like a utility, was the tech centerpiece of the Obama administration.

On Friday, the F.C.C. took its first steps to pull back those rules, analysts said. Mr. Pai closed an investigation into zero-rating practices of the wireless providers T-Mobile, AT&T and Verizon. Zero-rating is the offering of free streaming and other downloads that do not count against limits on the amount of data a consumer can download.

If a provider like AT&T offers free streaming of its DirecTV programs, does that violate net neutrality rules because it could put competing video services at a disadvantage? Under its previous leadership, the F.C.C. said in a report that it saw some evidence that made it concerned. But Mr. Pai said after closing the investigations into wireless carriers that zero-rating was popular among consumers, particularly low-income households.

"The speed of the ruling and the chairman's tone are very encouraging for internet service providers," said Paul Gallant, an analyst at Cowen. "I think it's a down payment on net neutrality, with much more to follow."

Last week, Mr. Pai said he disagreed with the move two years ago to declare broadband a utility. The reclassification of broadband into a service akin to telephones and electricity provided the legal foundation for net neutrality rules.

Mr. Pai said he had not decided how he would approach the overhaul of broadband classification and net neutrality rules, but he faces legal hurdles. A federal court upheld the rules last year, and the commission could end up in a lengthy legal battle if he tries to scrap the rules.

Mr. Pai will have the help of powerful members of Congress who have promised to attack the classification of broadband as a utility-like service. And he is popular among Republican leaders, including the Senate's majority leader, Mitch McConnell, who with other members viewed Mr. Pai as a loyal voice of dissent during the Obama years. Mr. Pai,

> **If a provider like AT&T offers free streaming of its DirecTV programs, does that violate net neutrality rules because it could put competing video services at a disadvantage?**

44, the child of immigrants from India who settled in Kansas, is a fresh face for the Republican Party.

Congress could introduce legislation that limits the agency's ability to regulate broadband providers and enforce net neutrality rules. Also under attack are privacy rules for broadband providers. "The agency has strayed from its core mission," said Marsha Blackburn, a Republican representative from Tennessee who oversees a telecommunications and tech subcommittee. She has called for a hearing within two weeks on the F.C.C. agenda under the new administration.

Democrats in Congress said they would fight legislation that waters down net neutrality rules. They said Mr. Pai, described as a straight-A student of telecom law, would be a tough adversary, and they face great opposition from Republicans who have promised to prioritize the overturning of net neutrality rules. "The key here is that it's already been tested in the courts and the court upheld this," said Representative Anna G. Eshoo, Democrat of California. "Ajit Pai is intelligent and genial, but he is not on the side of consumers and the public interest."

Most troubling to consumer advocates was the secrecy around Mr. Pai's early actions. That included a decision to rescind the permissions of nine broadband providers to participate in a federal subsidy plan for low-income consumers. None of the providers currently serve low-income consumers, but Mr. Pai's comments could foreshadow a shake-up of the Lifeline low-income subsidy program.

On Monday, the F.C.C. is scheduled to appear before a federal judge to defend its push to curb extraordinarily expensive phone call prices from prison. But it told a judge a few days ago that Mr. Pai disagreed with many aspects of the case.

Mignon Clyburn, the sole Democrat of the three sitting members of the F.C.C., warned that the actions would directly harm consumers. "Rather than working to close the digital divide, this action widens the gap," Ms. Clyburn said.

Print Citations

CMS: Kang, Cecelia. "Trump's F.C.C. Pick Quickly Targets Net Neutrality Rules." In *The Reference Shelf: Internet Abuses and Privacy Rights*, edited by Betsy Maury, 60-62. Ipswich, MA: H.W. Wilson, 2017.

MLA: Kang, Cecelia. "Trump's F.C.C. Pick Quickly Targets Net Neutrality Rules." *The Reference Shelf: Internet Abuses and Privacy* Ed. Betsy Maury. Ipswich: H.W. Wilson, 2017. 60-62. Print.

APA: Kang, C. (2017). Trump's F.C.C. pick quickly targets net neutrality rules. In Betsy Maury (Ed.), *The Reference Shelf: Internet Abuses and Privacy Rights* (pp. 60-62). Ipswich, MA: H.W. Wilson. (Original work published 2017)

Now It's Much Easier for Government Agencies to Get NSA Surveillance Data

By Robyn Greene
Slate, January 17, 2017

Just days before Donald Trump takes office, the director of national intelligence and attorney general have issued new procedures that undermine Americans' right to privacy and Fourth Amendment constitutional protections. These procedures will allow the NSA to share with other intelligence agencies "raw intelligence" that it collects while conducting mass surveillance under Executive Order 12333, which has been in effect since 1981. Raw intelligence is just what it sounds like—emails and phone calls and anything else that the NSA collects during its daily surveillance. These records aren't minimized or redacted to mask identifying information.

The previous procedures allowed for the NSA to share this information with other intelligence agencies, but only after it had been minimized to protect individuals' privacy, and only if it was pertinent to their mission.

These new, more lax procedures are extremely troubling because thanks to legal loopholes, EO 12333 is used to scoop up billions of communications around the world every day, including those of Americans, without a warrant or any judicial—or even congressional— oversight. The idea behind EO 12333 was that it governs NSA collection of purely foreign communications. That collection didn't need judicial or congressional oversight because if all the people in those communications were abroad, they weren't entitled to the protections of our laws.

That all made sense when President Reagan signed the order, but today, the NSA uses EO 12333 to tap the cables that connect the internet across the world. An email I send from my office to a colleague just one floor down could travel between servers in Japan and Brazil before getting to its destination, and could get picked up by the NSA along the way as a "foreign communication." Accordingly, the NSA has a virtually unchecked authority to warrantlessly collect Americans' communications.

All of this is troubling in and of itself, but it becomes even more concerning in light of the new procedures that allow the NSA to share the information it collects with other intelligence agencies, without first trying to screen out Americans' communications or identifying information. The procedures say that a high-level official at an agency like the FBI could make an application to the NSA for the communications that state the specific "authorized foreign intelligence or counter-intelligence missions that are the basis for the request."

This may seem reasonable, until you realize that "foreign intelligence" is really a catchall that can include most anything happening abroad. EO 12333 defines it as "information relating to the capabilities, intentions and activities of foreign powers, organizations or persons." Don't let the "organizations or persons" part of that definition hide behind the more important-seeming term "foreign powers."

That definition means that "foreign intelligence" includes communications about political and human rights activities, like if you send an email as part of an Amnesty International campaign to free a political prisoner. It can include anything impacting the economy—even a mom-and-pop coffee shop's email about a business trip to Europe to procure the finest French chocolate for their cookies. It can even be stretched to include social plans you make for your vacation abroad.

Accordingly, the NSA has a virtually unchecked authority to warrantlessly collect Americans' communications.

Now, is the FBI likely to ask to see the chocolate emails when it requests raw foreign intelligence information under these procedures? No. But despite some process-oriented protections built into the procedures, with no external oversight or transparency, it would be hard to know if abuse did happen.

Even without abuse, these procedures can serve as yet another work-around for the warrant requirement of our Constitution. If the communications the agency accesses only involve Americans, the procedures require that they be destroyed unless they have foreign intelligence or counterintelligence value. But they can be kept and disseminated if the agency thinks they include evidence of a crime. In that case, the communications could be shared, for example, with the Department of Justice or the FBI and used in a criminal investigation that would have otherwise required a warrant from a judge to obtain the same information.

While it's a big step forward in transparency that these procedures were made public in the first place, we still won't know enough information about how much information will get shared, how often, and when it will be used for non-foreign intelligence investigations or prosecutions. We may simply never know the full impact these new procedures will have on our privacy.

Print Citations

CMS: Green, Robyn. "Now It's Much Easier for Government Agencies to Get NSA Surveillance Data." In *The Reference Shelf: Internet Abuses and Privacy Rights*, edited by Betsy Maury, 63-65. Ipswich, MA: H.W. Wilson, 2017.

MLA: Green, Robyn. "Now It's Much Easier for Government Agencies to Get NSA Surveillance Data." *The Reference Shelf: Internet Abuses and Privacy Rights*. Ed. Betsy Maury. Ipswich: H.W. Wilson, 2017. 63-65. Print.

APA: Green, R. (2017). Now it's much easier for government agencies to get NSA surveillance data. In Betsy Maury (Ed.), *The Reference Shelf: Internet Abuses and Privacy Rights* (pp. 63-65). Ipswich, MA: H.W. Wilson. (Original work published 2017)

The Risks of Sending Secret Messages in the White House

By Kaveh Waddell

The Atlantic, **February 15, 2017**

By some accounts, the deluge of leaks detailing the hurdles and setbacks that have troubled the first weeks of the Trump administration have provoked panic among its highest ranks—and prompted top officials to try to identify the leaky staffers. President Trump has tweeted his dismay at the leaks several times, once calling them "illegal." That's why, according to a report in the *Washington Post*, some White House employees have turned to technology to cover their tracks.

The app of choice: Confide, a platform that encrypts messages end-to-end, so that they can only be seen by the sender and the recipient, and deletes every trace of a message as soon as it's read. (Axios reported last week that Confide has also been taken up in larger Republican circles looking to avoid the fate of Democrats who had their emails hung out to dry by WikiLeaks.)

There are two problems with using Confide to chat with your colleagues in the White House. One has to do with digital security; the other with the law of the land.

The legal question is more straightforward than the technological one. The law that governs the preservation of presidential records requires the president and his or her staff to retain copies of all sorts of documents, including electronic correspondence. If the White House wants to dispose of a record, it needs to ask permission from the U.S. Archivist first—and notify Congress, which will have 60 days to review the proposal.

"There are very clear rules regarding the retention and deletion of records under the Presidential Records Act," said Adam Marshall, an attorney at the Reporters Committee for Freedom of the Press. "The use of messaging apps that automatically delete communications by persons subject to the PRA is incredibly troubling."

The White House was not available to comment on its policies for retaining Confide messages.

Even if White House staffers were allowed to delete traces of their communication, however, Confide may not be the most secure app to use for doing so. Jonathan Zdziarski, a security researcher who specializes in digital forensics, took a brief look at the app's security features on Tuesday. He found that the app uses a combination of open-source encryption methods and some unvetted techniques of its own creation, leaving questions about their security. Some of the app's other functions are unusual—but not necessarily problematic.

"The application doesn't smell fully kosher, but at least it uses some standard encryption routines, which many other applications fail to do," Zdziarski wrote. "I did not see any obvious red flags in terms of forensics artifacts or other overtly nefarious behavior, but this was a quick once-over."

He recommended that the White House submit the app to a full cryptographic review before allowing staffers to use it. "On the whole, it may be fine for personal conversation, but I would recommend a more proven technology, such as Signal, if I were to have my pick of the litter," he wrote.

I asked one of Confide's co-founders, Jon Brod, whether the app had been vetted by an independent security researcher, but didn't get an answer. Brod did say that he was happy to hear that staffers were making use of his app. "We think it makes perfect sense, regardless of which side of the aisle they're on," he said, given the sensitive nature of their work.

Brod said it's up to users to play by any applicable rules that govern communication in their workplace. "We expect people to use Confide in a way that complies with any regulation that may be relevant to their particular situation, just like they would with other communication platforms," he said.

Confide isn't the first secure-communications app to find popularity among politicians and their aides. Signal, the gold standard of encrypted messaging and calling, is used by staffers who work for President Trump, Barack Obama, Hillary Clinton, New York Governor Andrew Cuomo, and New York City Mayor Bill de Blasio. But now the app has recently added optional features that allow messages to expire, which could bring up the same records-retention issues as Confide.

Communication apps with disappearing text could run afoul of presidential records laws—and might not be as secure as they seem.

The popularity of encrypted communications apps has caught the attention of Congress. This week, two members of the House Committee on Science, Space, and Technology—including its chairman—sent a letter to the inspector general of the Environmental Protection Agency, responding to reports that some of its employees were using encrypted-communication apps to discuss how they'd respond to certain actions from the Trump Administration. In the letter, the representatives wrote that the practice may "run afoul of federal record-keeping requirements" and shield important information from Freedom of Information Act requests or congressional inquiries.

Since the EPA is a federal agency, its records are subject to the Federal Records Act, not the Presidential Records Act. But the requirements are essentially the same.

A document published by the National Archives and Records Administration in 2015 clarifies guidance for how to manage electronic records other than email: Google chat, Skype, iMessage and SMS, Twitter direct messages, and Slack, to name a few. According to the document, these messages are federal records, and must be treated as such. Depending on the nature of the messages, they may need to be kept either temporarily or permanently. That includes official business conducted over personal accounts, the document says.

Consternation inside the government over disappearing messages—at the EPA, the White House, or elsewhere—seem motivated mostly by politics. The Republican-led Science, Space, and Technology Committee is wary of rebellious federal workers, and top White House officials hope to crack down on damaging leaks. But if it continues to spread, disappearing-message apps could become a black hole that sucks away important records that should, by law, be preserved.

Print Citations

CMS: Waddell, Kaveh. "The Risks of Sending Secret Messages in the White House." In *The Reference Shelf: Internet Abuses and Privacy Rights*, edited by Betsy Maury, 66-68. Ipswich, MA: H.W. Wilson, 2017.

MLA: Waddell, Kaveh. "The Risks of Sending Secret Messages in the White House." *The Reference Shelf: Internet Abuses and Privacy Rights*. Ed. Betsy Maury. Ipswich: H.W. Wilson, 2017. 66-68. Print.

APA: Waddell, K. (2017). The risks of sending secret messages in the White House. In Betsy Maury (Ed.), *The Reference Shelf: Internet Abuses and Privacy Rights* (pp. 66-68). Ipswich, MA: H.W. Wilson. (Original work published 2017)

3
New Challenges to Privacy

Credit: David Becker/Getty Images

An Amazon Echo device is displayed at the Ford booth at CES 2017 at the Las Vegas Convention Center on January 5, 2017 in Las Vegas, Nevada. Ford is incorporating the voice operating device into its vehicles.

Cyberthreats of Today and Tomorrow

Each year, tech analysts and rights watch dogs identify emerging cyberthreats that represent new challenges to digital privacy and security. Privacy threats can emerge from a variety of different domains, whether as a result of hackers and cybercriminals profiting from personal data, corporations using personal information for targeted marketing campaigns, or governments surveilling citizens in an effort to promote national security. In each case, those concerned about their digital privacy must realize that the current state of Internet regulation means that the freedom and convenience of the Web essentially come at the expense of at least some degree of personal privacy. This may change as consumers become more aware, demanding that governments and corporations do more to protect their privacy, but, in 2017, this fundamental sacrifice is the price that consumers pay for the freedom of digital tech. With new threats emerging every year, and no clear resolution in sight of debates over the ownership of digital data, the only recourse for the digital citizen is to stay abreast of current trends, to know the current dangers and those on the horizon, and to take part in the debate, voicing their concerns to politicians and corporations whose activities will define the future of digital privacy.

Zombies and Bots

From the birth of the digital age to 2017, one of the biggest threats to digital security and privacy has come in the form of automated programs known as Web robots or bots. Bots are software programs that perform automatic functions within a computer system. A 2017 article in the *Atlantic* describes bots at the "worker bees" of the Internet, performing a variety of benign actions that fuel much of the work of digital devices. Research shows that 52 percent of all Web activity consists of automated bot traffic. [1] Browsing the Web, for instance, depends on "Web spidering," which sends out bots to ping websites and collects information for search results. One of the most active types of helperbots is the feed fetcher bot, which is used to refresh a person's feed on sites like Facebook and Twitter. The Facebook feed fetcher alone accounted for more than 4 percent of Web traffic in 2016 and feed fetcher bots constituted 12 percent of all Web traffic in that same year.

Studies also indicate that as much as 29 percent of Web traffic consists of malicious bots, inadvertently installed on computer systems. There are many, many types of malicious bots that perform a variety of unwanted activities once inadvertently installed. Spam bots, for instance, hijack e-mail programs to send out mass blasts of spam mail to the computer-owners' contacts. Cybercriminals known as "botherders" use various types of bots to invade the privacy and steal information from computer users for fun or profit. Some bots install spyware, which is a type of program that gives another user access an infected computer. Using spyware, a cybercriminal can secretly watch another user browse the Web or can even access built-in cameras and microphones, allowing them to actively watch or listen to a computer user from their own computer. Bots can also be used to steal personal information, such as bank data, medical information, and credit card numbers. This information can then be sold through clandestine Web markets (known as the Dark Web) to buyers involved in credit card theft, identity theft, or other types of information brokering.

In many cases, bots and botherders target companies with their activities. Bots involved in "clickfraud," for instance, "click" on Web advertisements automatically, thus allowing individuals using bots to upcharge advertisers seeking to advertise on their sites.[2] A common method of attacking a website or corporation is to engage in a Distributed Denial of Service or DDoS attack uses bots to disable a site by overwhelming the site's servers with fake traffic. The cybercriminals then attempt to extort payment from the site's owners in return for returning control of the site.[3] In 2016, bots involved in DDoS attacks accounted for as much as 24 percent of total Web traffic. While attacks on corporations are more lucrative and thus more common than attacks against individual computer users, violating corporate security also leaves the company's users, subscribers, or customers vulnerable to privacy violations.

One increasingly common type of bot attack uses bots to secretly take over another user's computer, causing the computer to perform activities that may go unnoticed by the user for months, years, or indefinitely. Computers secretly taken over by bots can then send bot programs out to other users, creating networks of controlled computers, known as "zombie networks" or "botnets." Unknowingly, a user's computer has become part of a botherder's malicious network, distributing malware, viruses, or other programs to other computers attached to the same network. The botherder then benefits from the collective power of the many enslaved computers infected by his or her bots.

One way in which bot makers have been attempting to profit from their actions is through programs known as "ransomware," which use bots to lock up data or other functions on a user's computer. Once the bots have been unintentionally activated, the user's access to data, whether photos, files, or other functions, will be locked and then the botherder sends the user a message requesting a ransom to unlock the computer. Reports from 2016 indicated that ransomware users were increasingly attacking hospitals, universities, and corporations, thus increasing the potential for profit but also the danger of locking out key information.[4]

Botwarfare and the Internet of Things

Mirai is a botnet that first appeared in September of 2016 when the botnet was used to stage a DDoS attack against the Web company Dyn. This attack disabled a massive chunk of the Internet running across the eastern seaboard of the United States, preventing users from visiting sites like *Wired, New York Times, Reddit,* and *Spotify*. Dyn, which manages a DNS (Domain Name System) is one of the companies that helps users reach a specific site by resolving searches for a specific Web address. The DDoS attack essentially overwhelmed Dyn's servers by launching millions of lookup requests.[5]

What was especially unusual about Mirai was that it didn't just target computers, but used a variety of other Web-enabled devices to spread its malignant program. These devices are part of what is being called the Internet of Things or IoT, an emerging trend in which a variety of common objects, appliances, and features of the physical environment are equipped with technology that enables the objects to be linked into a network. For instance, when IoT devices are linked to create a home network or "smart home," users can remotely activate or deactivate lights, monitor their home through cameras and other sensors, and perform a variety of other activities. The Internet of Things doesn't just involve personal electronics, but also has the potential to stimulate development in a variety of other areas. For instance, sensors installed in concrete, creating what is called "smart concrete," can transmit information about the state of the concrete to police, emergency crews, and citizens using the concrete. In one possible manifestation, smart concrete can be linked to the computers integrated into vehicles so that the concrete itself can alert approaching vehicles of danger, such as potholes, structural weakness, the presence of ice, or even simply when the road is experiencing a traffic jam. The smart vehicle can then relay this information to the driver, in the form of a warning or by suggesting another route.[6]

The Mirai virus used routers to spread it's malicious message, marking the first time that botherders had effectively infiltrated the IoT, leading to the largest DDoS attack in history in which thousands of devices had become bots engaging in the attack. Once the botnet had been created, the individual(s) involved rented out access to the zombie network, essentially allowing others to pay to take down specific sites or services. In February 2017, police in London arrested a 29-year-old hacker, with the handle BestBuy, who was reportedly the primary engineer of the Mirai attack. BestBuy sold access to the Mirai botnet on the Dark Web, earning an unknown amount for taking down Dyn.[7]

The Future of Digital Privacy and Security

Recent attacks utilizing the IoT have brought the issue of corporate responsibility into the debate and many are asking why the companies involved in manufacturing Internet-capable devices aren't doing more to protect the security of their customers. In a February 2017 article posted on the *IoT Evolution* website, CEO of Zvelo Technology Jeff Finn argued that companies are not addressing IoT security because there is currently no financial incentive. If IoT threats become more common, however, the companies will likely be forced to invest more in security. Consumers also have the right to contact their service providers independently, objecting to violations of privacy and requesting that the company do more to protect their privacy.[8]

The IoT is still in its infancy, but, as the system continues to advance, with digital tech integrated into everything from concrete to smart watches, consumers become more vulnerable to attack. Complicating this controversial landscape is the fact that technology is still rapidly evolving and future threats to privacy and security may be far more dangerous than anything known in the 2010s. Consider that encryption (methods used to transform data into code such that only a user with the correct decryption code can translate the data) is the backbone of digital security and that virtually all current security measures are based on the ability to securely encrypt information. However, scientists note that the most advanced encryption available in 2017 will be completely obsolete in the coming age of quantum computing. Quantum computers use subatomic particles rather than electrical signals and this will make quantum computers fundamentally more powerful and potentially able to crack the most advanced military codes in seconds. Just as the Digital Revolution fundamentally changed the way that people engage in their social, financial, and personal lives, the coming quantum revolution could be every bit as transformative.

Supporters of digital privacy have suggested that government regulations could be established to demand that companies involved in the collection and transmission of digital data enact stronger security protocols to protect against cybercrime and to refrain from using customer data in ways not explicitly approved by consumers. Currently, the situation is one in which corporations offer Web services under the caveat that using them requires users to surrender their privacy. The US government, unchecked by laws to prevent the activity, has subsequently used corporate ownership of data as an excuse to engage in warrantless surveillance. A September 2016 Pew Research report found that 91 percent of American adults believe that citizens have lost control of how personal information is collected and used by companies. Research has shown that a vast majority of Americans are also deeply concerned about both governmental surveillance and criminal threats to their personal data.[9] Digital citizens concerned about privacy threats might consider supporting organizations like the Electronic Frontier Foundation (EFF), which is involved in the effort to promote digital privacy legislation. Ultimately, the need for digital privacy is subjective and cannot be reduced to a single set of variables that apply to all individuals and all situations. Each person must decide for him- or herself whether privacy is important to them and how much they feel they should fight for their rights to privacy.

Micah L. Issitt

Works Used

Bolton, Alexander. "Schiff: Trump's Attacks on the Intelligence Community Are 'Deeply Counterproductive.'" *The Hill*, Capitol Hill Publishing Corp. Feb 19 2017. Web. 27 Feb 2017.

"Bots and Botnets—A Growing Threat." *Norton*, Symantec Inc. 2016. Web. 27 Feb 2017.

Burrus, Daniel. "The Internet of Things Is Far Bigger Than Anyone Realizes." *Wired*, Condé Nast. Nov 2014. Web. 26 Feb 2017.

Ciluffo, Frank J. "Emerging Cyber Threats to the United States." *George Washington University*. Center for Cyber and Homeland Security. Feb 25 2016. Pdf. 27 Feb 2017.

"Cybersecurity Spotlight: The Ransomware Battle." *Tech Pro*, ZD Net. Aug 2016. Web. 27 Feb 2017.

Elgin, Ben, Riley, Michael, Kocieniewski, David, and Joshua Brustein. "How Much of Your Audience Is Fake?" *Bloomberg*, Bloomberg, L.P. Sep 24, 2015. Web. 25 Feb 2017.

Finn, Jeff. "Why Aren't IoT Manufacturers Doing More to Prevent Botnet Attacks?" *IoT Evolution*, IOT Evolution World. Feb 23, 2017. Web. 27 Feb 2017.

Franceschi-Bicchierai, Lorenzo. "Police Have Arrested a Suspect in a Massive 'Internet of Things' Attack." *Motherboard*, Vice Media. Feb 23 2017. Web. 27 Feb 2017.

Lafrance, Adrienne. "The Internet Is Mostly Bots." *The Atlantic*, Atlantic Monthly Group. Jan 31, 2017. Web. 26 Feb 2017.

Newman, Lily Hay. "What We Know About Friday's Massive East Coast Internet Outage." *Wired*, Condé Nast. Oct 21, 2016. Web. 25 Feb 2017.

Rainie, Lee. "The State of Privacy in Post-Snowden America." *Pew Research*, Pew Research Center. Sep 21 2016. Web. 27 Feb 2017.

Notes

1. Lafrance, "The Internet Is Mostly Bots."
2. Elgin, Riley, Kocieniewski, and Brustein, "How Much of Your Audience Is Fake?"
3. "Bots and Botnets—A Growing Threat," *Norton*.
4. "Cybersecurity Spotlight: The Ransomware Battle," *Tech Pro*.
5. Newman, "What We Know about Friday's Massive East Coast Internet Outage."
6. Burrus, "The Internet of Things Is Far Bigger Than Anyone Realizes."
7. Francheschi-Bicchierai, "Police Have Arrested a Suspect in a Massive 'Internet of Things' Attack."
8. Finn, "Why Aren't IoT Manufacturers Doing More to Prevent Botnet Attacks?"
9. Rainie, "The State of Privacy in Post-Snowden America."

The Privacy Threat from Always-On Microphones Like the Amazon Echo

By Jay Stanley

ACLU.org/blog, January 13, 2017

A warrant from police in Arkansas seeking audio records of a man's Amazon Echo has sparked an overdue conversation about the privacy implications of "alwayson" recording devices. This story should serve as a giant wakeup call about the potential surveillance devices that many people are starting to allow into their own homes.

The Amazon Echo is not the only such device; others include personal assistants like Google Home, Google Now, Apple's Siri, Windows Cortana, as well as other devices including televisions, game consoles, cars and toys. We can safely assume that the number of live microphones scattered throughout American homes will only increase to cover a wide range of "Internet of Things" (IoT) devices. (I will focus on microphones in this post, but these devices can include not just audio recorders but video as well, and the same considerations apply.)

The Insecurity of a Nearby Mic

I was at a dinner party recently with close friends where the conversation turned to some entirely theoretical, screenplaywritingtype speculations about presidential assassinations—speculations that would be pretty dicey should certain outside parties who did not know us and where we were coming from be listening in.

Realizing this as we spoke, the group thought of our host's Amazon Echo, sitting on a side table with its little light on. The group's conversation became self-conscious as we began joking about the Echo listening in. Joking or not, in short order our host walked over and unplugged it.

It is exactly this kind of selfconsciousness and chilling effects that surveillance—or even the most remote threat of surveillance—casts over otherwise freewheeling private conversations, and is the reason people need ironclad assurance that their devices will not—cannot—betray them.

Overall, digital assistants and other IoT devices create a triple threat to privacy: from government, corporations, and hackers.

It is a significant thing to allow a live microphone in your private space (just as it is to allow them in our public spaces). Once the hardware is in place, and receiving electricity, and connected to the Internet, then you're reduced to placing your trust in the hands of two things that unfortunately are less than reliable these days: (1) software, and (2) policy.

Software, once a mic is in place, governs when that microphone is live, when the audio it captures is transmitted over the Internet, and to whom it goes. Many devices are programmed to keep their microphones on at all times but only record and transmit audio after hearing a trigger phrase—in the case of the Echo, for example, "Alexa." Any device that is to be activated by voice alone must work this way. There are a range of other systems. Samsung, after a privacy dustup, assured the public that its smart televisions (like others) only record and transmit audio after the user presses a button on its remote control. The Hello Barbie toy only picks up and transmits audio when its user presses a button on the doll.

Software is invisible, however. Most companies do not make their code available for public inspection, and it can be hacked, or unscrupulous executives can lie about what it does (think Volkswagen), or government agencies might try to order companies to activate them as a surveillance device.

The *dumber* and more straightforward a user's control, the better. Depriving a microphone of electricity by unplugging it and/or removing any batteries provides ironclad assurance that it's not recording. A hardware switch is nearly as good, provided there's no software mediation that could be overcome by hackers. (Switches can be bought for just that purpose.) A verbal command is far less certain, and devices like Echo will sometimes misinterpret sounds as their "wake word" and record random snippets of conversation. It's easy to see how a sentence such as "He was driving a Lexus in a way she said was dangerous" could be heard by an Echo as "Alexa: Sin away she said—was dangerous." The constant potential for accidental recording means that users do not necessarily have complete control over what audio gets transmitted to the cloud.

Once their audio is recorded and transmitted to a company, users depend for their privacy on good policies—how it is analyzed; how long and by whom it is stored, and in what form; how it is secured; who else it may be shared with; and any other purposes it may be used for. This includes corporate policies (caveat emptor), but also our nation's laws and Constitution.

Access to Recordings by Law Enforcement

We fear that some government agencies will try to argue that they do not need a warrant to access this kind of data. We believe the Constitution is clear, and that, at a minimum, law enforcement needs a warrant based on probable cause to access conversations recorded in the home using such devices. But more protections are needed. Congress, recognizing the extremely invasive nature of traditional wiretaps, enacted safeguards that go beyond what the courts had ruled the Constitution requires. These include requirements that wiretaps be used only for serious crimes, or be permitted only when other investigative procedures have failed or are unlikely to succeed. We think that these additional privacy protections should also apply to invasive digital devices in the home.

Unfortunately the existing statutes governing the interceptions of voice communications are ridiculously tangled and confused and it's not clear whether or how data recorded by devices in the home are covered by them.

When it comes to law enforcement access, the key issues for us as a legal matter are:

- Breadth. Access needs to be no broader than necessary. Any warrant authorizing access to stored conversations should particularly and narrowly describe the data that law enforcement has probable cause to believe is related to a crime—for example, a specific time period, subject matter, and/or type of activity.

- Minimization. There need to be protections in place to limit the collection of information that is ultimately irrelevant. In the wiretap context these include rules requiring the police to stop listening when a conversation is irrelevant, and analagous rules should be developed for IoT device data.

- Notice. Historically, citizens served with search warrants have always received notice that their property is being searched—especially when that property is one's home—and that practice should not be ended just because it is moving into the electronic realm. (We discussed this issue in greater depth last year.) Notice of IoT searches should always be served on all affected parties.

In the Arkansas case, the police did serve Amazon with a warrant—but Amazon has fought it, apparently because of overbreadth. Our only information is what the company has said in a statement: that "Amazon objects to overbroad or otherwise inappropriate demands as a matter of course."

A Legal Contradiction

Digital assistants, like smart meters and many other IoT devices, split open a contradiction between two legal doctrines that both sit at the core of privacy law:

The sanctity of the home. The inside of the home has for centuries been sacred when it comes to privacy. The Supreme Court has refused to let police use thermal scanners on private homes, for example, despite government protests that it was only measuring the heat leaving the home. And although the Court has ruled that dog sniffs for drugs are not a search in cars or in public spaces, it refused to allow them near the home. As Justice Antonin Scalia pointed out in the thermal scanner case, "the Fourth Amendment draws a firm line at the entrance to the house."

The third-party doctrine. As strong as privacy jurisprudence has been in protecting the home, it has been very weak in another area. Under the court's socalled "third-party doctrine," the Constitution does not require police to get a warrant to get people's records from their bank, telephone company, internet service provider, Google, Amazon, or any other third party. As a result, law enforcement agencies have argued in recent years that they should be able to obtain information such as individuals' cell phone records, location history, even emails from companies without a warrant.

The contradiction arises when devices inside the home stream data about activities in that home to the servers of a thirdparty corporation. Because of the third party doctrine, to give just one example, police have been obtaining home energyuse data from utilities without a warrant. In a home with a "smart meter," that kind of data can be so minutely detailed that it can reveal all kinds of details about what people are doing inside their homes—which appliances they use, and when they use them—and even what television shows they watch (based on the pat-

> **When people depend on software to protect their privacy, transparent code is the only way to give people assurance a device is doing what it's supposed to and no more.**

terns of light and dark in a show, which changes a television set's electricity draw). In fact, in the very same Arkansas murder case in which the police are seeking data from the suspect's Amazon Echo, they built their case against him using warrantlessly obtained data from his smart water meter, which prosecutors say shows he used 140 gallons of water between 1 and 3 a.m. They allege he was trying to hose blood stains off his patio. (He says the AM/PM setting on the meter's clock was wrong and he used that water in the afternoon in order to fill his hot tub.)

The solution to the contradiction between the sanctity of the home and the third party doctrine is clear: the third-party doctrine must go. It is increasingly untenable in an era where much of the data created about people's lives sits on the servers of international corporations—and the growth of IoT devices like digital assistants will make its inadequacy in the information age even clearer.

Recommendations

In addition to rigorously applying constitutional privacy protections as outlined above, the following steps should be applied to IoT microphones:

- Speech fragments transmitted to companies should be retained for the minimal necessary period, should not be shared absent a warrant, and should not be used for other purposes.

- Companies should do whatever necessary to ensure their users have a clear understanding about what data is kept and for how long. That means fine print buried in a clickthrough agreement is not enough.

- Users should have access to any of their audio recordings that a company retains, and the option to delete them. Commendably, some companies (Google and Amazon, for example) already do this. It needs to become at minimum an expected, standard best practice.

- It should become standard for microphones to feature a hardwired, non-softwaremodifiable LED indicator light that turns on whenever a mic is on (defined as transmitting electrical signals to anywhere else). It might make sense for there to be another, separate indicator when software is recording and/or transmitting signals to the internet. The more transparency to the consumer, the better.

- It should also become standard to build in a hardware power switch that physically cuts off electricity to a microphone so that consumers can stop a microphone from recording. As much as possible, the power interruption that switch effects should be tangible or even visible, so that customers can feel complete certainty that the microphone cannot record, akin to the certainty that comes from putting a bandage (or ACLU sticker) over the camera on one's laptop.

- To the greatest extent possible, the code governing the operation of microphones should be public. When people depend on software to protect their privacy, transparent code is the only way to give people assurance a device is doing what it's supposed to and no more.

- Special attention should be paid to any capability for remote activation of recording. Best for privacy is for no such activation to be possible. If there is a strong case to be made that such capability may be desired by consumers, then it should be to the greatest extent possible designed to be something that only consumers themselves can activate, and that consumers can permanently disable if they wish. Consumers must also be given explicit warning where any such capabilities exist.

- Companies and policymakers need to address the raft of issues around the stability of IoT devices, especially inhome devices with microphones or cameras. When not regularly updated, for example, such devices quickly become security threats. And what happens when the company providing those updates goes out of business or is acquired—or just changes its privacy policy? Devices that start out as private and secure can become a toxic presence inside the home as a result of things happening in the outside world, and right now, consumers are on their own in a Wild West.

- One of the best things that can be done for privacy is for speech recognition capabilities to be embedded locally in a device, so there's no need to send audio clips to servers across the Internet. While that can work now for some simple commands, experts say that good recognition of a broader array of speech still requires processing in the cloud.

- Legislative privacy protections are also needed. In addition to broad privacy rules governing corporate use of private data, which would help in this area as in so many others, Congress should lay out strong and precise standards for when the government can access data from these new devices. As with wiretaps, the privacy and public interests at stake may require protections beyond a warrant and notice requirement.

Again, all of these principles should also apply to video that inhome devices may capture and potentially stream to the cloud, which carries the same threats and problems.

It is a healthy thing that this Arkansas story has sparked a public conversation about always-on devices. We and other privacy advocates have been watching this technology for some time—our allies at the privacy group EPIC wrote a letter to the FTC in 2015 requesting an investigation of alwayson devices and their privacy implications. And the Future of Privacy Forum, a DC think tank, produced a helpful report on the issue last year.

But if microphones are going to be part of our daily lives in our intimate spaces, we need broader awareness of the issues they raise, and to settle on strong protections and best practices as soon as possible.

Print Citations

CMS: Stanley, Jay. "The Privacy Threat from Always-on Microphones Like the Amazon Echo." In *The Reference Shelf: Internet Abuses and Privacy Rights*, edited by Betsy Maury, 77-82. Ipswich, MA: Salem Press, 2017.

MLA: Stanley, Jay. "The Privacy Threat from Always-on Microphones Like the Amazon Echo." *The Reference Shelf: Internet Abuses and Privacy Rights*. Ed. Betsy Maury. Ipswich: H.W. Wilson, 2017. 77-82. Print.

APA: Stanley, J. (2016). The privacy threat from always-on microphones like the Amazon Echo. In Betsy Maury (Ed.), *The Reference Shelf: Internet Abuses and Privacy Rights* (pp. 77-82). Ipswich, MA: H.W. Wilson. (Original work published 2017)

Incentives Need to Change for Firms to Take Cyber-Security More Seriously

The Economist, **December 20, 2016**

It has been a cracking year for hacking. Barack Obama and the CIA accused Russia of electronic meddling in an attempt to help Donald Trump win the presidency. Details emerged of two enormous data breaches at Yahoo!, one of the world's biggest internet companies; one, in 2013, affected more than a billion people. Other highlights include the hack of the World Anti-Doping Agency; the theft of $81m from the central bank of Bangladesh (only a typo prevented the hackers from making off with much more); and the release of personal details of around 20,000 employees of the FBI. The more closely you look at the darker corners of the internet, the more the phrase "computer security" looks like a contradiction in terms.

Why, two decades after the internet began to move out of universities and into people's homes, are things still so bad? History is one reason: the internet started life as a network for the convenient sharing of academic data. Security was an afterthought. Economics matters, too. Software developers and computer-makers do not necessarily suffer when their products go wrong or are subverted. That weakens the incentives to get security right.

Unfortunately, things are likely to get worse before they get better. The next phase of the computing revolution is the "internet of things" (IoT), in which all manner of everyday objects, from light bulbs to cars, incorporate computers connected permanently to the internet. Most of these gizmos are as insecure as any other computer, if not more so. And many of those making IoT products are not computer firms. IT companies have accumulated decades of hard-won wisdom about cyber-security; toaster-makers have rather more to learn.

In November cyber-security researchers revealed a malicious program that could take control of any smart light bulbs within 400 metres. A hacked light bulb does not sound too dangerous. But such unobtrusive computers can be recruited into remotely controlled "botnets" that can be used to flood websites with bogus traffic, knocking them offline. Routers, the small electronic boxes that connect most households to the internet, are already a popular target of bot-herders. Other targets are more worrying. At a computer-security conference in 2015, researchers demonstrated how wirelessly to hack a car made by Jeep, spinning its steering wheel or slamming on its brakes. As the era of self-driving cars approaches, the time to fix such problems is now.

One option is to leave the market to work its magic. Given the damage that cybercrime can do to companies, they have good commercial reasons to take it seriously. If firms are careless about security, they risk tarnished reputations and lost customers. A planned buy-out of Yahoo! by Verizon, an American telecoms firm, may be rethought after its hacks. But these incentives are blunted when consumers cannot make informed choices. Most customers (and often, it seems, executives) are in no position to evaluate firms' cyber-security standards. What is more, the epidemic of cybercrime is best tackled by sharing information. A successful cyber-attack on one company can be used against another. Yet it is tempting for firms to keep quiet about security breaches.

> **Software developers and computer-makers do not necessarily suffer when their products go wrong.**

That suggests a role for government. Researchers draw an analogy with public health, where one person's negligence can harm everyone else—which is why governments regulate everything from food hygiene to waste disposal. Some places are planning minimum computer-security standards, and will fine firms that fail to comply. The IoT has also revived the debate about ending the software industry's long-standing exemption from legal liability for defects in its products.

Neither Relax nor Chill

The problem is that regulation is often fragmented. America has a proliferation of state-level rules, for example, when a single, federal regime would be better. Regulation can also go too far. From January financial institutions in New York must comply with a new cyber-security law that many think sets the bar for breach notifications too low. Changing the liability regime for software could chill innovation by discouraging coders from trying anything new.

Rule-makers can, however, set reasonable minimum expectations. Many IoT devices cannot have their software updated, which means that security flaws can never be fixed. Products should not be able to operate with factory usernames and passwords. No software program can be made impregnable, but liability regimes can reflect firms' efforts to rectify flaws once they become apparent. Firms need to be encouraged to take internet security more seriously. But overly detailed prescriptions will just hack everyone off.

Print Citations

CMS: "Incentives Need to Change for Firms to Take Cyber-Security More Seriously." In *The Reference Shelf: Internet Abuses and Privacy Rights*, edited by Betsy Maury, 83-85. Ipswich, MA: H.W. Wilson, 2017.

MLA: "Incentives Need to Change for Firms to Take Cyber-Security More Seriously." *The Reference Shelf: Internet Abuses and Privacy Rights*. Ed. Betsy Maury. Ipswich: H.W. Wilson, 2017. 83-85. Print.

APA: The Economist. (2017). Incentives need to change for firms to take cyber-security more seriously. In Betsy Maury (Ed.), *The Reference Shelf: Internet Abuses and Privacy Rights* (pp. 83-85). Ipswich, MA: H.W. Wilson. (Original work published 2016)

Hacking, Cryptography, and the Countdown to Quantum Computing

By Alex Hutchinson
The New Yorker, September 26, 2016

Given the recent ubiquity of cyber-scandals—Colin Powell's stolen e-mails, Simone Biles's leaked medical records, half a billion plundered Yahoo! accounts—you might get the impression that hackers can already break into just about any computer they want. But the situation could be a lot worse. The encryption methods that protect everything from online shopping to diplomatic communications remain effectively impregnable when properly implemented, even if, in practice, there are frequent breaches—whistle-blowers, careless clicks, and so on. This relatively happy state of affairs will not, however, endure. Scientists around the world are inching toward the development of a fully functioning quantum computer, a new type of machine that would, on its first day of operation, be capable of cracking the Internet's most widely used codes. Precisely when that day will arrive is unclear, but it could be in as little as ten years. Experts call the countdown Y2Q: "years to quantum."

This looming but uncertain deadline hovered in the air at the Hilton Toronto last week, where government officials, cyber-security researchers, and representatives from companies like Amazon, Microsoft, and Intel gathered for an international workshop on "quantum-safe cryptography." Michele Mosca, a professor at the University of Waterloo's Institute for Quantum Computing and the co-host of the workshop, pegged the odds of reaching Y2Q by 2026 at one in seven, rising to one in two by 2031. But the exact date doesn't really matter, because the time needed to invent, battle-test, standardize, and roll out new security algorithms Internet-wide might be just as long. Brian LaMacchia, the head of security and cryptography at Microsoft Research, has a working estimate of 2030. "The people who try to build quantum computers, who sit on the floor upstairs from me, said fifteen years last year," he told me. "So I said, O.K., let's work backwards from that. And I'm out of time."

Classical computers encode information as a series of bits, which can be either 0 or 1, and then manipulate those bits according to simple rules. A quantum computer isn't just a faster or better classical computer; it's fundamentally different. Instead of bits, it stores information as qubits, which can be 0, 1, or both at once. That's a consequence of the quantum-mechanical property of superposition, which allows physical objects to exist in multiple states, or even be in different places, at one time. Thus, two qubits can represent four states simultaneously (00, 01, 10, 11), and a hundred qubits can represent 1.3 quadrillion quadrillion. This quantum peculiarity allows the computer to find patterns in huge data sets very quickly—to get detailed information about a forest without looking at all the trees, as Mosca put it. The main mathematical challenge in breaking current codes is factoring very large numbers, which for classical computers is the equivalent of trying combination after combination to see if it opens a lock. As the keys get longer, the locks get tougher. It took about two years on hundreds of computers to unlock a single instance of the RSA-768 algorithm, which, as its name suggests, requires a key that is seven hundred and sixty-eight bits long. Doing the same for its more secure cousin, RSA-1024, would take about a thousand times longer, and RSA-4096 is effectively out of reach. A quantum computer, on the other hand, would tackle such problems effortlessly.

When quantum computing was first proposed, in the nineteen-eighties, it was mostly a theoretical curiosity. That changed in 1994, when Peter Shor, then at AT & T's Bell Labs, demonstrated how it could apply to cryptography. Once the significance of Shor's work became clear, the race to actually build a quantum computer became one of the hottest tickets in physics. Among the biggest players was the U.S. government, which by 2007 was spending about sixty million dollars a year on quantum-computing research. It didn't just want to build one; it also needed to know whether anyone else was getting close. After all, top-secret messages sent today could still be embarrassing or dangerous if they were intercepted and stored, then decrypted by a device built a decade from now.

So far, the best quantum computers have just a handful of qubits—five, for example, in a system that I.B.M. announced earlier this year. The company expects to scale up to between fifty and a hundred qubits within the next decade, which would be powerful but still short of the thousand or so that LaMacchia estimates would represent a serious cryptographic threat. (D-Wave Systems, a Canadian company that caused a stir when it announced a thousand-qubit computer last year, uses an alternative approach to quantum computing that isn't suitable for code-breaking.) This may sound like painfully modest progress after two decades, but it has been steady enough in the past few years to shift the underlying question from if to when.

The "Y2Q" handle makes explicit the parallels between the quantum threat and the Y2K bug, which, at the turn of the millennium, was supposed to make the world's computers think it was 1900 again, bringing civilization to a grinding halt. In the popular imagination, Y2K has become a punch line, a prophecy of doom unfulfilled, like the Maya calendar turned out to be in 2012. But for many of the people at the cryptography workshop—those responsible for establishing international standards for safe computing or signing off on data-security protocols for hundred-billion-dollar companies—Y2K was a relatively minor event only because the hysteria that preceded it mobilized an estimated three hundred to five hundred billion dollars in preventive action by governments and corporations. So far, Y2Q has failed to generate quite that level of interest.

One big difference is that it was clear, if inconvenient, what needed to be done to avoid Y2K. The best way to ward off a quantum attack, on the other hand, is still very much up for debate. The simplest approach is basically mathematical: come up with new encryption algorithms that quantum computers can't break. That doesn't require big changes in technology, but it's very hard to know for sure which algorithms will be resistant, until they fail. The other approach is to directly harness the weirdness of quantum mechanics; since the mere act of observing a quantum system freezes it in one state, you can construct sophisticated communications links where it's impossible, even in theory, to eavesdrop on the message without destroying it or betraying your presence. This approach sounds great, but is far harder (and more expensive) to implement.

Both approaches have been making progress in the real world over the past few months. China, for instance, has nearly completed a twelve-hundred-mile fibre-optic "quantum backbone" that will link Shanghai and Beijing, allowing signals to travel from one end to the other without losing their quantum properties. And the world's first quantum satellite, launched from the Gobi Desert in August, will allow the country to send fully quantum-encrypted messages over much longer distances. For most of the companies and other governments represented at the workshop, though, quantum-resistant algorithms remain the focus. In July, Google announced that it would test a candidate algorithm dubbed New Hope in a small fraction of Chrome browsers. Soon afterward, the National Institute of Standards and Technology put out a public call for input on how it should evaluate such algorithms in the future. The organization may be ready to issue standards in draft form, a NIST cryptographer at the workshop estimated, by 2022 or 2023. Some members of the crowd reacted with audible consternation.

> **Scientists around the world are inching toward the development of a fully functioning quantum computer, a new type of machine that would, on its first day of operation, be capable of cracking the Internet's most widely used codes.**

In a sense, then, the fundamental question isn't whether we should do something to prepare for Y2Q. It's how we balance the seeming necessity of doing something right now with the inconvenient fact that we don't yet know what to do. The most persuasive answer to this dilemma came from Vadim Makarov, an exuberantly bearded, Hagrid- like figure who heads the University of Waterloo's Quantum Hacking Lab. He and his colleagues work with companies to test their quantum-cryptography systems before they go public, and have demonstrated that even "theoretically perfect" setups can be hacked when they're actually implemented—for example, by blinding the receiving device with a bright laser that makes it unable to distinguish between quantum and classical signals. Such vulnerabilities may suggest that quantum-safe systems aren't yet ready for prime time, but Makarov, during a panel discussion, drew the opposite conclusion. "It's a bit of chicken-and-an-egg problem," he said in a thick Russian accent. It will be impossible to know which systems can resist attacks until they're out there, in the real world, inviting attacks. Waiting for a perfect solution just brings the arrival of a quantum computer closer and closer, at which point it will be too late to fix things. "So, folks, please deploy more," Makarov said. "We want real hackers, not the toy ones like me and my students." He smiled, not quite reassuringly.

Print Citations

CMS: Hutchinson, Alex. "Hacking, Cryptography, and the Countdown to Quantum Computing." In *The Reference Shelf: Internet Abuses and Privacy Rights*, edited by Betsy Maury, 86-89. Ipswich, MA: H.W. Wilson, 2017.

MLA: Hutchinson, Alex. "Hacking, Cryptography, and the Countdown to Quantum Computing." *The Reference Shelf: Internet Abuses and Privacy Rights*. Ed. Betsy Maury. Ipswich: H.W. Wilson, 2017. 86-89. Print.

APA: Hutchinson, A. (2017). Hacking, cryptography, and the countdown to quantum computing. In Betsy Maury (Ed.), *The Reference Shelf: Internet Abuses and Privacy Rights* (pp. 86-89). Ipswich, MA: H.W. Wilson. (Original work published 2016)

The Dyn DDoS Attack and the Changing Balance of Online Cyber Power

By Kalev Leetaru
Forbes.com, October 31, 2016

As the denial of service (DDOS) attack against Dyn shook the internet a little over a week ago, it brought to the public forefront the changing dynamics of power in the online world. In the kinetic world of the past, the nation state equivalent was all-powerful, since it alone could raise the funds necessary to support the massive military and police forces necessary to command societies. In the online world, however, the "armies" being commanded are increasingly used against their will, massive networks of infected drone machines formed into botnets. The cost of acquiring, powering, cooling, connecting and operating these virtual soldiers are borne by private individuals and corporations, with criminal enterprises able to co-opt them into massive attack botnets. What does this suggest is in store for the future of the online world?

The notion of using large botnets to launch globally distributed DDOS attacks is by no means a new concept and in fact has become a hallmark of the modern web. Indeed, I remember as a freshman in college 16 years ago seeing a new Linux server installed where I worked one morning and seeing the same machine being carted off by the security staff that afternoon after it had been hacked and converted into a botnet drone just a few hours after being plugged in. What makes the attack against Dyn so interesting is the scale at which it occurred and its reliance on compromised Internet of Things devices, including DVRs and webcams, allowing it to command a vastly larger and more distributed range of IP addresses than typical attacks. Making the attack even more interesting is the fact that it appears to have relied on open sourced attack software that makes it possible for even basic script kiddies to launch incredibly powerful attacks with little knowledge of the underlying processes.

This suggests an immense rebalancing in the digital era in which anyone anywhere in the world, all the way down to a skilled teenager in his or her parent's basement in a rural village somewhere in a remote corner of the world, can take down some of the web's most visible companies and wreak havoc on the online world. That preliminary assessments suggest that the attack was carried out by private actors rather than a nation state only reinforces this shift in online power.

Warfare as a whole is shifting, with conflict transforming from nations attacking nations in clearly defined and declared geographic battlespaces to ephemeral flagless organizations waging endless global irregular warfare. In the cyber domain, as the battleground of the future increasingly places individuals and corporations in the cross hairs, this raises the fascinating question of how they can protect themselves?

> **The notion of using large botnets to launch globally distributed DDoS attacks is by no means a new concept and in fact has become a hallmark of the modern web.**

In particular, the attack against Dyn largely mirrored an attack against Brian Krebs' *Krebs on Security* blog last month, which raises the specter of criminals and nations being able to increasingly silence their critics, extort businesses and wreak havoc on the online world, perhaps even at pivotal moments like during an election day.

In the physical world, the nation state offers protection over the physical assets of companies operating in its territories, with military and police forces ensuring the sanctity of warehouses, office buildings and other tangible assets. However, in the digital world, state hackers from one country can easily compromise and knock offline the ecommerce sites of companies in other nations or leak their most vital secrets to the world.

In the case of Brian Krebs' site, his story thankfully has a happy ending, in which Alphabet's Jigsaw (formerly Google Ideas) took over hosting of his site under their Project Shield program. Project Shield leverages Google's massive global infrastructure to provide free hosting for journalistic sites under sustained digital attack, protecting them from repressive governments and criminal enterprises attempting to silence their online voices.

Looking to the future, what options do companies have to protect themselves in an increasingly hostile digital world? Programs such as the Project on Active Defense by George Washington University's Center for Cyber & Homeland Security are exploring the gray space of proactive countering and highly active response to cyberattacks. For example, what legal and ethical rights does a company have to try and stop an incoming cyberattack? Can it "hack back" and disable key command and control machines in a botnet or take other active approaches to disrupt the incoming traffic? What happens if a company remotely hacks into a control machine to disable it and it turns out it is an infected internet-connected oven in someone's house and in the process of disabling it, the oven malfunctions and turns to maximum heat and eventually catches fire and burns the house down? Is the company responsible for the damage and potential loss of life? What legal responsibilities and liabilities do device manufacturers have to develop a more secure Internet of Things? If a company in 2016 still sells devices with default administrative passwords and well-known vulnerabilities that make them easy prey for botnets, should the companies bear the same burden as any other consumer safety issue? As over-the-air remote security updates become more common, should legislation be passed to require all consumer devices have the ability to be remotely updated with security patches?

As the modern web celebrates more than 20 years of existence, somewhere over those last two decades the web has gone from a utopia of sharing and construction of a brighter future to a dystopia of destruction and unbridled censorship. Will the web grow up and mature to a brighter security future or will it descend into chaos with internet users fleeing to a few walled gardens like Facebook that become the "safe" version of the web? Only time will tell.

Print Citations

CMS: Leetaru, Kaley. "The Dyn DDoS Attack and the Changing Balance of Online Cyber Power." In *The Reference Shelf: Internet Abuses and Privacy Rights*, edited by Betsy Maury, 90-92. Ipswich, MA: H.W. Wilson, 2017.

MLA: Leetaru, Kaley. "The Dyn DDoS Attack and the Changing Balance of Online Cyber Power." *The Reference Shelf: Internet Abuses and Privacy Rights*. Ed. Betsy Maury. Ipswich: H.W. Wilson, 2017. 90-92. Print.

APA: Leetaru, K. (2017). *The Dyn DDoS attack and the changing balance of online cyber power*. In Betsy Maury (Ed.), *The Reference Shelf: Internet Abuses and Privacy Rights* (pp. 90-92). Ipswich, MA: H.W. Wilson. (Original work published 2016)

The Internet of Things Is a Cyberwar Nightmare

By James Stavridis and Dave Weinstein

Foreignpolicy.com, November 3, 2016

The world got a glimpse of the future last month when a large-scale cyberattack prevented access to hundreds of key websites, including Twitter, the online *New York Times*, and Amazon. The "distributed denial of service" attack against the New Hampshire-based DNS provider Dyn, which blocked access to major online services for users as far away as Europe, fulfilled the direst predictions of technologists and security researchers alike.

The attack exposed the clear reasons for concern about the coming age of an Internet of Things, in which ever more household devices are connected to the web. What's less immediately clear is what should be done to ensure the internet's most likely future iteration remains safe.

Cyberattacks

To date, the vast majority of disruptive and even destructive cyberattacks have been the work of militaries, foreign intelligence services, or other state-sponsored hackers. These actors are usually operating under some degree of political direction and interests and tend to moderate their use of malicious code for disruptive or destructive purposes.

But according to America's top intelligence official, Director of National Intelligence James Clapper, last month's attack was "likely" the work of a nonstate actor, and his assessment has been backed up by reports from the private cybersecurity firm Flashpoint.

This marks an important shift. The barriers to entry are becoming low enough that hackers no longer need the backing of a government to carry out crimes or even acts of warfare in cyberspace. These nonstate actors are especially destabilizing because they are not subject to traditional means of diplomacy or law enforcement. They operate beyond legal jurisdictions and without regard for geographic political boundaries, so the instruments of deterrence that have largely kept nation-states from projecting disruptive or destructive cyberforce are increasingly obsolete.

The first factor driving these low barriers to entry is the internet's rapidly expanding digital real estate, which nonstate hackers view as their battlefield. The rapidly expanding Internet of Things consists of normal household devices like surveillance cameras, thermostats, baby monitors, televisions, and refrigerators to which an IP address has been affixed and that can communicate with one another and other devices. It is already massive and is expected to more than triple in size by 2020 to nearly 21 billion devices. For a cyber-defender, this means that hackers will not only have three times as many targets—they will also have three times as many vectors from which to attack any given target. This creates vast new challenges for network security and complicates the already murky legal and technical landscape for attributing who is responsible for an attack.

The second factor bolstering this threat is the ubiquity of the tools used to conduct such attacks. The Mirai malware that was used last month to compromise 50,000 internet-connected devices is a powerful new threat. Botnets, or armies of zombie computers infected with malware, are not a new phenomenon; what is new, however, is the act of transforming the Internet of Things into a distributed zombie network—an Internet of Botnets. But

> **But we can still prevent our household appliances from becoming an army of malicious computer zombies out to destroy the web.**

the source code for Mirai is not secured in a government vault, but rather shared in forums on deep, dark corners of the web for sympathetic, force-multiplying hackers to copy and deploy with the stroke of a key.

Finally, last month's attack demonstrated our need for a more redundant internet. Dyn, which is akin to a large digital phonebook, is one of many companies that connect a web address typed in a browser to a website's IP address. By flooding its servers in New Hampshire with dummy traffic from random devices, amateurs effectively shut down popular online services like Twitter and Netflix for millions of their customers. Ultimately, the effects of that attack were quite limited. The effects, however, of a similar style attack directed against more critical services during a local, regional, or national emergency could be catastrophic.

Preventing Attacks

Such hypotheticals are entirely reasonable to contemplate. They will also undoubtedly encourage a chorus of criticism about the viability of the Internet of Things. Technology skeptics will ask, "Why does my refrigerator need an internet connection?" But that's the wrong question. There are too many benefits to linking our world together to slow that process down. The real question is: How can we prevent such attacks?

First, we need to require higher levels of security in any device that will be connected to the web. Some of this will be done because manufacturers are self-incentivized to do so. For example, last week, Chinese camera manufacturer Hangzhou Xiongmai was quick to recall millions of its products sold in the United States that were vulnerable to the Mirai malware. More will follow voluntarily to avoid legal liability in the event of an attack.

Second, we need better technology to manage in real time the vulnerability of Internet of Things devices. Just as technology vendors (or at least the more reliable ones) deploy software patches when a bug is discovered, Internet of Things manufacturers should include device-based auto-updates as a standard security measure in their new products. And there are plenty of other viable low-cost solutions for these devices—after all, we're not talking about nuclear weapons. An entire secondary cybersecurity market to protect relatively simple devices attached to the Internet of Things is already gaining speed.

And third, we all have to recognize that we have a broad responsibility to protect the internet as consumers of it. While it's easy to place blame on device manufacturers, in the end, perhaps the more appropriate culprit is the user. Think about how we fully embrace our responsibilities to prevent the spread of the flu: We take shots, wash our hands, cover our mouths when we cough, and stay home and self-isolate when we are sick (at least most of us do). That same mentality must be inculcated in the public when it comes to the web. When we attach a device to the internet, we need to change the password, allow security updates, and monitor for trouble. Technology can help, but in the end we own the internet—all of us—and it's our job to keep it safe and secure.

In October, the United States observed National Cybersecurity Awareness Month. How appropriate that the largest single attack on the internet came rolling through it like a line of squalls. It neatly demonstrated the basic facts of our present cybersecurity state: Everything is hackable, and in the digital age of nonstate threats, cybersecurity is a collective responsibility. Now we need to heed those facts.

Print Citations

CMS: Stavridis, James, and Dave Weinstein. "The Internet of Things Is a Cyberwar Nightmare." In *The Reference Shelf: Internet Abuses and Privacy Rights*, edited by Betsy Maury, 93-95. Ipswich, MA: H.W. Wilson, 2017.

MLA: Stavridis, James, and Dave Weinstein. "The Internet of Things Is a Cyberwar Nightmare." *The Reference Shelf: Internet Abuses and Privacy Rights*. Ed. Betsy Maury. Ipswich: H.W. Wilson, 2017. 93-95. Print.

APA: Stavridis, J., & D. Weinstein. (2017). The internet of things is a cyberwar nightmare. In Betsy Maury (Ed.), *The Reference Shelf: Internet Abuses and Privacy Rights* (pp. 93-95). Ipswich, MA: H.W. Wilson. (Original work published 2016)

The Biggest Security Threats Coming in 2017

Wired staff, January 2, 2017

Whether it was a billion compromised Yahoo! accounts or state-sponsored Russian hackers muscling in on the US election, this past year saw hacks of unprecedented scale and temerity. And if history is any guide, next year should yield more of the same.

It's hard to know for certain what lies ahead, but some themes began to present themselves toward the end of 2016 that will almost certainly continue well into next year. And the more we can anticipate them, the better we can prepare. Here's what we think 2017 will hold.

Consumer Drones Get Weaponized

Given how frequently the US has used massive flying robots to kill people, perhaps it's no surprise that smaller drones are now turning deadly, too—this time in the hands of America's enemies. In October the *New York Times* reported that in the first-known case, US-allied Kurdish soldiers were killed by a small drone the size of a model airplane, rigged with explosives. As drones become smaller, cheaper, and more powerful, the next year will see that experiment widened into a full-blown tactic for guerrilla warfare and terrorism. What better way to deliver deadly ordnance across enemy lines or into secure zones of cities than with remote-controlled accuracy and off-the-shelf hardware that offers no easy way to trace the perpetrator? The US government is already buying drone-jamming hardware. But as with all IEDs, the arms race between flying consumer grade bombs and the defenses against them will likely be a violent game of cat-and-mouse.

Another iPhone Encryption Clash

When the FBI earlier this year demanded that Apple write new software to help crack its own device—the iPhone 5c of dead San Bernadino terrorist Rizwan Farook—it fired the first shots in a new chapter of the decades-long war between law enforcement and encryption. And when it backed off that request, saying it had found its own technique to crack the phone, it only delayed any resolution. It's only a matter of time until the FBI or other cops make another legal demand that an encryption-maker assist in cracking its protections for users, setting the conflict in motion again. In fact, in October the FBI revealed in October that another ISIS-linked terrorist, the man who stabbed ten people in a Minnesota mall, used an iPhone. Depending on what model iPhone it is, that locked device could spark Apple vs. FBI, round two, if the bureau is determined enough to access the terrorist's data. (It took three months after the San Bernadino attack for the FBI's conflict with Apple to become public, and that window hasn't passed in the Minnesota case.) Sooner or later, expect another crypto clash.

Russian Hackers Run Amok

Two months have passed since the Office of the Director of National Intelligence and the Department of Homeland Security stated what most of the private sector cybersecurity world already believed: That the Kremlin hacked the American election, breaching the Democratic National Committee and Democratic Congressional Campaign Committee and spilling their guts to WikiLeaks. Since then, the White House has promised a response to put Russia back in check, but none has surfaced. And with less than a month until the inauguration of Putin's preferred candidate—one who has buddied up to the Russian government at every opportunity and promised to weaken America's NATO commitments—any deterrent effect of a retaliation would

> This was the year of Internet of Things (IoT) botnets, in which malware infects inconspicuous devices like routers and DVRs and then coordinates them to overwhelm an online target with a glut of internet traffic, in what's known as a distributed denial of service attack (DDoS).

be temporary at best. In fact, the apparent success of Russia's efforts—if, as CIA and FBI officials have now both told the *Washington Post*, Trump's election was the hackers' goal—will only embolden Russia's digital intruders to try new targets and techniques. Expect them to replicate their influence operations ahead of elections next year in Germany, the Netherlands, and France, and potentially to even try new tricks like data sabotage or attacks on physical infrastructure.

A Growing Rift between the President and the Intelligence Community

Though the US intelligence community—including the FBI, NSA, and CIA—has unanimously attributed multiple incidents of political hacking to Russian government-sponsored attackers, President-elect Donald Trump has remained skeptical. Furthermore, he has repeatedly cast doubt on digital forensics as an intelligence discipline, saying things like, "Once they hack, if you don't catch them in the act you're not going to catch them. They have no idea if it's Russia or China or somebody." Trump has also caused a stir by declining daily intelligence briefings. Beyond just the current situation with Russia, Trump's casual dismissal of intelligence agency findings is creating an unprecedented dissonance between the Office of the

President and the groups that bring it vital information about the world. Current and former members of the intelligence community told *Wired* in mid-December that they find Trump's attitude disturbing and deeply concerning. If the President-elect permanently adopts this posture, it could irrevocably hinder the role of intelligence agencies in government. President Obama, for one, says he is hopeful that the situation is temporary, since Trump has not yet felt the full responsibility of the presidency. "I think there is a sobering process when you walk into the Oval Office," Obama said recently in a press conference. "There is just a whole different attitude and vibe when you're not in power as when you are in power." If Trump does eventually embrace the intelligence community more fully, the next question will be whether it can move on from what has already transpired.

DDoS Attacks Will Crash the Internet Again (and Again, and Again)

This was the year of Internet of Things (IoT) botnets, in which malware infects inconspicuous devices like routers and DVRs and then coordinates them to overwhelm an online target with a glut of internet traffic, in what's known as a distributed denial of service attack (DDoS). Botnets have traditionally been built with compromised PCs, but poor IoT security has made embedded devices an appealing next frontier for hackers, who have been building massive IoT botnets. The most well-known example in 2016, called Mirai, was used this fall to attack and temporarily bring down individual websites, but was also turned on Internet Service Providers and internet-backbone companies, causing connectivity interruptions around the world. DDoS attacks are used by script kiddies and nation states alike, and as long as the pool of unsecured computing devices endlessly grows, a diverse array of attackers will have no disincentive from turning their DDoS cannons on internet infrastructure. And it's not just internet connectivity itself. Hackers already used a DDoS attack to knock out central heating in some buildings in Finland in November. The versatility of DDoS attacks is precisely what makes them so dangerous. In 2017, they'll be more prevalent than ever.

Ransomware Expands Its Targets

Ransomware attacks have become a billion-dollar business for cybercriminals and are on the rise for individuals and institutions alike. Attackers already use ransomware to extort money from hospitals and corporations that need to regain control of their systems quickly, and the more success attackers have, the more they are willing to invest in development of new techniques. A recent ransomware version called Popcorn Time, for example, was experimenting with offering victims an alternative to paying up—if they could successfully infect two other devices with the ransomware. And more innovation, plus more disruption, will come in 2017. Ransomware attacks on financial firms have already been rising, and attackers may be emboldened to take on large banks and central financial institutions. And IoT ransomware could crop up in 2017, too. It may not make sense for a surveillance camera, which might not even have an interface for users to pay the ransom, but could be effective for devices that sync with smartphones or tie in to a corporate network. Attackers could also demand money in exchange for ceasing an IoT botnet-driven DDoS attack. In other words, ransomware attacks are going to get bigger in every possible sense of the word.

Print Citations

CMS: "The Biggest Security Threats Coming in 2017." In *The Reference Shelf: Internet Abuses and Privacy Rights*, edited by Betsy Maury, 96-99. Ipswich, MA: H.W. Wilson, 2017.

MLA: "The Biggest Security Threats Coming in 2017." *The Reference Shelf: Internet Abuses and Privacy Rights*. Ed. Betsy Maury. Ipswich: H.W. Wilson, 2017. 96-99. Print.

APA: Wired. (2017). The biggest security threats coming in 2017. In Betsy Maury (Ed.), *The Reference Shelf: Internet Abuses and Privacy Rights* (pp. 96-99). Ipswich, MA: H.W. Wilson. (Original work published 2017)

Why Does Our Privacy Really Matter?

By Evan Selinger

The Christian Science Monitor, **April 22, 2016**

In his new book, *The Internet of Us: Knowing More and Understanding Less in the Age of Big Data,* philosophy professor Michael P. Lynch argues that the vast majority of people still fail to grasp the true importance of privacy.

Mr. Lynch, who teaches at the University of Connecticut, says privacy is a critical component in society because it is essential for respecting autonomy. Without privacy, he says, individuals lack the ability to freely make their own decisions, and therefore are stripped of a core value in a free and democratic society.

I recently spoke with him about the core reasons privacy invasions are harmful. Edited excerpts follow.

Selinger: *What's the The Internet of Us about?*

Lynch: *It's about knowledge in the Information Age—in particular, the philosophical problems that arise due to the pervasiveness and power of information technology. We often hear that we live in a new knowledge economy now, and that's clearly true in many ways: thanks to the digital devices we carry in our pockets, how we acquire, distribute and produce knowledge has changed.*

But what sort of knowledge should we be acquiring and what sort of knowledge should we be producing? Those are the hard questions. The gap between what we're actually doing and what we should be doing forms the critical, and often ethical, parts of the book.

Selinger: *What's wrong with information technology?*

Lynch: *In itself, nothing. Information technology allows us to know more about the world than ever before. But it also allows the world to know more about us. The Internet, in other words, is a window from which we can look both ways—and from which others can, too. That's why it's so crucial to understand why privacy is important. Appropriate privacy norms tell us quite a bit about how all kinds of information should be handled.*

Selinger: *With so many conversations occurring today about privacy, what don't people still understand about it?*

Lynch: *Lots of people don't grasp the core reasons why privacy matters. Perhaps this isn't surprising. It's fundamentally a philosophical problem. Consequently, people presume they know why privacy matters, and so readily jump to matters of figuring out how to secure it, or else combat advocates by insisting privacy protections are outweighed by tradeoffs.*

But the harms that come from having your privacy unjustly invaded aren't limited to the difficulties that many expect: consequential or instrumental matters. There's also intrinsic harms and in-principle problems. Both matter tremendously, but can be difficult to appreciate until they're spelled out clearly.

Selinger: *So, why does privacy matter?*

Lynch: *Privacy matters in principle because it's connected to the autonomy of decision making. When we talk about information as private it exemplifies two different hallmarks: One is our ability to control the information and the other is our ability to protect the information from intrusion. Let's focus on the control aspect. When I decide to share information with you or others on the Internet, this behavior tends to be thought of as an autonomous decision.*

Part of the problem with privacy invasions is that they can undermine these decisions. For example, if you hacked into all the photos on my phone and shared them with your friends (who will be really bored), you've taken away my decision to select who to share the photos with and who to withhold them from. You've made that issue moot and in the process undermined my autonomy of decision. To clarify further, here's an analogy. The situation is much like a paternalistic doctor deciding to give a patient a drug without asking for permission. The doctor makes a decision on behalf of another, removing that person out of the decision-making process.

Selinger: *In the case of the phone hack, one reason you'd be upset is that people might somehow be able to use your photos against you. But what about people who could never exploit, extort, harass you with this data and the knowledge it conveys? On this topic, you've proposed a thought experiment about telepathic Martians who can read our minds but will never ever interact with any earthlings. Given their practical impotence, are these extraterrestrials committing privacy invasions?*

> **Philosophy professor Michael Lynch says that privacy violations erode individuals' rights to autonomously make their own decisions and exercise individual power.**

Lynch: *Let's start closer to home and then consider the thought experiment. Imagine someone reads your e-mails but opts to never to do anything with that information. You never find out about the incident and nothing bad ever happens as a result. Has a harm been committed? Yes. We can see that this person superseded part of your autonomy. They abused their power by taking you out of the decision-making equation.*

The same goes with the people on the faraway planet. They have taken power from us, and this matters because autonomy enables us to shape our own decisions and make ones that are in line with our deepest preferences and convictions. Autonomy lies at the heart of our humanity.

Selinger: *Are you saying that having access to someone's private information without their permission is itself a deprivation of their autonomy, and that it's the type of deprivation which makes for an asymmetric exercise in power?*

Lynch: *That would be precisely how I'd put it. That said, let me be clear that someone who accesses your information without your permission and doesn't do anything about it is violating your privacy less than someone who takes the information and causes negative consequential outcomes, like reputational damage. And yet—and this is the key point—the moral residue of autonomy lies at the basis of all privacy violations.*

Selinger: *Is this a fundamentally existential view? Would you object to someone taking a picture of a wild animal and posting it on the Internet without its permission?*

Lynch: *I'd be fine with that. But there are gray areas, like parents posting photos of their kids online without asking for permission. As my daughter grows older, my wife and I have started letting her determine when a photograph is appropriate to post. This is because we believe that as children become older they become more autonomous.*

Selinger: *To put this in the grandest way possible, does this mean the deprivation of our autonomy in the Digital Age is a divestment in our humanity?*

Lynch: *Yes, although, of course, it depends on how technology is used. Plenty of digital technology improves the quality of our lives. But the privacy violations we've been discussing do indeed erode our humanity.*

Selinger: *And to put this in the most practical way possible, what are the policy implications of your view?*

Lynch: *Well, the first thing is to recognize that laws protecting citizens' information privacy aren't there just to protect those citizens from the criminal misuse of their data—just as laws promoting informed consent in healthcare aren't there to just protect us from the misuse of drugs or other treatments.*

In both cases such protections are an important part of the story, but not the only part. And that means our policies—legal or otherwise—need to be crafted to recognize that in both cases, we are also protecting a citizen's basic right to autonomy. That means that governments and companies have a pretty high bar if they are going to argue that it is justified in certain cases to violate our privacy. This is a point we need to start recognizing should apply universally to information privacy.

Print Citations

CMS: Selinger, Evan. "Why Does Our Privacy Really Matter." In *The Reference Shelf: Internet Abuses and Privacy Rights*, edited by Betsy Maury, 100-103. Ipswich, MA: H.W. Wilson, 2017.

MLA: Selinger, Evan. "Why Does Our Privacy Really Matter." *The Reference Shelf: Internet Abuses and Privacy Rights*. Ed. Betsy Maury. Ipswich: H.W. Wilson, 2017. 100-103. Print.

APA: Selinger, E. (2017). *Why does our privacy really matter*. In Betsy Maury (Ed.), *The Reference Shelf: Internet Abuses and Privacy Rights* (pp. 100-103). Ipswich, MA: H.W. Wilson. (Original work published 2016)

4

Internet News and Accountability

Jared Peterson leaves a sign outside Comet Ping Pong on Monday December 5, 2016 in Washington, DC. A man identified as Edgar Maddison Welch was arrested Sunday after coming to the restaurant armed. The incident was linked to a series of fake news stories that have been dubbed 'Pizzagate'.

Internet News and the Fight for Legitimacy

Journalism has been called the "fourth estate," an unofficial branch of the government entrusted with providing information to the populace and holding world leaders accountable for their actions. Thomas Jefferson famously wrote that "whenever the people are well informed, they can be trusted with their own government." This is the goal of the free press and the reason that freedom of the press was enshrined in the Constitution. However, the work of the press has always been hindered by those who use misinformation and propaganda for personal or political gain, placing their own needs and beliefs ahead of the welfare of the people. In the Digital Age, the viral spread of fake news and the myopic view of the world created through social media news feeds have compromised the effectiveness of the press and made it difficult for citizens to tell fact from fiction when learning about current events. While digital news and media have made this problem more daunting, Web- research tools also make it easier for computer users to detect misinformation, preventing both the problem and the solution.

Fake News Goes Mainstream

In January 2017, the *New York Times* profiled fake news writer Cameron Harris, a conservative college student who wrote a fictional news story entitled "BREAKING: 'Tens of thousands' of fraudulent Clinton votes found in Ohio warehouse." Harris, who reportedly makes more than $1,000 per hour based on the number of clicks his articles receive, was inspired by Trump's claims that the national vote was going to be "rigged" against him. Harris wrote a story in which he imagined someone had discovered evidence of voter fraud. Within a week, the story had been circulated millions of times and even caught the attention of more mainstream news.[1]

Harris and others like him craft fake news stories for profit or to promote a political viewpoint, with seemingly little concern for how their work misleads people or damages the lives of the individuals who are the target of their inflammatory accusations. One of the most well-known examples, the so-called #Pizzagate controversy, occurred after a fake news site published information that Comet Ping Pong pizza, in Washington D.C., was a front for a child sex ring run by Hillary Clinton. As incredulous as it might seem, the headline convinced thousands who Tweeted, e-mailed, texted, and phoned the pizzeria with threats or demanded a police intervention. One especially excitable North Carolina man even went so far as to travel to the restaurant with an assault rifle to uncover the plot and free the trapped children. He was immediately arrested and has since stated he will take a more critical approach to news he reads on the Internet.[2]

Fake news is not a new phenomenon and even the often-mythologized founding fathers like John Adams and Benjamin Franklin purposefully created and published false news stories to discredit their political opponents or to sway public opinion on key issues.[3] Despite playing a venerable role in American politics, little attention was paid to fake news until the 2016 election. One reason is that Donald Trump liberally quoted fictional claims and statistics from fake news in his campaign. For instance, in his presidential campaign Trump repeated an allegation that appeared in the *National Enquirer*, claiming that Republican candidate Ted Cruz's father had been friends with Lee Harvey Oswald, the assassin who killed President John F. Kennedy. Though the claim was disproven, Trump never acknowledged that the story had been false. In another example, Trump Tweeted claims that more than 3 million undocumented migrants had cast votes for Hillary Clinton in the election based on an article published by *Infowars*, a website known for publishing conspiracy theories aimed at extreme right-wing readers. Trump's voter fraud claim was immediately and convincingly disproven by journalists utilizing widely available public information.[4]

Another reason that fake news has become a major topic is that Internet publishing and social media have made it easier for fake news' peddlers and propagandists to masquerade as journalists. In the past, journalists were judged by the reputation of their newspaper, magazine, or broadcaster and these media institutions were responsible for fact checking submissions and preventing misinformation. In 2017, with thousands of alleged news websites and millions of people taking news and information directly from the Web and social media, an important layer of oversight has been lost.

A study by University of California, Los Angeles social scientist Daniel Fessler found that while all people are vulnerable to being fooled by fake news, conservative Americans and Trump supporters are especially vulnerable because of the same worldview that leads them to embrace the conservative platform. Essentially, individuals in these categories are hyperattuned to the dangers in their world and so especially likely to believe news that confirms their suspicions about real or imagined dangers around them. Individuals identifying as liberals or progressives are less likely to be concerned about conspiracies and hidden dangers and so tend to be more suspicious of inflammatory or extreme-sounding headlines.[5]

Shaping the Bubble

In late 2016, a study found that 40 percent of news shared on Facebook pages belonging to rightwing/conservative individuals/organizations and 19 percent of news shared by left-leaning individuals/groups during the election was either false or misleading. Given that as many as 44 percent of adults get news from Facebook or other social media sites, the growth of fake news on social media poses a serious problem for those seeking to maintain a well-informed electorate.[6] The controversy became so damaging to Facebook's reputation that the company announced plans to add filters to media feeds, to take steps to promote legitimate media, and permanently banned more than 200 publishers from advertising on the site.[7]

Individuals getting news from social media may also be getting a misleading picture of the world because of the social media "bubble," which is a phenomenon in which the information a person receives depends on the beliefs/ideologies of the person's friends/connections and on the fact that social media companies use automated algorithms to select news/information items to be presented on a person's page. These recommended items align with the interests that the individual displays when browsing online and the result is that individuals are more likely to encounter information that supports rather than challenges their existing views or provides a more moderate perspective.

Unlike the fake news phenomenon, the bubble is created by the user her- or himself. Repeated memes and snippets of unverified information reinforce a person's beliefs, shaping their views of the world and creating unrealistic ideas about how other people are thinking about the same issues. A person can actively shape their own bubble by demonstrating diverse interests but the most effective solution is also far simpler: Consider social media a form of entertainment and go elsewhere for news.

Focusing on Facts

So, how can a person navigate a media environment filled with manipulative information and avoid the social media bubble? The first step might be to consider one's sources. A 2012 study from Fairleigh Dickinson University found that respondents' ability to answer political questions depended on where the individual got his or her news. Those who reported getting most of their news from NPR were the most informed, while those getting their news from MSNBC or from Fox News (both known to be highly biased) were less informed than those who reported using no news media at all.[8]

Corroboration is also key to avoiding misinformation and experts typically recommend never basing one's beliefs on a single article. If the author lists sources for the claims made within the article, readers can follow those sources to find out more. If the article does not list sources, this might mean that the article is a fake. For instance, claims that there were 3-million illegal votes in 2016 were repeated widely by Trump and supporters but no articles on the issue cited a source of authority for the claim, except for Trump, who most likely based his belief on the original *Infowars* post, which also did not list any sources.

The website *Snopes.com*, which investigates and fact checks political statements, Internet rumors, and urban legends (such as the one about a mother who named her children *lemonjello* and *orangejello*), warns consumers that articles by anonymous authors should usually be avoided. *Snopes.com* also recommends that readers take the time to search the Web for information about the author as some fake news' authors will attempt to make their articles seem legitimate by using a fake bio or fake credentials. Simple Web searches may even reveal that the alleged author is an entirely fictitious persona created by the original, anonymous author. In addition, *Snopes.com* warns that many illegitimate news sites attempt to convince readers that their site is associated with legitimate news organizations. The URL abcnews.com.co, for instance, is a fake news site and is not associated with the American Broadcasting Company (ABC).

Fact-checking websites like *Politifact*, *FactCheck.org*, and *Snopes.com*, can also help readers check the facts behind political claims and statements made by politicians. Some conservative pundits have alleged that the website *Politifact* is biased against conservatives, however, bias does not matter because *Politifact* always provides links or descriptions of the sources used to fact-check a claim or statement. If the user thinks that *Politifact* is biased, he or she needs only to follow the links provided to check the information for themselves.

It should also be noted that bias and political truth are often relative. In many cases, controversial issues are controversial precisely because the facts available are disputed or because information exists to support both sides. For those interested in connecting with or hearing commentary from those who have the same or similar values or opinions, the bubble is largely meaningless and ideological news sources, like Fox News or MSNBC, are appropriate choices. On some level, legitimate media only really matters to those who value having verifiable facts to *develop* their opinions. The media reflects and creates what citizens demand, and can either be a tool to strengthen and maintain democracy or a marketplace where clever deception sells and political leaders use misinformation to gain or maintain power.

Micah L. Issitt

Works Used

Borchers, Callum. "Donald Trump Wonders Why the *National Enquirer* Didn't Win a Pulitzer Prize: Here's Why." *The Washington Post.* Jul 22 2016. Web. 27 Feb 2017.

Calderone, Michael. "Donald Trump Boosts the *National Enquirer* as Likely Showdown with Hillary Clinton Looms." The *Huffington Post*, Huffington Post Co. May 4 2016. Web. 27 Feb 2017.

Khazan, Olga. "Why Fake News Targeted Trump Supporters." *The Atlantic*, Atlantic Monthly Group. Feb 2 2017. Web. 27 Feb 2017.

Maheshwari, Sapna. "10 Times Trump Spread Fake News." *The New York Times*, The New York Times Co. Jan 18 2017. Web. 27 Feb 2017.

Mitchell, Amy, Gottfried, Jeffrey, Barthel, Michael, and Elisa Shearer. "The Modern News Consumer." *Pew Research*, Pew Research Center. Jul 7 2016. Web. 27 Feb 2017.

Parkinson, Robert G. "Fake News? That's a Very Old Story." *The Washington Post*, Nash Holdings. Nov 25 2016. Web. 27 Feb 2017.

Patterson, Thomas E. "News Coverage of the 2016 Presidential Primaries: Horse Race Reporting Has Consequences." *Shorentein Center*, Harvard Kennedy School. Jul 11 2016. Web. 27 Feb 2017.

Quackenbush, Daniel. "Public Perceptions of Media Bias: A Meta-Analysis of American Media Outlets during the 2012 Presidential Election." *The Elon Journal of Undergraduate Research in Communications*. Vol. 4, No. 2, 2013.

Samuelson, Robert J. "Robert Samuelson: Media Bias Explained in Two Studies." *The Washington Post.* Apr 23 2014. Web. 27 Feb 2017.

Romano, Aja "The Scariest Part of Facebook's Fake News Problem: Fake News Is More Viral Than Real News." *Vox*, Nov 16, 2016. Web. 27 Feb 2017.

Shane, Scott. "From Headline to Photograph, a Fake News Masterpiece." *The New York Times*, The New York Times Co. Jan 18 2017. Web. 27 Feb 2017.

Siddiqui, Faiz and Susan Svrluga. "N.C. Man Told Police He Went to D.C. Pizzeria with Gun to Investigate Conspiracy Theory." *The Washington Post.* Dec 5, 2016. Web. 27 Feb 2017.

"The Last Lap." *Pew Research*, Pew Research Center. Oct 31 2000. Web. 27 Feb 2017.

Wakabayashi, Daisuke and Mike Isaac. "In Race against Fake News, Google and Facebook Stroll to the Starting Line."*The New York Times*, The New York Times Co. Jan 25 2017. Web. 27 Feb 2017.

Wallace, Tim and Alicia Parlapiano. "Crowd Scientists Say Women's March in Washington Had 3 Times as Many People as Trump's Inauguration." *The New York Times*, The New York Times Media Co. Jan 22 2017. Web. 27 Feb 2017.

"What you know depends on what you watch: Current events knowledge across Popular News Sources." *Public Mind*, Fairleigh Dickinson University. May 3 2012. Web. 27 Feb 2017.

Notes

1. Shane, "From Headline to Photograph, a Fake News Masterpiece."
2. Siddiqui and Svrluga. "N.C. Man Told Police He Went to D.C. Pizzeria with a Gun to Investigate Conspiracy Theory."
3. Parkinson, "Fake News? That's a Very Old Story."
4. Maheshwari, "10 Times Trump Spread Fake News."
5. Khazan, "Why Fake News Targeted Trump Supporters."
6. Romano, "The Scariest Part of Facebook's Fake News Problem: Fake News Is More Viral Than Real News." *Vox*, Vox Media. Nov 16, 2016. Web. 27 Feb 2017.
7. Wakabayashi and Isaac, "In Race against Fake News, Google and Facebook Stroll to the Starting Line."
8. "What You Know Depends on What You Watch: Current Events Knowledge across Popular News Sources," Fairleigh Dickinson University.

Fake News Expert on How False Stories Spread and Why People Believe Them

NPR Fresh Air, December 14, 2016

Craig Silverman of BuzzFeed News has spent years studying media inaccuracy. He explains how false stories during the presidential campaign were spread on Facebook and monetized by Google AdSense.

DAVE DAVIES, HOST: *This is Fresh Air. I'm Dave Davies in for Terry Gross. So do you remember reading that Hillary Clinton paid Jay Z and Beyonce $62 million dollars for performing at a rally in Cleveland before the election? You might have, but the story is false, one of many posted on hyperpartisan websites and spread by aggressive social media campaigns during the presidential election.*

Our guest, Craig Silverman, has spent much of his career as a journalist writing about issues of accuracy in media. He wrote a column for the Poynter Institute called "Regret the Error" and later a book of the same name on the harm done by erroneous reporting. He also launched a webbased startup called Emergent devoted to crowdsourcing the factchecking of fake news.

He's now the media editor for the website BuzzFeed, and he spent much of this year writing about fake news, rumors and conspiracy theories that gained currency in the presidential campaign—where they came from, why they got so much engagement on social media and what should be done to reduce their impact on public discourse. I spoke to Craig Silverman yesterday.

Well, Craig Silverman, welcome to Fresh Air. You did an analysis comparing how stories done by, you know, mainstream major news organizations like the New York Times, *the* Washington Post *did it in terms of engagement on Facebook. You compared those stories to other stories done by essentially fake websites or fake election stories. What did you find?*

CRAIG SILVERMAN: *Something pretty surprising. So what we did was we looked at 19 major media organizations and we found sort of the election content from them that had performed best on Facebook. And to kind of define what that means, Facebook doesn't give us a lot of data. That's I think one of the frustrations overall that a lot of researchers and other people have. But what Facebook will give you is one number for* *a piece of content that gives you the total count of the number of shares and comments and reactions for that one piece of content.*

And so what we did was we looked across 19 major media organizations and we picked out the best-performing stuff about the election. And then because I'd been looking at fake news for so long, I have lists of more than 50 websites that completely publish fake information. I looked at what had performed best from them about the election, and I also did some searches to try and find other things about conspiracy theories that I knew had spread.

So at the end of the day, when we kind of looked at the numbers we saw that nine months before the election, six months before the election, the overall Facebook engagement for those top election stories from the mainstream outlets was greater than the fake news that was spreading. But when we went three months before the election, that critical time, we actually saw the fake news spike. And we saw the mainstream news engagement on Facebook for those top 20 stories decline.

And so at the end of the day, in that critical moment, the fake news of those top 20 stories was getting more engagement on Facebook than some of the stories from the biggest media outlets in the U.S. And that was incredibly surprising. I didn't actually expect fake news to win out in that sense.

DAVIES: *So what does that tell us?*

SILVERMAN: *Something was going on there where, one, you can conclude that the stuff that they were creating and spreading was really resonating with voters. But two, I think you also have to look at Facebook itself and wonder how is it that these sites that have for so long been so marginal, how is it that these sites that in many cases had only been launched in the previous, you know, six to 12 months, how is it possible that they're getting stuff out there on this massive platform, Facebook, that is getting more engagement than, you know, opeds and commentary pieces from major media, than, you know, big stories about the Trump campaign, about the Clinton campaign? It just didn't make sense to me.*

But there's no question that these fake stories resonated with people. There's no question that they saw them and they shared them or they commented on them and they liked them, and that created tremendous velocity on Facebook. And a lot of people saw them, and that's a really surprising thing and it's a distressing thing.

DAVIES: *When you looked at the fake news stories, did they tend to help one side more than another?*

SILVERMAN: *Yeah. Overwhelmingly, when you looked at the stories that performed really well on Facebook, they were proTrump or they were antiClinton. And that was a very clear trend. The stuff that was antiTrump was just not getting the same traction. And so I think what happened is that a lot of people creating fake news looked at this and said, well, let's go allin on Trump.*

DAVIES: *You've discovered that there are more than a hundred websites peddling false news stories for the American voting public from a single town in Macedonia in the Balkans. Tell us about this place. Who's pushing this stuff?*

SILVERMAN: *There's a town in central Macedonia called Veles, you know, population is roughly around 40 to 50,000 people. And, you know, to back up for a second, myself and a researcher named Lawrence Alexander were interested in pro Trump movements outside of the United States and outside of North America. And so working with Lawrence, we kind of went from, you know, one European country in particular to the next to sort of see, you know, are there other pro Trump Facebook pages? Are there pro Trump websites? Who are the people running these? You know, what messaging are they using?*

We were interested in that element of it, and we were interested for a couple of reasons. The first reason is that a lot of pro Trump content online was getting really good engagement. And so we figured that there might be people from other countries around the world who are sort of trying to grab a piece of that. And then the second piece was that we were interested to see if there were any other foreign entities that were helping push pro Trump messaging outside of the U.S.

And, obviously, one of the ones that comes to mind when you think about that would be Russia. Are there any sites pushing pro Trump messaging in Europe that had connections perhaps to Russian interests? So we went looking and we found some sites in different places. And we found this small cluster initially in Macedonia, and that was sort of, of interest. You know, why would people in Macedonia be running sites that seemed very pro Trump in English?

And we looked a little bit closer and did more research and we found that actually the Guardian months earlier had pointed to over a hundred websites about U.S. politics in this small town of Veles. So we did our own research and we turned up a number of 140 sites. And I went and I visited every single one of these 140 sites personally. And we started to build a spreadsheet to sort of see like, OK, so what kind of content are they publishing and do they lean right or left or do they seem kind of, you know, in the middle?

And as I filled out the spreadsheet it became very clear that they were overwhelmingly pro Trump. And as I visited the websites and read their content, I saw that a lot of the stuff that they were pushing was misleading, was to the extreme of partisanship and also occasionally was false. And so we dug in even more and realized that among the top shared articles from, you know, these range of sites, the majority of, like, the top five were actually completely false. So at that point, once we understood the content that they were publishing and how many there were, we really wanted to understand so who are the people behind these sites?

DAVIES: *OK, so you got in contact with these folks. Who were they?*

SILVERMAN: *Yeah, I shot out a lot of emails. You know, the sites that we had found, we found sort of who was registered as the owner of the sites. And most people didn't respond to me. Some people got back to me and politely declined saying that they weren't interested in talking to me.*

But a few people through email or through finding them on Facebook and talking to them did speak to me. And one of the things that stood out right away was that a lot of them were very young. In fact, a lot of the people I spoke to were still in their teens or in their 20s and in university. And, you know, the biggest question is why. You know, why run politics sites, why proTrump politics sites and how would a teenager in Macedonia think to do this?

And I think there were probably still some unanswered questions there. But the answer that they always gave me was that, you know, it was simply for money. There are a lot of sites run out of Veles, run out of Macedonia in general that we found. In particular, there's a huge cluster of websites in English about health issues because they find that that content does really well.

And if they sign up, for example, for Google AdSense, an ad program, they can get money as people visit their sites and it's pretty straightforward. So they tried election sites, and over time they all came to realize that the stuff that did the best was proTrump stuff. They got the most traffic and most traction.

DAVIES: *So these are young people, teenagers in some cases, who aren't driven by ideology. They're making a buck. Do they make money from doing well on Facebook?*

SILVERMAN: *Facebook directly doesn't really earn them a lot of money. But the key thing about Facebook—and this is true whether you're running a politics site out of Macedonia or whether you run a very large website in the U.S. —Facebook is the biggest driver of traffic to, you know, news websites in the world now. You know, 1.8 billion people log into Facebook every month. And they'll...*

DAVIES: *They see stuff they like, they hit the link and they go to the site, right?*

SILVERMAN: *That's it. And so the key thing there is you have to get your content onto Facebook. You have to get in front of people so that they start sharing it and clicking on it. And so Facebook is the driver. And what we've found in subsequent investigations was that a lot of the folks running these sites in Macedonia also have these—sometimes they're creating or buying fake Facebook accounts which they then use to go online and to drop links to the stories on their websites into, for example, proTrump Facebook groups that exist online. Maybe they have thousands or tens of thousands of members. If you put your story in there, hopefully you're going to get some clicks. And so that's what they were doing. They were using Facebook to drive the traffic to the website where they had ads from Google and where they would earn money from that traffic.*

DAVIES: *Right. Now, these young people in Macedonia I don't expect know enough* *about American politics to produce convincing fake election stories. Where were they getting the content?*

SILVERMAN: *This is, again, one of the key things you wonder because, I mean, the English of some of the folks that I interviewed, you know, was OK, but not enough for them to kind of create this content themselves. And so as we were looking at the sites, we realized that, you know, if you, for example, would place the headline for a particular article on a Macedonian site in Google, you would probably find that exact headline on a site run out of the U.S. maybe a day or two earlier.*

And so in the end, what they were doing was paying attention to the content that was doing well on Facebook, you know, looking in those proTrump Facebook groups to see what people were sharing. And then they would, you know, copy that text completely or just kind of pick a little piece out of it and link back. And so it was a very easy thing for them to do. They didn't have to come up with stories. They certainly weren't doing reporting. They were kind of copying and pasting and getting their stuff onto Facebook.

And the key here is it speaks to kind of what happens on Facebook, which is that it doesn't matter who necessarily created the story first. It matters who was able to get it to move the most on Facebook. That's who would earn the most money.

DAVIES: *So these guys figured out there was money to be made from pushing this. When you talked to them, did you say hey, this isn't true, voters are being misinformed? Did they care?*

SILVERMAN: *There wasn't a huge amount of concern over that. And I think part of it is that, you know, Veles, it's a small place. It's—economically, it's not doing very well. Used to be heavy industry there. A lot of those jobs are gone now. And I think there was an element almost— in some of the people I was speaking to, there was almost an element of pride saying, you know, we're here in this small country that most Americans probably don't even think about, and we're able to, you know, put stuff out and earn money and to run a business. And I think there was a bit of pride in that. One of the people that I spoke to, who was a bit older—he was in his 20s—you know, he said that yeah, I mean, people know that a lot of the content is false. But that's what works.*

And that's, again, one of the really big takeaways, I think, from this election, is—and I heard this not only from people in Macedonia, but from people in the U.S. who run very large—what people sort of refer to as hyperpartisan conservative Facebook pages. You know, meaning that their content is very, very slanted and very much appealing to their core audience there. They all said that when it came down to it, the fake stuff performed better on Facebook. And if you weren't doing some stuff that was misleading or fake, you were going to get beat by people who were.

DAVIES: *You actually did an analysis where you looked at the accuracy of stories done by hyper-partisan sites on the right, hyperpartisan sites on the left and mainstream sites. What did you find about how well accurate stuff played and how well false stuff played?*

SILVERMAN: *So a team of us at BuzzFeed, you know, we spent seven consecutive weekdays looking at all of the posts that went up on the Facebook pages of a selection of, as you said, pages on the right, pages on the left. And then we also looked at three mainstream pages as well as kind of, you know, a base of comparison. And what we found overall is that the content that performed best was—you know, fell into two categories. So one is—was sort of misleading or false completely. That would get high engagement, meaning high shares on Facebook. That's—we really zeroed in on shares because that's how you drive the most traffic.*

And then the other type of content that performed really well was, you know, memes, like a photo that just sort—kind of expressed a very partisan opinion. These—you know, they weren't necessarily factually based, but they really kind of riled up the base. And for the pages that were partisan pages on the right and the left, if you had stuff that really appealed to people's existing beliefs—really appealed to, you know, a negative perception of Hillary Clinton, a negative perception of Donald Trump—even if it, you know, completely bent the truth, that would perform much better than a sort of purely factual thing.

And when we looked at the performance of the mainstream pages, you know, the engagement for the partisan pages was much better. And I don't think that's only because we did find false and misleading stuff on the partisan pages. I think it's also because frankly, you know, the mainstream pages weren't posting as many memes. They weren't posting as many videos. And that stuff does really well on Facebook. It's strange, but you would think the media—big media companies are better at kind of running their Facebook pages. But honestly, these partisan pages on the right and the left were just much better at understanding what does well on Facebook.

DAVIES: *Craig Silverman is the media editor for BuzzFeed. We'll continue our conversation in just a moment. This is* Fresh Air.

DAVIES: *This is* Fresh Air, *and we're talking about fake news in the presidential campaign with BuzzFeed media editor Craig Silverman. When we left off, we were talking about BuzzFeed's analysis of how false, highly partisan content did better on Facebook than stories reported by mainstream media.*

SILVERMAN: *So at the core of this is—there's two factors that are at play here. So one is a human factor and one is kind of a platform or algorithmic factor. So on the human side, there's a lot of research out there going back a very long time that looks at sort of how humans deal with information. And one of the things that we love as humans— and this, this affects all of us. We shouldn't think of this as just being something for people who are very partisan. We love to hear things that confirm what we think and what we feel and what we already believe. It's—it makes us feel good to get information that aligns with what we already believe or what we want to hear.*

And on the other side of that is when we're confronted with information that contradicts what we think and what we feel, the reaction isn't to kind of sit back and consider it. The reaction is often to double down on our existing beliefs. So if you're feeding people information that basically just tells them what they want to hear, they're probably going to react strongly to that. And the other layer that these pages are very good at is they bring in emotion into it, anger or hate or surprise or, you know, joy. And so if you combine information that aligns with their beliefs, if you can make it something that strikes an emotion in them, then that gets them to react.

And that's where the kind of platform and algorithms come in. Which is that on Facebook, you know, the more you interact with certain types of content, the more its algorithms are going to feed you more of that content. So if you're reading stuff that aligns perfectly with your political beliefs, it makes you feel really good and really excited and you share it, Facebook is going to see that as a signal that you want more of that stuff. So that's why the false misleading stuff does really well is because it's highly emotion-driven. It tells people exactly what they want to hear. It makes them feel very comforted and it gets them to react on the platform. And the platform sees that content does really well and Facebook feeds more of it to more people.

DAVIES: *There are plenty of stories that debunk inaccurate information and you looked at how they do. How do they compare to the false stories?*

SILVERMAN: *They don't, unfortunately. And this goes back to a research project I did a couple of years ago where I was really very focused, one, on the spread of rumors and misinformation online and two, also how media organizations deal with this new world where it's very easy for something, you know, that's simply a tweet claiming something to suddenly get huge exposure and huge distribution. And the same obviously happens on Facebook on an even bigger scale. So when you're a journalist and you see something out there, you're not sure whether it's true or false, how do you deal with it? Do you wait and do your work? Or because potentially millions of people have already seen it, do you kind of write about it?*

So I did a research project where we kind of identified rumors that we saw out there. We looked at how media coverage was of it. And this is how I started to encounter a lot of fake news stories and started to realize that there were entire websites that existed that just had completely fake stuff. So when I would see that completely fake stuff circulating, I would—we would look at the Facebook and other types of social engagement for it. And then we would also try to find any debunking of it from Snopes or from other sources. And honestly during that research project, we really only found I think one example where the debunkings actually had actually gotten more engagement on social, and in particular Facebook, than the false information.

DAVIES: *It's just not as much fun?*

SILVERMAN: *Yeah. There's a few things going on there. And again, psychology comes into it a little bit. So one, when people create the false stuff and if they're smart about it—if I put it that way—you know, they know that it needs to appeal to emotion. They know that maybe if it can have a sense of urgency, if it can be tied to things people care* *about, that's probably going to do well in terms of fake stuff. Whereas when you come in as the debunker, what you're doing is actively going against information that people are probably already, you know, willing to believe and that gets them emotionally. And to tell somebody I'm sorry that thing you saw and shared is not true is you coming in a very negative way unfortunately.*

And so the reaction is often for people to get defensive and to disagree with you. And just in general you just seem like kind of a spoil sport. You're ruining the fun or you're getting in the way of their beliefs. And a lot of times when I put debunkings out there, you know, some of the reactions I get are people saying, well, it might as well be true. You know, he could have said that or that could have happened. Or, of course, you get accusations that, you know, you're biased. And so the debunkings just don't appeal as much to us on a psychological level. There's some emotional resistance to wanting to be wrong. That's a very natural human thing. And they're just not as shareable because the emotion there isn't as real and raw as something that makes you angry, for example.

DAVIES: *Craig Silverman is media editor for* BuzzFeed. *After a break, he'll talk about how Facebook handles fake news and what it might do better. I'm Dave Davies and this is Fresh Air.*

DAVIES: *This is* Fresh Air. *I'm Dave Davies in for Terry Gross. We're speaking with BuzzFeed media editor Craig Silverman about the spread of fake news in the presidential campaign. Silverman spent a lot of this year investigating fake news, reporting that a torrent of false web stories came from a small town in Macedonia and discovering that late in the campaign fake news did better on Facebook than stories from mainstream media sources.*

As the campaign proceeded, did the campaigns themselves or Donald Trump through his tweets have any role in building an audience for these fake news stories?

SILVERMAN: *Yeah. I think the Trump campaign was so remarkable for so many reasons when we talk about this specific area. So the first that I think needs to be mentioned is that, you know, the Trump campaign itself helped circulate false news stories, 100 percent fake news stories from 100 percent fake news websites.*

DAVIES: *Give us an example.*

SILVERMAN: *So the one that comes to mind right away, this is a story that was on a website that is made to look like ABC News but its domain is slightly different. And the story that was published, you know, long before the election claimed that a protester had been paid $3,500 to go and protest at a Trump rally. And this fed into perceptions that the people who are against Trump were being paid by big interests.*

And that story did pretty well on Facebook. It got a fair amount of engagement. But it was tweeted by Eric Trump. It was tweeted by Corey Lewandowski, who was a campaign manager for Donald Trump, and it was tweeted by Kellyanne Conway, who was his campaign manager, not that long before the election. So when you have people in positions of power and influence putting out fake news—and I want to say, you know, there's no evidence that they knew it was fake and put it out there to fool people. I think in each case they genuinely believed it was true because, as we've discussed, I think it fed into the message their campaign wanted to put

> **And when you have somebody who is in that position of power, with that amount of influence, with that amount of people who are very passionate about him and what they think he can bring to the country, putting out false information—you know, I think it lays the groundwork for other false information to get out there.**

out. And it's really kind of unprecedented to think of people that high in a campaign actively putting out misinformation and it happening from several people. You would have thought that after one or two of them did it, your people would have talked to them. So that piece is really, really remarkable.

The other one that I think has to be mentioned is that Donald Trump, on a very frequent basis throughout the campaign and now that he is the president-elect, says things that are not true and things that are demonstrably false. And when you have somebody who is in that position of power, with that amount of influence, with that amount of people who are very passionate about him and what they think he can bring to the country, putting out false information—you know, I think it lays the groundwork for other false information to get out there. And it creates a fertile environment for folks to start kind of making things up because the door is wide open. And I think that there is something unique about the Trump campaign in that respect.

DAVIES: *Did you see any of this kind of activity among Democrats?*

SILVERMAN: *So there certainly was false information circulating that was, you know, antiTrump or proClinton. I certainly can't think of an example from the Clinton campaign of them actively falling for fake news or what have you. But there's no question that there were things that were false that spread about Donald Trump.*

I can think of one meme that I saw where people had misquoted him. One that was really popular actually was one that falsely claimed he had given a quote to People magazine many years ago basically saying that if I ever ran for president, I would run as a Republican because conservatives are so stupid they'll believe anything. And this was turned into a meme.

It spread a lot on Facebook. It was debunked so many times. We debunked it at BuzzFeed. Snopes has debunked it. And it just kept going and going and going because this is something I think a lot of Democrats wanted to believe. But it also has to be said, I mean, all of the analysis that we've done about misinformation related to the election has shown that proTrump misinformation and antiClinton misinformation far outperformed anything that came from the other side.

DAVIES: *Do we have any idea what the effect of this was on this election? Has anybody tried to figure out how many minds were changed, how many votes might have been affected?*

SILVERMAN: *I don't think anybody's going to get a definitive answer on that. It's really tough to conclude the effect of media on people's voting habits because there are so many factors. But—so I think anyone who believes that fake news won Trump the election is wrong. There's no data to support that. And I say this as somebody who's been looking at this data in a lot of different ways. There's no smoking gun. There's—I don't think we'll ever get it.*

But when we look at some of the data about the impact of misinformation, it's really significant. So we at BuzzFeed partnered with Ipsos to do a survey of 3,000 Americans. And one of the things we wanted to find out was their familiarity with fake news headlines about the election. And what we found in the end after testing a group of five fake news headlines that went really big during the election and six real news headlines that went really big during the election is that 75 percent of the time, the Americans who were shown a fake news headline and had remembered it from the election believed it to be accurate.

And that's a really shocking thing. It's impossible to go the next step and say, well, they voted because of that. But I think one of the things this election has shown is that people will believe fake news, misinformation will spread and people will believe it and it will become part of their worldview.

DAVIES: *Yeah, but did I hear that right, three quarters of us will believe a fake headline, think it's true?*

SILVERMAN: *This is—this was a pretty high number, a shocking number. And that number is based on more than 1,500 judgments about fake news headlines from people in this sample of 3,000 people. So it's a pretty good sample size. It's not definitive, but it's a high number. And it is shocking because, I mean, for example, one of these headlines that we tested claimed that Hillary Clinton had been proven to have sold weapons to ISIS. I mean, that was one of the headlines and people did believe that.*

DAVIES: *We're speaking with Craig Silverman. He is the media editor for* BuzzFeed. *We'll continue our conversation after a short break. This is* Fresh Air.

DAVIES: *This is* Fresh Air. *And we're speaking with Craig Silverman. He is the media editor for BuzzFeed. He's been writing about accuracy in reporting and factchecking for many years. And he spent a lot of time this election season writing about fake news.*

Let's talk about Facebook's role here. Now, Facebook founder Mark Zuckerberg has said a number of different things about this. At one point, he said, you know, we're a tech company, not a media company. And that's what Facebook does—right? —it allows millions of people to share content and is kind of reluctant maybe to regulate it. What have its own policies done to propagate or limit the spread of false information?

SILVERMAN: *One of the core things that Facebook does or I suppose what it doesn't do as much as it can tries to not act as kind of a censor or a control point on what people are sharing. And I think overall, you know, that's a good thing. I don't want Facebook deciding whether what I put up is good enough to be shown to other people or not.*

And this goes into what you mentioned about it sees itself as a platform, meaning it's a place where you can put stuff out and they help it reach lots of people and help you connect with other people. But, of course, that cuts both ways. So me sharing stuff about my family, me sharing news stories I've read that I care about can get just as much attention and can move just as easily as somebody who's consciously created something false and is working to get it to spread on Facebook. So the platform mentality creates the opportunity there.

And the scale of Facebook, which I think people should never get comfortable with how big it is because it's unlike anything in human history. There are almost 2 billion people logging in every month around the world. We've never had a communications system where people are connected in this way that has reached that amount of scale.

And so I think along with, you know, the platform mentality, there's also the scale piece of it that is a huge factor in false information spreading because there's just so many people there. And there's so much potential for information to move and to spread. And Facebook at the scale it's at to a certain extent I feel is almost unknowable. You can't even fathom understanding what's happening on it at any given moment. I think that's not only true for us, but it's also true for them because I think from what we've seen Mark Zuckerberg say, I think he's been really taken aback by what happened, to be honest.

DAVIES: *Taken aback by the volume of fake news stories that spread during the election, you mean?*

SILVERMAN: *Yeah. I mean, his first comments were very dismissive. You know, the first thing he said publicly about it was at a tech conference and he talked about it being, you know, just a crazy idea that fake news had an effect on the election. And, you know, I agree with him. I'm not ready to say that fake news decided the election for Trump. But I also think that completely dismissing, you know, the growing evidence that we have that fake news got huge, huge engagement on his platform, you know, it doesn't make any sense. And he got a lot of blowback for that comment. And I think over time they have come to realize inside Facebook that, you know, this is actually a big issue. And they faced a lot of criticism. And now, you know, the most recent thing from Mark Zuckerberg is they announced seven things they're going to do to try and reduce the spread of misinformation on their platform.*

DAVIES: *What are they? And do you think they're effective?*

SILVERMAN: *So one of the things that they're going to do, for example, is to make it easier for average users of Facebook if they see something that's false to be able to kind of flag it and say, hey, this is a false piece of content and signal to Facebook that this is something that you don't want to see but also something that they should look at and prevent from spreading further. Now, that's a feature that actually already exists in some ways. The problem is that it's very hidden. So they want to make that a little more evident for people. And I think that's a good thing. The downside as always is that how many people are going to use that? And would people use it to kind of flag stuff they simply just disagree with rather than things that are false?*

They've also acknowledged that there's a role of their algorithms in this. And they're looking at ways of having algorithms be able to recognize stuff that might be misinformation. And that may sound like a simple thing to say. It's incredibly complicated to do. And I've spoken to a lot of researchers who were very focused in this area of trying to automatically identify misinformation or automatically identify rumors and there is no algorithm that exists today that can do that at a high level of accuracy. So the opportunity is for Facebook to really do huge amounts of leadership in this area and do some innovation.

The downside is for them to hand too much over to an algorithm that starts suppressing free speech and suppressing other things it's not supposed to. One of the last things he mentioned that's probably worth noting is they've announced that they are not going to allow fake news websites to have access to the advertising tools on Facebook. So if you run a fake news website, they're going to try and stop you from, for example, paying to promote that post to more people on Facebook. And that's a good thing. And I think if we can cut off some of the financial incentives around fake news, that overall it can be quite powerful.

DAVIES: *Right. And, of course, that requires somebody to make a judgment about what a fake new site is.*

SILVERMAN: *Yeah. Now, this is where things are getting very tricky. And as much as we talk about algorithms when we talk about Facebook, you know, there are humans who are involved in the review of content. When you flag something as offensive on Facebook, it's possible that it may automatically then be scanned by an algorithm and realize that that is an image, for example, maybe they've already banned. But a lot of the time it ends up in front of a person on their content review team who has to make a judgment call. And I can tell you from speaking to people in conservative media, they are extremely concerned.*

One, they view Facebook as a liberal organization. They think it's biased against conservative points of view. And two, they're extremely concerned that if Facebook starts trying to weed out fakes, they're going to have people with a liberal point of view who disagree with an article potentially suppressing it. And so there is risk now of suppression of free speech and suppression of different points of view if these things were to go in the wrong direction.

DAVIES: *Do you have a view yourself about what they should be doing?*

SILVERMAN: *You know, the first thing in terms of what should be done is that—is the answer is kind of a lot of things. And that's an unsatisfying answer to give, but it speaks to the complexity of this problem. When people started circulating lists of fake news websites, it was a huge problem because a lot of the sites on those lists, sure, they may publish some stuff that's misleading or false but they weren't publishing stuff a hundred percent in those areas. And there were a lot of simply ideologicallydriven sites that were on these lists. And so if, for example, Facebook wanted to just implement a big bad blacklist, get rid of lots of sites, that would be a terrible, terrible outcome. So it's not as simple as I think some people have suggested it can be.*

I would like to see them make flagging more of—more easy for people and to make sure that it can't be abused. I think they absolutely need to innovate in the area of algorithmic detection of misinformation. I also think, frankly, they do need to increase the amount of people who are reviewing content, whether it's for being offensive or other things because the scale of their platform is so big that I don't think they've put the human element in there in the right places. So them figuring out where that can be applied and how to guard against ideologicallydriven decisions is a big thing. And to be honest, I think that they should figure out ways to identify the sites that are a hundred percent fake news and to see how they're sharing. Are they just being shared among small groups of people who all sort of think the same way and realize that that probably isn't a story that should spread further. So I'm not a huge proponent of blacklists but I think that analyzing the content and knowing what it is and knowing how it's being shared is really important.

The other unsexy thing finally, I think, is that we need to put this in our education system. There are a lot of people being fooled by fake news. There are a lot of people who don't know how to kind of check out the story they're reading online and that's understandable. It's not a matter of intelligence. We're consuming media in very different ways. We're having a whole menu of links and things from all different kinds of sources fed to us every day by Facebook. And that's very different from opening up a newspaper and knowing where everything was coming from. So I think we do in our schools need to start thinking about how we integrate more media literacy and critical thinking education so that people can make better judgments for themselves.

DAVIES: *What's Google's role in all of this?*

SILVERMAN: *Well, Google is in a lot of ways the financial engine for fake news. And similar to Facebook, Google is—considers itself a technology company, not a media company, and considers itself in many ways a platform, which means they're not there, you know, to decide what should or shouldn't be published. They're there to facilitate these things.*

The biggest piece for Google—aside from obviously the search element which can send a lot of traffic to these sites—the biggest piece is AdSense, which is their very big advertising network, which you can sign up for very quickly. If you put up a website and you've got some content on it and you submit to AdSense to apply to put ads on it, you can get approved relatively quickly. They do review the site to see if it goes against any of their terms of service. But once you have the ads up there, that's how you make the money.

And I have to say, I mean, the vast majority of the fake news websites and kind of dubious websites that I come across are running AdSense. And oftentimes they're doing things that are in direct opposition to the terms of service that Google says it applies to the sites that are supposed to be in that program.

DAVIES: How would they violate Google's terms of service?

SILVERMAN: Well, let's take the Macedonian sites as an example. One of the things that Google looks for in approving a site for AdSense is that they're adding value in some way. So if you, for example, set up a site and all you did was copy and paste content from other sites and you added nothing to it, you should not be approved for AdSense.

But that's what a lot of the Macedonia's sites that I looked at were doing. They were either completely plagiarizing or just quickly taking from elsewhere and copying it almost completely. There's no reason why those sites should have been approved. They violate Google's own terms of service for AdSense, and they just shouldn't be able to make money that way, but they do.

And so these review processes, whether it's Facebook, you know, trying to review a piece of content to figure out whether it's false or offensive or Google trying to figure out whether a site is in line with its advertising standards, you know, there's always going to be mistakes. There's always going to be things that slip through cracks because when you're a platform, you have reached such massive scale that it's very hard to do quality control.

DAVIES: Well, Craig Silverman, thanks so much for speaking with us.

SILVERMAN: Thank you.

DAVIES: Craig Silverman is media editor of BuzzFeed and author of the book Regret the Error. This is Fresh Air.

Print Citations

CMS: "Fake News Expert on How False Stories Spread and Why People Believe Them." In *The Reference Shelf: Internet Abuses and Privacy Rights*, edited by Betsy Maury, 113-127. Ipswich, MA: H.W. Wilson, 2017.

MLA: "Fake News Expert on How False Stories Spread and Why People Believe Them." *The Reference Shelf: Internet Abuses and Privacy Rights*. Ed. Betsy Maury. Ipswich: H.W. Wilson, 2017. 113-127. Print.

APA: NPR Fresh Air. (2017). Fake news expert on how false stories spread and why people believe them. In Betsy Maury (Ed.), *The Reference Shelf: Internet Abuses and Privacy Rights* (pp. 113-127). Ipswich, MA: H.W. Wilson. (Original work published 2016)

Who Controls Your Facebook Feed

By Will Oremus
Slate, January 3, 2016

Every time you open Facebook, one of the world's most influential, controversial, and misunderstood algorithms springs into action. It scans and collects everything posted in the past week by each of your friends, everyone you follow, each group you belong to, and every Facebook page you've liked. For the average Facebook user, that's more than 1,500 posts. If you have several hundred friends, it could be as many as 10,000. Then, according to a closely guarded and constantly shifting formula, Facebook's news feed algorithm ranks them all, in what it believes to be the precise order of how likely you are to find each post worthwhile. Most users will only ever see the top few hundred.

No one outside Facebook knows for sure how it does this, and no one inside the company will tell you. And yet the results of this automated ranking process shape the social lives and reading habits of more than 1 billion daily active users—one-fifth of the world's adult population. The algorithm's viral power has turned the media industry upside down, propelling startups like *BuzzFeed* and *Vox* to national prominence while 100-year-old newspapers wither and die. It fueled the stratospheric rise of billion-dollar companies like Zynga and LivingSocial—only to suck the helium from them a year or two later with a few adjustments to its code, leaving behind empty-pocketed investors and laid-off workers. Facebook's news feed algorithm can be tweaked to make us happy or sad; it can expose us to new and challenging ideas or insulate us in ideological bubbles.

And yet, for all its power, Facebook's news feed algorithm is surprisingly inelegant, maddeningly mercurial, and stubbornly opaque. It remains as likely as not to serve us posts we find trivial, irritating, misleading, or just plain boring. And Facebook knows it. Over the past several months, the social network has been running a test in which it shows some users the top post in their news feed alongside one other, lower-ranked post, asking them to pick the one they'd prefer to read. The result? The algorithm's rankings correspond to the user's preferences "sometimes," Facebook acknowledges, declining to get more specific. When they don't match up, the company says, that points to "an area for improvement."

"Sometimes" isn't the success rate you might expect for such a vaunted and feared bit of code. The news feed algorithm's outsize influence has given rise to a strand of criticism that treats it as if it possessed a mind of its own—as if it were some runic form of intelligence, loosed on the world to pursue ends beyond the ken of human understanding. At a time when Facebook and other Silicon Valley giants increasingly filter our choices and guide our decisions through machine-learning software, when tech titans like Elon Musk and scientific laureates like Stephen Hawking are warning of the existential threat posed by A.I., the word itself—*algorithm*—has begun to take on an eerie affect. Algorithms, in the popular imagination, are mysterious, powerful entities that stand for all the ways technology and modernity both serve our every desire and threaten the values we hold dear.

The reality of Facebook's algorithm is somewhat less fantastical, but no less fascinating. I had a rare chance recently to spend time with Facebook's news feed team at their Menlo Park, California, headquarters and see what it actually looks like when they make one of those infamous, market-moving "tweaks" to the algorithm— why they do it, how they do it, and how they decide whether it worked. A glimpse into its inner workings sheds light not only on the mechanisms of Facebook's news feed, but on the limitations of machine learning, the pitfalls of data-driven decision making, and the moves Facebook is increasingly making to collect and address feedback from individual human users, including a growing panel of testers that are becoming Facebook's equivalent of the Nielsen family.

Facebook's algorithm, I learned, isn't flawed because of some glitch in the system. It's flawed because, unlike the perfectly realized, sentient algorithms of our sci-fi fever dreams, the intelligence behind Facebook's software is fundamentally human. Humans decide what data goes into it, what it can do with that data, and what they want to come out the other end. When the algorithm errs, humans are to blame. When it evolves, it's because a bunch of humans read a bunch of spreadsheets, held a bunch of meetings, ran a bunch of tests, and decided to make it better. And if it does keep getting better? That'll be because another group of humans keeps telling them about all the ways it's falling short: us.

A Visit to Menlo Park

When I arrive at Facebook's sprawling, Frank Gehry–designed office in Menlo Park, I'm met by a lanky 37-year-old man whose boyish countenance shifts quickly between an earnest smile and an expression of intense focus. Tom Alison is director of engineering for the news feed; he's in charge of the humans who are in charge of the algorithm.

Alison steers me through a maze of cubicles and open minikitchens toward a small conference room, where he promises to demystify the Facebook algorithm's true nature. On the way there, I realize I need to use the bathroom and ask for directions. An involuntary grimace crosses his face before he apologizes, smiles, and says, "I'll walk you there." At first I think it's because he doesn't want me to get lost. But when I emerge from the bathroom, he's still standing right outside, and it occurs to me that he's not allowed to leave me unattended.

For the same reason—Facebook's fierce protection of trade secrets—Alison cannot tell me much about the actual code that composes the news feed algorithm.

He can, however, tell me what it does, and why—and why it's always changing. He starts, as engineers often do, at the whiteboard.

"When you study computer science, one of the first algorithms you learn is a sorting algorithm," Alison says. He scribbles a list of positive integers in dry erase:

4, 1, 3, 2, 5

The simple task at hand: devise an algorithm to sort these numbers into ascending order. "Human beings know how to do this," Alison says. "We just kind of do it in our heads."

Computers, however, must be told precisely how. That requires an algorithm: a set of concrete instructions by which a given problem may be solved. The algorithm Alison shows me is called "bubble sort," and it works like this:

1. For each number in the set, starting with the first one, compare it to the number that follows, and see if they're in the desired order.
2. If not, reverse them.
3. Repeat steps 1 and 2 until you're able to proceed through the set from start to end without reversing any numbers.

The virtue of bubble sort is its simplicity. The downside: If your data set is large, it's computationally inefficient and time-consuming. Facebook, for obvious reasons, does not use bubble sort. It does use a sorting algorithm to order the set of all posts that could appear in your news feed when you open the app. But that's the trivial part—a minor subalgorithm within the master algorithm. The nontrivial part is assigning all those posts a numerical value in the first place. That, in short, is the job of the news feed ranking team: to devise a system capable of assigning any given Facebook post a "relevancy score" specific to any given Facebook user.

That's a hard problem, because what's relevant to you—a post from your childhood friend or from a celebrity you follow—might be utterly irrelevant to me. For that, Alison explains, Facebook uses a different kind of algorithm, called a prediction algorithm. (Facebook's news feed algorithm, like Google's search algorithm or Netflix's recommendation algorithm, is really a sprawling complex of software made up of smaller algorithms.)

"Let's say I ask you to pick the winner of a future basketball game, Bulls vs. Lakers," Alison begins. "Bulls," I blurt. Alison laughs, but then he nods vigorously. My brain has taken his input and produced an immediate verbal output, perhaps according to some impish algorithm of its own. (The human mind's algorithms are far more sophisticated than anything Silicon Valley has yet devised, but they're also heavily reliant on heuristics and notoriously prone to folly.)

Random guessing is fine when you've got nothing to lose, Alison says. But let's say there was a lot of money riding on my basketball predictions, and I was making them millions of times a day. I'd need a more systematic approach. "You're probably going to start by looking at historical data," he says. "You're going to look at the win-loss record of each team, the records of the individual players, who's injured, who's on a streak." Maybe you'll take into account environmental factors: Who's the home team? Is one squad playing on short rest, or after a cross-country flight? Your prediction algorithm might incorporate all of these factors and more. If it's good, it will not only predict the game's winner, but tell you its degree of confidence in the result.

That's analogous to what Facebook's news feed algorithm does when it tries to predict whether you'll like a given post. I ask Alison how many variables—"features," in machine-learning lingo—Facebook's algorithm takes into account. "Hundreds," he says.

It doesn't just predict whether you'll actually hit the like button on a post based on your past behavior. It also predicts whether you'll click, comment, share, or hide it, or even mark it as spam. It will predict each of these outcomes, and others, with a certain degree of confidence, then combine them all to produce a single relevancy score that's specific to both you and that post. Once every possible post in your feed has received its relevancy score, the sorting algorithm can put them in the order that you'll see them on the screen. The post you see at the top of your feed, then, has been chosen over thousands of others as the one most likely to make you laugh, cry, smile, click, like, share, or comment.

> **Who controls your Facebook feed? A small team of engineers in Menlo Park. A panel of anonymous power users around the world. And, increasingly, you.**

Yet no matter how meticulously you construct an algorithm, there are always going to be data to which you aren't privy: the coaches' game plans, how Derrick Rose's knee is feeling that day, whether the ball is properly inflated. In short, the game isn't played by data. It's played by people. And people are too complex for any algorithm to model.

Facebook's prediction algorithm faces still another complication, this one a little more epistemological. The relevancy score is meant to be analogous to the likelihood that the Bulls will win the game. That's a discrete outcome that's fully measurable: They either win or they don't. Facebook's ranking algorithm used to try to predict a similarly measurable outcome: whether you'd interact in some way with the post in question. Interactions, the humans behind Facebook's news feed figured, are a good indicator that a given post has struck a chord. They also happen to be the fuel that drives the Facebook economy: clicks, likes, shares, and comments are what make posts go viral, turn individual users into communities, and drive traffic to the advertisers that Facebook relies on for revenue.

But those interactions are only a rough proxy for what Facebook users actually want. What if people "like" posts that they don't really like, or click on stories that turn out to be unsatisfying? The result could be a news feed that optimizes for virality, rather than quality— one that feeds users a steady diet of candy, leaving them dizzy and a little nauseated, liking things left and right but gradually growing to hate the whole silly game. How do you optimize against that?

Facebook's News Feed

It was late 2013, and Facebook was the hottest company in the world. The social network had blown past 1 billion users and gone public at a valuation of more than $100 billion. It had spent the past year building a revamped mobile app that quickly surpassed Google Search and Google Maps as the nation's most popular. No longer just a way to keep in touch with friends, Facebook had become, in effect, the global newspaper of the 21st century: an up-to-the-minute feed of news, entertainment, and personal updates from friends and loved ones, automatically tailored to the specific interests of each individual user.

Inside the company, the people in charge of the news feed were thrilled with the growth. But while users' engagement was skyrocketing, it wasn't clear whether their overall satisfaction with Facebook was keeping pace. People were liking more things on Facebook than ever. But were they liking Facebook less?

To understand how that question arose, you have to rewind to 2006. Facebook— which was originally little more than a massive compendium of profile pages and groups, something like Myspace—built the news feed in that year as a hub for updates about your friends' activities on the site. Users bristled at the idea that their status updates, profile picture changes, and flirtatious notes on one another's pages would be blasted into the feeds of all of their friends, but Facebook pressed on.

Even then, not everything your friends did made it into your news feed. To avoid overwhelming people with hundreds of updates every day, Facebook built a crude algorithm to filter them based on how likely they were to be of interest. With no real way to measure that— the like button came three years later—the company's engineers simply made assumptions based on their own intuition. Early criteria for inclusion of a post in your news feed included how recent it was and how many of your friends it mentioned. Over time, the team tried tweaking those assumptions and testing how the changes affected the amount of time users spent on the site. But with no way to assess which sorts of posts were delighting people and which were boring, offending, or confusing them, the engineers were essentially throwing darts.

The like button wasn't just a new way for users to interact on the site. It was a way for Facebook to enlist its users in solving the problem of how best to filter their own news feeds. That users didn't realize they were doing this was perhaps the most ingenious part. If Facebook had told users they had to rank and review their friends' posts to help the company determine how many other people should see them, we would have found the process tedious and distracting. Facebook's news feed algorithm was one of the first to surreptitiously enlist users in personalizing their experience—and influencing everyone else's.

Suddenly the algorithm had a way to identify the most popular posts—and make them go "viral," a term previously applied to things that were communicated from person to person, rather that broadcast algorithmically to a mass audience. Yet Facebook employees weren't the only ones who could see what it took for a given post to go viral. Publishers, advertisers, hoaxsters, and even individual users began to glean the elements that viral posts tended to have in common—the features that seemed to trigger reflexive likes from large numbers of friends, followers, and even random strangers. Many began to tailor their posts to get as many likes as possible. Social-media consultants sprung up to advise people on how to game Facebook's algorithm: the right words to use, the right time to post, the right blend of words and pictures. "LIKE THIS," a feel-good post would implore, and people would do it, even if they didn't really care that much about the post. It wasn't long before Facebook users' feeds began to feel eerily similar: all filled with content that was engineered to go viral, much of it mawkish or patronizing. Drowned out were substance, nuance, sadness, and anything that provoked thought or emotions beyond a simple thumbs-up.

Engagement metrics were up—way up—but was this really what the news feed should be optimizing for? The question preoccupied Chris Cox, an early Facebook employee and the news feed's intellectual architect. "Looking at likes, clicks, comments, and shares is one way of determining what people are interested in," Cox, 33, tells me via email. (He's now Facebook's chief product officer.) "But we knew there were places where this was imperfect. For example, you may read a tragic post that you don't want to click like, comment on, or share, but if we asked you, you would say that it really mattered to you to have read it. A couple of years ago, we knew we needed to look at more than just likes and clicks to improve how News Feed worked for these kinds of cases."

An algorithm can optimize for a given outcome, but it can't tell you what that outcome should be. Only humans can do that. Cox and the other humans behind Facebook's news feed decided that their ultimate goal would be to show people all the posts that really matter to them and none of the ones that don't. They knew that might mean sacrificing some short-term engagement—and maybe revenue— in the name of user satisfaction. With Facebook raking in money, and founder and CEO Mark Zuckerberg controlling a majority of the voting shares, the company had the rare luxury to optimize for long-term value. But that still left the question of how exactly to do it.

Media organizations have historically defined what matters to their audience through their own editorial judgment. Press them on what makes a story worthwhile, and they'll appeal to values such as truth, newsworthiness, and public interest. But Cox and his colleagues at Facebook have taken pains to avoid putting their own editorial stamp on the news feed. Instead, their working definition of what matters to any given Facebook user is just this: what he or she would rank at the top of their feeds given the choice. "The perfect way to solve this problem would be to ask everyone which stories they wanted to see and which they didn't, but that's not possible or practical," Cox says. Instead, Facebook decided to ask some people which stories they wanted to see and which they didn't. There were about 1,000 of those people, and until recently, most of them lived in Knoxville, Tennessee. Now they're everywhere.

Adam Mosseri, Facebook's 32-year-old director of product for news feed, is Alison's less technical counterpart—a "fuzzie" rather than a "techie," in Silicon Valley parlance. He traffics in problems and generalities, where Alison deals in solutions and specifics. He's the news feed's resident philosopher.

The push to humanize the news feed's inputs and outputs began under Mosseri's predecessor, Will Cathcart. (I wrote about several of those innovations here.) Cathcart started by gathering more subtle forms of behavioral data: not just whether someone clicked, but how long he spent reading a story once he clicked on it; not just whether he liked it, but whether he liked it before or after reading. For instance: Liking a post before you've read it, Facebook learned, corresponds much more weakly to your actual sentiment than liking it afterward.

The Feed Quality Panel

After taking the reins in late 2013, Mosseri's big initiative was to set up what Facebook calls its "feed quality panel." It began in summer 2014 as a group of several hundred people in Knoxville whom the company paid to come in to an office every day and provide continual, detailed feedback on what they saw in their news feeds. (Their location was, Facebook says, a "historical accident" that grew out of a pilot project in which the company partnered with an unnamed third-party subcontractor.) Mosseri and his team didn't just study their behavior. They also asked them questions to try to get at why they liked or didn't like a given post, how much they liked it, and what they would have preferred to see instead. "They actually write a little paragraph about every story in their news feed," notes Greg Marra, product manager for the news feed ranking team. (This is the group that's becoming Facebook's equivalent of Nielsen families.)

"The question was, 'What might we be missing?'" Mosseri says. "'Do we have any blind spots?'" For instance, he adds, "We know there are some things you see in your feed that you loved and you were excited about, but you didn't actually interact with." Without a way to measure that, the algorithm would devalue such posts in favor of others that lend themselves more naturally to likes and clicks. But what signal could Facebook use to capture that information?

Mosseri deputized product manager Max Eulenstein and user experience researcher Lauren Scissors to oversee the feed quality panel and ask it just those sorts of questions. For instance, Eulenstein used the panel to test the hypothesis that the time a user spends looking at a story in her news feed might be a good indicator that she likes it, even if she didn't actually click like. "We speculated that it might be, but you could think of reasons why it wouldn't be, too," Eulenstein tells me. "It might be that there are scary or shocking stories that you stare at, but don't want to see." The feed quality panelists' ratings allowed Eulenstein and Scissors to not only confirm their hunch, but to examine the subtleties in the correlation, and to begin to quantify it. "It's not as simple as, '5 seconds is good, 2 seconds is bad,'" Eulenstein explains. "It has more to do with the amount of time you spend on a story relative to the other stories in your news feed." The research also revealed the need to control for the speed of users' Internet connections, which can make it seem like they're spending a long time on a given story when they're actually just waiting for the page to load. Out of that research emerged a tweak that Facebook revealed in

June, in which the algorithm boosted the rankings of stories that users spent more time viewing in their feeds.

Within months, Mosseri and his team had grown so reliant on the panel's feedback that they took it nationwide, paying a demographically representative sample of people around the country to rate and review their Facebook feeds on a daily basis from their own homes. By late summer 2015, Facebook disbanded the Knoxville group and began to expand the feed quality panel overseas.

Mosseri's instinct was right: The news feed algorithm had blind spots that Facebook's data scientists couldn't have identified on their own. It took a different kind of data—qualitative human feedback—to begin to fill them in.

Crucial as the feed quality panel has become to Facebook's algorithm, the company has grown increasingly aware that no single source of data can tell it everything. It has responded by developing a sort of checks-and-balances system in which every news feed tweak must undergo a battery of tests among different types of audiences, and be judged on a variety of different metrics.

That balancing act is the task of the small team of news feed ranking engineers, data scientists, and product managers who come to work every day in Menlo Park. They're people like Sami Tas, a software engineer whose job is to translate the news feed ranking team's proposed changes into language that a computer can understand. This afternoon, as I look over his shoulder, he's walking me through a problem that might seem so small as to be trivial. It is exactly the sort of small problem, however, that Facebook now considers critical.

Most of the time, when people see a story they don't care about in their news feed, they scroll right past it. Some stories irk them enough that they're moved to click on the little drop-down menu at the top right of the post and select "Hide post." Facebook's algorithm considers that a strong negative signal and endeavors to show them fewer posts like that in the future.

Not everyone uses Facebook the same way, however. Facebook's data scientists were aware that a small proportion of users—5 percent—were doing 85 percent of the hiding. When Facebook dug deeper, it found that a small subset of those 5 percent were hiding almost every story they saw—even ones they had liked and commented on. For these "superhiders," it turned out, hiding a story didn't mean they disliked it; it was simply their way of marking the post "read," like archiving a message in Gmail.

Yet their actions were biasing the data that Facebook relied on to rank stories. Intricate as it is, the news feed algorithm does not attempt to individually model each user's behavior. It treats your likes as identical in value to mine, and the same is true of our hides. For the superhiders, however, the ranking team decided to make an exception. Tas was tasked with tweaking the code to identify this small group of people and to discount the negative value of their hides.

That might sound like a simple fix. But the algorithm is so precious to Facebook that every tweak to the code must be tested—first in an offline simulation, then among a tiny group of Facebook employees, then on a small fraction of all Facebook users—before it goes live. At each step, the company collects data on the change's effect on metrics ranging from user engagement to time spent on the site to ad revenue to page-load time. Diagnostic tools are set up to detect an abnormally large change on any one of these crucial metrics in real time, setting off a sort of internal alarm that automatically notifies key members of the news feed team.

Once a change like Tas' has been tested on each of these audiences, he'll present the resulting data at one of the news feed team's weekly "ranking meetings" and field a volley questions from Mosseri, Allison, Marra, and his other colleagues as to its effect on various metrics. If the team is satisfied that the change is a positive one, free of unintended consequences, the engineers in charge of the code on the iOS, Android, and Web teams will gradually roll it out to the public at large.

Even then, Facebook can't be sure that the change won't have some subtle, longer-term effect that it had failed to anticipate. To guard against this, it maintains a "holdout group"—a small proportion of users who don't see the change for weeks or months after the rest of us.

To speak of Facebook's news feed algorithm in the singular, then, can be misleading. It isn't just that the algorithm is really a collection of hundreds of smaller algorithms solving the smaller problems that make up the larger problem of what stories to show people. It's that, thanks to all the tests and holdout groups, there are more than a dozen different versions of that master algorithm running in the world at any given time. Tas' "hide stories" tweak was announced July 31, and his post about it on Facebook's "News Feed FYI" blog passed largely unnoticed by the public at large. Presumably, however, the superhiders of the world are now marginally more satisfied with their news feeds, and thus more likely to keep using Facebook, sharing stories with friends, and viewing the ads that keep the company in business.

Facebook's feed quality panel has given the company's news feed team richer, more human data than it ever had before. Tas and the rest of the ranking team are growing more skillful at finding and fixing the algorithm's blind spots. But there is one other group of humans that Facebook is turning to more and more as it tries to keep the news feed relevant: ordinary users like you and me.

The survey that Facebook has been running over the past six months—asking a subset of users to choose their favorite among two side- by-side posts—is an attempt to gather the same sort of data from a much wider sample than is possible through the feed quality panel. But the increasing involvement of ordinary users isn't only on the input side of the equation. Over the past two years, Facebook has been giving users more power to control their news feeds' output as well.

Fine-Tuning Your Own Feeds

The algorithm is still the driving force behind the ranking of posts in your feed. But Facebook is increasingly giving users the ability to fine-tune their own feeds—a level of control it had long resisted as onerous and unnecessary. Facebook has spent seven years working on improving its ranking algorithm, Mosseri says. It has machine-learning wizards developing logistic regressions to interpret how users' past behavior predicts what posts they're likely to engage with in the future. "We could spend 10 more years—and we will—trying to improve those [machine-learning techniques]," Mosseri says. "But you can get a lot of value right now just by simply asking someone: 'What do you want to see? What do you not want to see? Which friends do you always want to see at the top of your feed?' "

Those are now questions that Facebook allows every user to answer for herself. You can now "unfollow" a friend whose posts you no longer want to see, "see less" of a certain kind of story, and designate your favorite friends and pages as "see first," so that their posts will appear at the top of your feed every time you log in. How to do all of these things is not immediately obvious to the casual user: You have to click a tiny gray down arrow in the top right corner of a post to see those options. Most people never do. But as the limitations of the fully automated feed have grown clearer, Facebook has grown more comfortable highlighting these options via occasional pop-up reminders with links to explanations and help pages. It is also testing new ways for users to interact with the news feed, including alternate, topic-based news feeds and new buttons to convey reactions other than like.

Future Challenges

The shift is partly a defensive one. The greatest challenges to Facebook's dominance in recent years—the upstarts that threaten to do to Facebook what Facebook did to Myspace—have eschewed this sort of data-driven approach altogether. Instagram, which Facebook acquired in 2012 in part to quell the threat posed by its fast-growing popularity, simply shows you every photo from every person you follow in chronological order. Snapchat has eclipsed Facebook as teens' social network of choice by eschewing virality and automated filtering in favor of more intimate forms of digital interaction.

Facebook is not the only data-driven company to run up against the limits of algorithmic optimization in recent years. Netflix's famous movie-recommendation engine has come to rely heavily on humans who are paid to watch movies all day and classify them by genre. To counterbalance the influence of Amazon's automated A/B tests, CEO Jeff Bezos places outsize importance on the specific complaints of individual users and maintains a public email address for that very purpose. It would be premature to declare the age of the algorithm over before it really began, but there has been a change in velocity. Facebook's Mosseri, for his part, rejects the buzzword "data-driven" in reference to decision making; he prefers "data-informed."

Facebook's news feed ranking team believes the change in its approach is paying off. "As we continue to improve news feed based on what people tell us, we are seeing that we're getting better at ranking people's news feeds; our ranking is getting closer to how people would rank stories in their feeds themselves," says Scissors, the user experience researcher who helps to oversee the feed quality panel.

There's a potential downside, however, to giving users this sort of control: What if they're mistaken, as humans often are, about what they really want to see? What if Facebook's database of our online behaviors really did know us better, at least in some ways, than we knew ourselves? Could giving people the news feed they say they want actually make it less addictive than it was before?

Mosseri tells me he's not particularly worried about that. The data so far, he explains, suggest that placing more weight on surveys and giving users more options have led to an increase in overall engagement and time spent on the site. While the two goals may seem to be in tension in the short term, "We find that qualitiative improvements to the news feed look like they correlate with long-term engagement." That may be a happy coincidence if it continues to hold true. But if there's one thing that Facebook has learned in 10 years of running the news feed, it's that data never tell the full story, and the algorithm will never be perfect. What looks like it's working today might be unmasked as a mistake tomorrow. And when it does, the humans who go to work every day in Menlo Park will read a bunch of spreadsheets, hold a bunch of meetings, ran a bunch of tests—and then change the algorithm once again.

Print Citations

CMS: Oremus, Will. "Who Controls Your Facebook Feed." In *The Reference Shelf: Internet Abuses and Privacy Rights*, edited by Betsy Maury, 128-138. Ipswich, MA: H.W. Wilson, 2017.

MLA: Oremus, Will. "Who Controls Your Facebook Feed." *The Reference Shelf: Internet Abuses and Privacy Rights*. Ed. Betsy Maury. Ipswich: H.W. Wilson, 2017. 128-138. Print.

APA: Oremus, W. (2016). Who controls your Facebook feed. In Betsy Maury (Ed.), *The Reference Shelf: Internet Abuses and Privacy Rights* (pp. 128-138). Ipswich, MA: H.W. Wilson. (Original work published 2016)

The Very Real Consequences of Fake News Stories and Why Your Brain Can't Ignore Them

By Nsikan Akpan
PBS News Hour, December 5, 2016

On Sunday afternoon, a 28-year-old man walked into a Washington, D.C. ping-pong bar and pizzeria. He was carrying an AR-15 assault rifle—hardly standard-issue hardware for a round of table tennis. He fired one or more shots, as people fled Comet Ping Pong, before surrendering to police officers. No one was injured.

Edgar Maddison Welch told police he had traveled from his home in Salisbury, N.C. to the nation's capital to investigate a pre-election conspiracy theory, wherein Democratic presidential nominee Hillary Clinton allegedly led a child-trafficking ring out of Comet Ping Pong.

A false claim started by, you guessed it, fake news. (Here's a brief history on how #Pizzagate was born.)

Fake news, once confined to satire or the fringe bowels of the internet, has quickly become a contender for the most influential phrase of the year. Following Donald Trump's surprise election, story after story has questioned the role that fake news played in swaying voters—and for good reason. A *BuzzFeed* analysis found fake election news outperformed total engagement on Facebook when compared to the most popular election stories from 19 major news outlet combined. Facebook CEO Mark Zuckerberg described this allegation as "a pretty crazy idea" before ultimately announcing a move to deter misleading news. Later, Facebook and Google took steps to keep fake news sites from collecting revenue from their ad platforms.

To some degree, Zuckerberg's initial stance was warranted. A panel of experts told the *NewsHour* that it would be nearly impossible to prove that phony stories swayed the U.S. election in one direction or another, based on current research. On the flip side, they said incidents like the #Pizzagate shooting signify just one step in a long, dark trail of real world consequences caused by fake news—one that started well before this year. They argued that emerging technology may stem the tide of garbage news in the near future. And they highlighted one solution that already exists.

Before Pizzagate, Came Ebola

Fake news comes in many flavors, like satire or intentional hoaxes, but computer scientist Filippo Menczer said sensational news and social media campaigns filled with mistruths—like the PizzaGate story—started to surge on the internet around 2010.

"That is the first time that we started studying it actively, and at that time, we found several cases of websites that were publishing completely fake and fabricated news, purely for political propaganda," said Menczer, who designs algorithms to track political messaging as director of Indiana University's Center for Complex Networks and Systems Research.

Menczer recalled an example that occurred in 2010 during the special election to fill the vacancy created by the death of Massachusetts Senator Ted Kennedy. Researchers at Wellesley College found that, in the hours before the election, a Republican group from Iowa used thousands of Twitter bots to spread misinformation about the Democratic candidate Martha Coakley. At the time, search engines prioritized "real-time information" from social media platforms, so these fake posts topped search results just as people headed to the polls.

Six years ago, few fake news websites featured ads for their content, Menczer said. Their main goal was political gain. By his estimation, the cottage industry for phony stories appeared to take off during the 2014 Ebola crisis. The websites for places like *National Report*, which self-identifies as political satire, began to resemble legitimate news sources. False stories on *National Report* like "Texas Town Quarantined after Family of Five Test Positive for the Ebola Virus" feature elements like author biographies and video shorts embedded in the page to give the feel of authenticity, Menczer said. Whether those attributes or the "satirical writing" mislead people is hard to say. But the Texas story, which lacks a disclaimer in the body of the text that clearly identifies it as satire, was shared more than 330,000 times on Facebook according to MuckRack's WhoShared algorithm.

Irrational fears of the Ebola virus in the U.S. arguably drove web interest in this fake news story, as it likely did for any number of legitimate articles written during the outbreak. When the dust settled, America notched four imported cases and one death during the entire course of the epidemic, while in contrast Africa experienced around 30,000 cases and 11,000 deaths.

Yet the American news machine had its share of media casualties during the Ebola crisis. One example involved Kaci Hickox, a Doctors Without Borders nurse who volunteered to treat people in West Africa.

Upon returning on a flight through Newark, she was quarantined for 80 hours by the New Jersey Department of Health and Gov. Chris Christie, despite showing no conclusive symptoms. Even after an Ebola test came back and she was released, Gov. Christie reportedly said Hickox may be "tested for that again, because sometimes it takes a little bit longer to make a definitive determination," and that "There's no question the woman is ill, the question is what is her illness."

From Hickox's perspective, the modern news cycle did the rest.

"The statements were completely untrue, but they were printed and published.

Interviews with Chris Christie were playing on the news," Hickox told *NewsHour.* "It was another example of when you have a politician who really has access to say

> **Blaming readers for spreading fake news from a cognitive perspective is somewhat equivalent to blaming a baby for soiling itself. They can't help it.**

whatever they want, even though it was completely inaccurate."

The negative ramifications occurred immediately. As Hickox journeyed home to Maine, her landlord left a voicemail on her partner's cell phone, asking them to move out. "Before I left for Sierra Leone, she was very supportive, and she told me how amazing it was that I had the skills to go help respond to the Ebola outbreak," Hickox recalled. "Then all of a sudden this woman doesn't want you to return home, even though I never had Ebola, I wasn't symptomatic and there was no reason for anyone to fear."

Those public fears ballooned when Maine Gov. Paul LePage followed in Christie's tracks and tried to enforce a similar quarantine. Maine police officers complained about fielding phone calls from concerned residents who had been duped by fake news articles. Hickox heard rumors from the police department about physical threats against her, and her partner ended up dropping out of nursing school because they wouldn't allow him to attend while he was living with her, she said. The couple opted to ultimately go on a widely publicized bike ride to, in essence, force a judge to make a decision about the quarantine, a point that was missed by the mainstream media, she said.

"The state hadn't met the burden of proof to say that I needed to be quarantined. No one really explained that," Hickox said. A Reuters headline at the time, for instance, read "Bike-riding nurse defies Ebola quarantine, on collision course with governor"—even though no court had issued an official quarantine at the time.

Hickox, who ultimately left Maine, said outside Christie and LePage, she wasn't sure who to blame for the unjustified hype around her story.

"Is it the media that causes public panic, or is it that we, the public, just desire drama and fear, and that therefore feeds into the media," Hickox asked.

Based on research, the answer is both, as Menczer detailed recently in an OpEd for the *Conversation.* Trending news stories, both fake and real, buy into what's called the attention economy, whereby "if people pay attention to a certain topic, more information on that topic will be produced."

Why Your Brain Loves Fake News

Tell me if you've heard this common refrain since the election: "If people were smarter, fake news wouldn't be a problem," or "Readers are responsible for telling fake news from the real stuff. Don't blame Facebook."

But to communications psychologist Dannagal Young, blaming readers for spreading fake news from a cognitive perspective is somewhat equivalent to blaming a baby for soiling itself. They can't help it.

This takeaway comes after a decade of studying how the human mind responds to political satire. Satire is arguably the most prevalent variety of fake news and arguably the best studied. The mental processing of satire is unique compared to other types of information, Young said, because it requires audience participation.

"So compared to what we see in traditional communication, there is this enhanced attention, enhanced interest and enhanced processing that happens," said Young, who works at the University of Delaware. "So things that you hear in the context of humor will be more on the top of your mind."

But here's where problem lies with fake news and the human mind. Our brains have a finite capacity for processing information and for remembering, so our minds make value judgments about what to keep. Humor tips the scales in favor of being remembered and recalled, even when counterarguments are strong.

"The special sauce of humor is that you might get people to entertain ideas of constructs that they otherwise might reject out of hand," she said, and this powerful mode of persuasion extends to sensational fake news as well. "When you have exposure to fake news or satire, or any content at all, as soon as those constructs have been accessed and brought into working memory, they are there. You can't un-think them."

> **Trending news stories, both fake and real, buy into what's called the attention economy, whereby "if people pay attention to a certain topic, more information on that topic will be produced."**

This mental reflex may explain why caricature traits—"Al Gore is stiff and robotic" or "George W. Bush is dumb"—persist in the zeitgeist for so long despite being untrue, Young said.

These days, the trouble arises from people being unable to recognize irony in online satire, Young said. She offered the example of a recent Change.org petition—Allow Open Carry of Firearms at the Quicken Loans Arena during the RNC Convention in July. The petition was written as if real, and news outlets like *USA Today* assumed as much, but its gun control-supporting author was actually trying to portray what he viewed as hypocrisy from conservative politicians. Young argued spoken irony—think John Oliver—creates less confusion because it's easier to recognize the tones of intent.

How to Beat Fake News

So, what happens next in the wild west of phony tales? Some are looking to robots to save the day. For example, the verbal themes of satire are so distinctive, so salient, that linguists like Victoria Rubin can engineer machine-learning algorithms to filter this brand of fake news from legitimate articles.

"We were able to reach about 86 percent accuracy, which means definitely eight out of 10 would be pinpointed as satire," said Rubin, who studies information and media at the University of Western Ontario. These algorithms are trained to spot the hallmarks of satire, like extra-long sentences or unexpected juxtapositions of random people and places, locations.

These programs, however, still struggle when it comes to identifying the type of misinformation present in sensational news items. Their attempts at a deception detector yielded a 63 percent success rate, which is better than the human ability to spot lies—54 percent on average—but not by much.

In recent weeks, many have called on Facebook to develop such programs or other methods to stop fake news, but Young said the social media platform had tried long before fake news became a mainstream problem.

A year and a half ago, Young said Facebook rolled out satire labeling for stories from satirical sources like the *Onion*. She said readers disliked this option because part of the allure of satire is getting momentarily swept up before realizing the story is a joke.

Next, Facebook tried a button in the right corner of posts that allowed readers to flag posts as fake, but then satirical content producers like the *Daily Currant* protested, based on research to be published by Young in an upcoming book in 2017. Facebook appeared to change how flagged stories were distributed, and referrals from Facebook to the *Daily Currant* dropped by 95 percent within a few months.

Though this crowdsourced option for reporting fake news still exists, Young said its influence on the distribution of stories into news feeds may have been supplanted by the "reaction emojis" that Facebook introduced in February. But she wonders if a "Ha-ha" or "sad" emoji carries the weight in crowdsourcing remarks about misinformative news.

Both she and Menczer also question whether crowdsourcing is the best path to defeating fake news on social media.

"I have been a huge advocate of digital technologies as an inherently democratizing medium that's going to change everything. Now I'm like, 'Oh my God, we have destroyed ourselves," Young said, somewhat in jest.

Since the election, many have tossed blame on Facebook for creating "filter bubbles" or "echo chambers" in users' news feed. But this notion rings hollow because these platforms are designed to cater to a people's choices. These decisions, Young said, are driven by confirmation bias and motivated reasoning. In other words, people share articles after reading only the headline, because they want to think they're right, she said. She votes for bringing back human gatekeepers to tailor trending news and to prevent fake stories from running amok.

Menczer recommended that social media users who want to avoid echo chambers should follow moderate news sources or organizations that don't necessarily match their most intimate viewpoints. Or, "don't unfollow people just because they post something you disagree with," he said. "Unfollowing is one of the most efficient techniques to put yourself inside an echo chamber."

Having lived through the consequences of such public behavior, Hickox is now cautious about how she views others in the news.

"I would encourage people to always be questioning whether they're only getting part of a story," Hickox said. "To make snap judgments that lead to fear and to discrimination against someone is not the right way, and will not get us anywhere."

Print Citations

CMS: Akpan, Nsikan. "The Very Real Consequences of Fake News Stories and Why Your Brain Can't Ignore Them." In *The Reference Shelf: Internet Abuses and Privacy Rights*, edited by Betsy Maury, 139-144. Ipswich, MA: H.W. Wilson, 2017.

MLA: Akpan, Nsikan. "The Very Real Consequences of Fake News Stories and Why Your Brain Can't Ignore Them." *The Reference Shelf: Internet Abuses and Privacy Rights*. Ed. Betsy Maury. Ipswich: H.W. Wilson, 2017. 139-144. Print.

APA: Akpan, N. (2017). The very real consequences of fake news stories and why your brain can't ignore them. In Betsy Maury (Ed.), *The Reference Shelf: Internet Abuses and Privacy Rights* (pp. 139-144). Ipswich, MA: H.W. Wilson. (Original work published 2016)

Why Do We Fall for Fake News?

By Shyam Sundar

The Conversation, **December 7, 2016**

In recent weeks, the amount of online fake news that circulated during the final months of the presidential race is coming to light, a disturbing revelation that threatens to undermine the country's democratic process. We're already seeing some real-world consequences. After fake news stories implicated a Washington, D.C. pizza shop as the site of a Clinton coordinated child sex ring, a man wielding an AR15 assault rifle entered the store on Dec. 4 to "investigate" and fired shots.

Much of the analysis, however, has focused on the people who create these false articles—whether it's teenagers in Macedonia or satirical news sites—and what Facebook and Google can do to prevent its dissemination.

But fake news wouldn't be a problem if people didn't fall for it and share it. Unless we understand the psychology of online news consumption, we won't be able to find a cure for what the *New York Times* calls a "digital virus."

Some have said that confirmation bias is the root of the problem—the idea that we selectively seek out information that confirms our beliefs, truth be damned. But this doesn't explain why we fall for fake news about nonpartisan issues.

A more plausible explanation is our relative inattention to the credibility of the news source. I've been studying the psychology of online news consumption for over two decades, and one striking finding across several experiments is that online news readers don't seem to really care about the importance of journalistic sourcing—what we in academia refer to as "professional gatekeeping." This laissez faire attitude, together with the difficulty of discerning online news sources, is at the root of why so many believe fake news.

Do people even consider news editors credible?

Since the earliest days of the internet, fake news has circulated online. In the 1980s there were online discussion communities called Usenet newsgroups where hoaxes would be shared among cliques of conspiracy theorists and sensationmongers.

Sometimes these conspiracies would spill out into the mainstream. For example, 20 years ago, Pierre Salinger, President Kennedy's former press secretary, went on TV to claim that TWA Flight 800 was shot down by a U.S. Navy missile based on a document he had been emailed. But these slipups were rare due to the presence of

TV and newspaper gatekeepers. When they did happen, they were quickly retracted if the facts didn't check out.

Today, in the age of social media, we receive news not only via email, but also on a variety of other online platforms. Traditional gatekeepers have been cast aside; politicians and celebrities have direct access to millions of followers. If they fall for fake news, any hoax can go viral, spreading via social media to millions without proper vetting and factchecking.

Back in the 1990s, as part of my dissertation, I conducted the firstever experiment on online news sources. I mocked up a news site and showed four groups of participants the same articles, but attributed them to different sources: news editors, a computer, other users of the online news site and the participants themselves (through a pseudoselection task, where they thought they had chosen the news stories from a larger set).

When we asked the participants to rate the stories on attributes tied to credibility—believability, accuracy, fairness and objectivity—we were surprised to discover that all the participants made similar evaluations, regardless of the source.

They did disagree on other attributes, but none favored journalistic sourcing. For example, when a story was attributed to other users, participants actually liked reading it more. And when news editors had selected a story, participants thought the quality was worse than when other users had selected ostensibly the same story. Even the computer as the gatekeeper scored better on story quality than news editors.

The Problem of Layered Sources

When it comes to internet news, it seems that the standing of professional news agencies—the original gatekeepers—has taken a hit. One reason could be the amount of sources behind any given news item.

Imagine checking your Facebook news feed and seeing something your friend has shared: a politician's tweet of a newspaper story. Here, there's actually a chain of five sources (newspaper, politician, Twitter, friend and Facebook). All of them played a role in transmitting the message, obscuring the identity of the original source. This kind of "source layering" is a common feature of our online news experience.

Which of these sources is most likely to resonate with readers as the "main source?"

My students and I approached this issue by analyzing news aggregator sites of varying credibility, such as Yahoo! News (high credibility) and Drudge Report (low). These sites will often republish or link to articles that have originated somewhere else, so we wanted to know how often readers paid attention to original sources in the stories appearing on these websites.

We found readers will usually pay attention to the chain of sourcing only if the topic of the story is really important to them. Otherwise, they'll be swayed by the source or website that republished or posted the story—in other words, the vehicle that directly delivered them the story. It's not surprising, then, to hear people say they got their news from "sources" that don't create and edit news articles: Verizon, Comcast, Facebook and, by proxy, their friends.

When Friends—and the Self —Become the Source

When reading online news, the closest source is often one of our friends. Because we tend to trust our friends, our cognitive filters weaken, making a social media feed fertile ground for fake news to sneak into our consciousness.

The persuasive appeal of peers over experts is compounded by the fact that we tend to let our guard down even more when we encounter news in our personal space. Increasingly, most of our online destinations—whether they're portal sites (such as Yahoo! News and Google News), social media sites, retail sites or search

> **Because we tend to trust our friends, our cognitive filters weaken, making a social media feed fertile ground for fake news to sneak into our consciousness.**

engines—have tools that allow us to customize the site, tailoring it to our own interests and identity (for example, choosing a profile photo or a news feed about one's favorite sports team).

Our research shows that internet users are less skeptical of information that appears in these customized environments. In an experiment published in the current issue of the journal *Media Psychology*, a former student, Hyunjin Kang, and I found that study participants who customized their own online news portal tended to agree with statements like "I think the interface is a true representation of who I am" and "I feel the website represents my core personal values."

We wanted to see if this enhanced identity changed how they processed information. So we introduced fake health news stories—about the negative effects of applying sunscreen and drinking pasteurized milk—into their portal.

We discovered that participants who had customized their news portal were less likely to scrutinize the fake news and more likely to believe it. What's more, they showed a higher tendency to act on the advice offered in the stories ("I intend to stop using sunscreen") and recommend that their friends do the same.

These findings explain why fake news thrives on Facebook and Twitter, social media sites where we're connected with our friends and have curated our own pages to reflect ourselves. Lulled into a false sense of security, we become less likely to scrutinize the information in front of us.

We can't distinguish between real news and fake news because we don't even question the credibility of the source of news when we are online. Why would we, when we think of ourselves or our friends as the source?

Print Citations

CMS: Sundar, Shyam. "Why Do We Fall for Fake News?" In *The Reference Shelf: Internet Abuses and Privacy Rights*, edited by Betsy Maury, 145-148. Ipswich, MA: H.W. Wilson, 2017.

MLA: Sundar, Shyam. "Why Do We Fall for Fake News?" *The Reference Shelf: Internet Abuses and Privacy Rights*. Ed. Betsy Maury. Ipswich: H.W. Wilson, 2017. 145-148. Print.

APA: Sundar, S. (2017). Why do we fall for fake news? In Betsy Maury (Ed.), *The Reference Shelf: Internet Abuses and Privacy Rights* (pp. 145-148). Ipswich, MA: H.W. Wilson. (Original work published 2016)

The Trump Administration Plays Right into Russia's Information Warfare Strategy

By David Fidler

Net Politics, **February 13, 2017**

In discussing what President Trump might do in cybersecurity, an acquaintance sent me a hyperlink to a story supporting his perspective. The link contained an article from *RT*, formerly known as *Russia Today*—a tool of the Russian government. The link appeared during our robust sharing of ideas, not as a warning about Russian propaganda. But, there, in my email inbox was a manifestation of Russian information warfare.

Lest you think me paranoid, look at the *Handbook of Russian Information Warfare*. Keir Giles of Chatham House wrote the Handbook for NATO personnel who have not "studied Russian principles of war fighting" but who should understand "current and projected Russian operations in the information and cyber domains." The *Handbook* deserves a broader audience. By drawing on Russian and Western sources, Giles explains basic concepts, objectives, historical development, implementation, and likely future of Russian information warfare. With the 2016 election "hack and leak" campaign fading from headlines, the *Handbook* is a warning about an information conflict Russia is waging to obtain strategic advantage over the United States.

Particularly valuable are Giles' efforts to demonstrate how differently Russia thinks about information warfare compared to the United States and its NATO allies. The *Handbook* shows that, for Russia, information communicated through all media is simultaneously a weapon, target, and operational domain in peace and war. Giles quotes a Russian expert arguing that winning "information confrontations" achieves strategic victory "in the defeat of an enemy's armed forces[,] . . . the capture of his territory, destruction of his economic potential, and overthrow of his political system." Here, "information" has no independent value.

Facts and lies, truth and deceit are equally valuable.

Russia's approach does not privilege cyberenabled information, but the internet makes Moscow's information operations "cheaper, simpler, and more permanent than in previous decades when the primary medium was newspapers." Russia exploits the internet through "sock puppet media outlets," troll farms and campaigns, and automated botnets in order to engage in information warfare at an unprecedented scale, speed, sophistication, and intensity.

The *Handbook* details how Russia integrates information warfare techniques into its political, diplomatic, and military toolkits. This integration is manifest in spheres of armed conflict (e.g., Crimea, Ukraine, and Syria) and in nonmilitary contestation over power and influence. As Giles observes, in Russian thinking, "there are no rear areas" in information warfare. Equally worrying is the Handbook's conclusion that Russia is constantly developing its capabilities, tactics, and targets such that "future campaigns will not resemble the ones seen to date."

The *Handbook* does not develop a policy agenda for responding to Russian information warfare. However, Giles observes that "EuroAtlantic . . . 'postfact' or 'post-truth' political environments" mean that, for Russian information operations against the West, "much of its work has already been done." Giles does not pursue this point, but President Trump and his administration do, indeed, unwittingly function as a troll farm and botnet for Russian information warfare.

As a candidate, president-elect, and president, Trump has attacked Congress, the judiciary, civil servants, the intelligence community, the media, American corporations, NATO, European Union, and U.S. allies. This onslaught has involved a torrent of deceit, distortion, deception, and "alternative facts" from the president and his advisors. Meanwhile, President Trump declares his respect for Vladimir Putin, seeks better relations with Russia, ignores the implications of Russian interference in the U.S. elections, and equates Russian state violence at home and abroad with U.S. behavior.

These attacks on American institutions and allies, the political falsehoods, and the pro-Russian views spread through all media channels, including those in the United States and abroad that proliferate "fake news" over the internet and provide sustenance for the divisive echo chambers of social media. Like Russian information operations, the Trump administration's behavior damages the legitimacy of American leadership and power, sows doubt and confusion about what is actually happening, and dilutes resistance to Russian actions, interests, and influence.

> **The *Handbook* details how Russia integrates information warfare techniques into its political, diplomatic, and military toolkits.**

This environment proves deleterious for the infrequent administration statements that take a firmer line against Russia, such as those from Nikki Haley, the U.S. ambassador to the United Nations. In particular, these statements project dissonance within the administration rather than solidarity in the White House and between the United States and its allies on a strategy for addressing the threats Russia presents.

As the *Handbook* emphasizes, Russian information warfare thinking anticipates that trolls and bots not under Kremlin control will amplify the messages and effects of Russia's own information operations.

However, having a U.S. president, his administration, and his own networks of disinformation playing these roles is probably beyond the wildest dreams of Russian strategists and tacticians of information warfare.

Putin will not squander this opportunity.

Print Citations

CMS: Fidler, David. "The Trump Administration Plays Right into Russia's Information Warfare Strategy." In *The Reference Shelf: Internet Abuses and Privacy Rights*, edited by Betsy Maury, 149-151. Ipswich, MA: H.W. Wilson, 2017.

MLA: Fidler, David. "The Trump Administration Plays Right into Russia's Information Warfare Strategy." *The Reference Shelf: Internet Abuses and Privacy Rights*. Ed. Betsy Maury. Ipswich: H.W. Wilson, 2017. 149-151. Print.

APA: Fidler, D. (2017). The Trump administration plays right into Russia's information warfare strategy. In Betsy Maury (Ed.), *The Reference Shelf: Internet Abuses and Privacy Rights* (pp. 149-151). Ipswich, MA: H.W. Wilson. (Original work published 2017)

5

The Power and Influence of Technology

Wikileaks founder Julian Assange prepares to speak from the balcony of the Ecuadorian embassy on February 5, 2016 in London, England. Assange's organization Wikileaks released classified information from official US presidential campaigns and government agencies in 2016 and 2017.

Black Hats and White Hats: The Hacking Phenomenon

Hacking as a form of cybercrime has been a controversial issue since the 1970s, but concern over the influence of hackers spiked in the United States after it was revealed that Russian hackers stole sensitive information from US political agencies and used it to support Donald Trump in the 2016 election. However, hacking isn't just a criminal enterprise or a tool of cyberwarfare, it is an art and science that challenges and advances digital design, helping to create better security and new advances in Web engineering. Both maligned and celebrated, the hacking subculture has produced epic criminal exploits, dangerous threats to national security, and has been the substrate for a new genre in television, film, and other fiction. Hackers are both the most dangerous threat of the Digital Age and the pioneers of cyberspace, exploring and pushing the boundaries of what is possible in the virtual world.

The Evolution of a Subculture

Hacking has become so well-known (and yet often misunderstood) in popular culture that the word "hack" has taken on new meanings. In general, "hacking" has come to mean either subverting standard procedures to arrive at a novel solution to a problem (e.g., Lifehacks) or breaking down complex systems into smaller constituent parts in an effort to understand or control a complex system (hacking a genome). The term was originally used to refer to working on a technology problem in a unique way.[1]

In 2017, the term "hacker" is often seen as synonymous with cybercriminals who use their knowledge of computer/network security to steal and manipulate data for fun, profit, or other purposes, such as to manipulate the outcome of an election in a foreign nation. Within the hacking subculture, individuals who specialize in breaking through encryption and infiltrating protected systems are called "crackers"; ; some are also called "black hat hackers" or "black hats." Black hats are the anarchists of the hacking world, challenging themselves and each other to defy any attempt to protect data and stealing and selling information through secret encrypted websites on the "Dark Web."

In 1998, as the Internet was just beginning to gain sufficient importance to be seen as a public utility, the Boston-based hacking collective L0pht Heavy Industries discovered that, with about 30 minutes of work, they would be able to effectively disable the entire Web. L0pht hackers Weld Pond, Mudge, Brian Oblivion, Kingpin, Tan, Stefan Von Neumann, and Space Rogue, decided to alert the authorities and testified before the US Senate's Committee on Governmental Affairs.[2] Hackers were already earning a reputation as the villains in the cyberworld, but L0pht decided to use their knowledge to warn the world about the potential dangers that hackers could pose. By protecting citizens from Webmisconduct, L0pht established themselves as what are sometimes called "white hat hackers" or "white hats," tech and security experts who use their abilities to test security systems or to derail the efforts of the black hats who cause mayhem and commit Web crimes.[3] White hat hackers often work for specific companies, helping to engineer security systems or analyzing various types of malicious programs; independent white hats can earn between $500 and $200,000 by selling information to companies offering payment to individuals who discover vulnerabilities in their software or hardware, called "bug bounty programs."[4]

Of course, not all hackers fit neatly into the black or white hat molds, and those who participate in unauthorized intrusion, but are not doing so for personal gain, may be called "gray hats." Some gray hats called "hacktivists" use their expertise to expose the perceived wrongdoings of corporations or politicians. The hacker group Anonymous, for instance, targets banks, financial institutions, and government officials, and disrupts their systems to call attention to their allegedly unethical or immoral activities. As a rule, gray hats do not sell information to criminals (like black hats), but rather sell their data to governments, law enforcement, and intelligence agencies, providing data that those agencies can then use to exploit the weaknesses of their enemies.[5]

Hackers use a variety of tools to infiltrate secure networks and devices and the data they obtain can be used in many different ways. Black hats may be directly involved in identity or credit card theft or may sell the data needed to perpetrate these crimes to other criminals. To bypass security, hackers have created an ever growing fauna of malicious programs (malware) including Web robots or "bots" that can perform a variety of malignant processes when inadvertently installed on a computer. For instance, some black hats use their bots, viruses, or other forms of malware to disable a computer or a network, then keep the system locked until the owner agrees to pay a ransom in return for regaining control, a subfield of cybercrime now known as "ransomware." Sometimes, hackers make and sell tools that empower others to engage in hacking. This has created the sub-subculture of "script kiddies," who are typically juveniles experimenting in cybercrime and who lack the ability to create their own hacking programs but use scripts (programs) made by others to infiltrate security or cause other havoc on computers and/or networks.[6]

Often portrayed as a criminal underworld by the media, the core of the subculture has always been one of creativity and curiosity blended with a tendency to defy or at least challenge authority. For all the bad press, hackers have not only helped to advance technology in many beneficial and unexpected ways, but the danger of cybercrime itself provides an important motivator that keeps engineers and security experts working diligently to protect their products from those who would exploit even the most minor flaws in their design.

Hacking Turns to Political Warfare

In June of 2016, it was revealed that Russian hackers infiltrated the Democratic National Committee (DNC) and the Republican National Committee (RNC) using a technique called "phishing," in which the hacker sends an e-mail or message to another computer user attempting to trick the user into clicking a link or otherwise performing some voluntary action that results in a program being installed on the user's computer. Two Russian hacker groups, known as Cozy Bear and Fancy Bear, were later identified as the ones responsible. The website WikiLeaks, known for making confidential government documents public, posted tens of thousands of e-mails from the DNC in late July. The leaked e-mails portrayed members of Hillary Clinton's campaign in an unfavorable light and gave fuel to Trump's long-standing tactic of portraying Clinton as untrustworthy with regard to sensitive or classified data.[7]

Despite propagandistic claims by Trump and associates that his electoral victory was a "landslide win," numerous sources have demonstrated—using nothing more sophisticated than Web searches of publicly available documents and statistics collected by nonpartisan organizations operating in the public trust—that Trump's electoral win amounted to less than 100,000 votes in three key swing states and that Trump lost the popular vote by nearly 2.9 million votes with no evidence of voter fraud.[8] The narrow margin of Trump's victory is important to understanding the level of concern over the Russian hacking scandal as any change in voter preference that might have favored Clinton could easily (though not necessarily) have resulted in a different outcome in the election.[9]

Soon after Trump's victory, it was revealed in statements issued by the Central Intelligence Agency (CIA), Federal Bureau of Investigation (FBI), and National Security Agency (NSA) that Russian hackers had hacked both the DNC and the RNC and appeared to have selectively used data they obtained to increase the likelihood that Trump would be elected. Furthermore, the intelligence community report stated that the hackers were acting on behalf of the Russian government, essentially meaning that the effort to influence the election could be considered an act of cyberwarfare. It is important to note, however, that Russian intervention was not the only factor affecting the outcome of the election and there is no definitive evidence to suggest that Trump would not have been able to win the electoral vote *without* Russian assistance.

The Russian hacking incident is a form of "political warfare," a process that uses indirect methods, such as propaganda or psychological manipulation, to affect a foreign nation in a way that is advantageous to a political rival or enemy nation. As of March 2017, the motivations of the Russian government remain unclear, though it appears that some of Trump's close advisers had close contact with the Russian government and significant investment in Russian industry. The United States has levied sanctions against Russia for human rights abuses related to Russia's activities in the Crimean Peninsula and Trump, during his campaign, criticized these efforts and supported a more cooperative relationship with Vladimir Putin's government.[10]

It was later revealed that two close advisers to Trump, former NSA Adviser Mike Flynn and Attorney General Jeff Sessions, had both had inappropriate contact with Russian ambassadors leading up to the election and had both either denied of obfuscated this in meetings with other officials. Flynn resigned as the result of investigative reports by the *Washington Post* and other newspapers exposing his actions, while Sessions agrees to recuse himself from any investigation of Russian hacking. Questions remain as to whether Trump himself has any ongoing economic ties to Russia or whether he or members of his campaign staff knew about the hacking attack before it was revealed through intelligence investigations.[11] Trump has called the Russian scandal "fake news" and has suggested that the Democratic Party and mainstream media are conspiring against him. However, for this to be true, the entire intelligence community, including the NSA, CIA, and FBI, would also have to be involved in the conspiracy as all three groups confirmed that hacking occurred and that the data stolen was used to assist Trump's chances of being elected.

The Growing Threat

Hackers are one of the greatest threats of the Digital Age. Black hats can bring down massive corporations, wreaking billions in financial damage and affecting millions who depend on the Web in their daily lives. When those same skills are used for political machination, hackers can effectively shift the global balance of power. But what happens when the government hacks its own? This too has become reality in the form of warrantless NSA, CIA, and FBI surveillance, with intelligence agencies using hacking tools to intercept audio, text, and visual data from thousands of American citizens in an effort to detect national security threats. In an era of political divisiveness and misinformation, addressing complex threats that ultimately require cooperation between branches of society becomes more difficult. With a lack of effective government regulation or corporate oversight and a government divided over whether or not foreign cyberespionage is a real or imagined problem, digital citizens must protect themselves and each other, learning about these developing threats and adopting the behavioral and technological tools that can help keep them safe in the rapidly evolving digital world.

Micah L. Issitt

Works Used

"2016 Presidential Campaign Hacking Fast Facts." *CNN*, Cable News Network. Feb 26 2017. Web. 3 Mar 2017.

Dewan, Angela and Kara Fox. "Trump and Russia: What the Fallout Could Be." *CNN*, Cable News Network. Mar 5 2017. Web 5 Mar 2017.

Graves, Allison. "Fact-Check: Did 3 Million Undocumented Immigrants Vote in This Year's Election?" *Politifact*, Politifact. Nov 18 2016. Web. 3 Mar 2017.

"Hanging Out with the Script Kiddies," *BBC News*, BBC. Feb 17 2016. Web. 3 Mar 2017.

Newman, Lily Hay. "Apple's Finally Offering Bug Bounties—With the Highest Rewards Ever." *Wired*, Condé Nast. Aug 4 2016. Web. 3 Mar 2017.

Timberg, Craig. "A Disaster Foretold—And Ignored." *The Washington Post*, Nash Holdings. Jun 22 2015. Web. 3 Mar 2017.

Valeriano, Brandon, Maness, Ryan C.. and Benjamin Jensen. "5 Things We Can Learn from the Russian Hacking Scandal." *The Washington Post*, Nash Holdings. Jan 9 2017. Web. 3 Mar 2017.

Ward, Mark. "Exposing the Hidden History of Computer Hacking." *BBC News*, BBC. Oct 27 2014. Web. 3 Mar 2017.

Wing, Nick. "Final Popular Vote Total Shows Hillary Clinton Won Almost 3 Million More Ballots Than Donald Trump." *The Huffington Post*, Huffington Post Co. Dec 20 2016. Web. 3 Mar 2017.

Yagoda, Ben. "A Short History of 'Hack.'" *The New Yorker*, Condé Nast. Mar 6 2014. Web. 2 Mar 2017.

Zetter, Kim. "Hacker Lexicon: What Are White Hat, Gray Hat, and Black Hat Hackers?" *Wired,* Condé Nast. Apr 13 2014. Web. 3 Mar 2017.

Notes

1. Yagoda, "A Short History of 'Hack.'"
2. Timberg, "A Disaster Foretold—And Ignored."
3. Ward, "Exposing the Hidden History of Computer Hacking."
4. Newman, "Apple's Finally Offering Bug Bounties—With the Highest Rewards Ever."
5. Zetter, "Hacker Lexicon: What Are White Hat, Gray Hat, and Black Hat Hackers?"
6. "Hanging Out with the Script Kiddies," *BBC*.
7. "2016 Presidential Campaign Hacking Fast Facts," *CNN*.
8. Graves, "Fact-Check: Did 3 Million Undocumented Immigrants Vote in This Year's Election?"
9. Wing, "Final Popular Vote Total Shows Hillary Clinton Won Almost 3 Million More Ballots Than Donald Trump."
10. Valeriano, Maness, and Jensen, "5 Things We Can Learn from the Russian Hacking Scandal."
11. Dewan and Fox, "Trump and Russia: What the Fallout Could Be."

The Perfect Weapon: How Russian Cyberpower Invaded the U.S.

By Eric Lipton, David E. Sanger, and Scott Shane
The New York Times, December 13, 2016

WASHINGTON—When Special Agent Adrian Hawkins of the Federal Bureau of Investigation called the Democratic National Committee in September 2015 to pass along some troubling news about its computer network, he was transferred, naturally, to the help desk.

His message was brief, if alarming. At least one computer system belonging to the DNC had been compromised by hackers federal investigators had named "the Dukes," a cyberespionage team linked to the Russian government.

The FBI knew it well: The bureau had spent the last few years trying to kick the Dukes out of the unclassified email systems of the White House, the State Department and even the Joint Chiefs of Staff, one of the government's best-protected networks.

Yared Tamene, the tech-support contractor at the D.N.C. who fielded the call, was no expert in cyberattacks. His first moves were to check Google for "the Dukes" and conduct a cursory search of the D.N.C. computer system logs to look for hints of such a cyberintrusion. By his own account, he did not look too hard even after Special Agent Hawkins called back repeatedly over the next several weeks—in part because he wasn't certain the caller was a real F.B.I. agent and not an impostor.

It was the cryptic first sign of a cyberespionage and information-warfare campaign devised to disrupt the 2016 presidential election, the first such attempt by a foreign power in American history. What started as an information-gathering operation, intelligence officials believe, ultimately morphed into an effort to harm one candidate, Hillary Clinton, and tip the election to her opponent, Donald J. Trump.

Like another famous American election scandal, it started with a break-in at the D.N.C. The first time, 44 years ago at the committee's old offices in the Watergate complex, the burglars planted listening devices and jimmied a filing cabinet. This time, the burglary was conducted from afar, directed by the Kremlin, with spear-phishing emails and zeros and ones.

An examination by the *Times* of the Russian operation—based on interviews with dozens of players targeted in the attack, intelligence officials who investigated it and Obama administration officials who deliberated over the best response—reveals a series of missed signals, slow responses and a continuing underestimation of the seriousness of the cyberattack.

The D.N.C.'s fumbling encounter with the F.B.I. meant the best chance to halt the Russian intrusion was lost. The failure to grasp the scope of the attacks undercut efforts to minimize their impact. And the White House's reluctance to respond forcefully meant the Russians have not paid a heavy price for their actions, a decision that could prove critical in deterring future cyberattacks.

The low-key approach of the F.B.I. meant that Russian hackers could roam freely through the committee's network for nearly seven months before top D.N.C. officials were alerted to the attack and hired cyberexperts to protect their systems. In the meantime, the hackers moved on to targets outside the D.N.C., including Mrs. Clinton's campaign chairman, John D. Podesta, whose private email account was hacked months later.

Even Mr. Podesta, a savvy Washington insider who had written a 2014 report on cyberprivacy for President Obama, did not truly understand the gravity of the hacking.

By last summer, Democrats watched in helpless fury as their private emails and confidential documents appeared online day after day—procured by Russian intelligence agents, posted on WikiLeaks and other websites, then eagerly reported on by the American media, including the *Times*. Mr. Trump gleefully cited many of the purloined emails on the campaign trail.

The fallout included the resignations of Representative Debbie Wasserman Schultz of Florida, the chairwoman of the D.N.C., and most of her top party aides. Leading Democrats were sidelined at the height of the campaign, silenced by revelations of embarrassing emails or consumed by the scramble to deal with the hacking. Though little-noticed by the public, confidential documents taken by the Russian hackers from the D.N.C.'s sister organization, the Democratic Congressional Campaign Committee, turned up in congressional races in a dozen states, tainting some of them with accusations of scandal.

In recent days, a skeptical president-elect, the nation's intelligence agencies and the two major parties have become embroiled in an extraordinary public dispute over what evidence exists that President Vladimir V. Putin of Russia moved beyond mere espionage to deliberately try to subvert American democracy and pick the winner of the presidential election.

Many of Mrs. Clinton's closest aides believe that the Russian assault had a profound impact on the election, while conceding that other factors—Mrs. Clinton's weaknesses as a candidate; her private email server; the public statements of the F.B.I. director, James B. Comey, about her handling of classified information—were also important.

While there's no way to be certain of the ultimate impact of the hack, this much is clear: A low-cost, high-impact weapon that Russia had test-fired in elections from Ukraine to Europe was trained on the United States, with devastating effectiveness. For Russia, with an enfeebled economy and a nuclear arsenal it cannot use short of all-out war, cyberpower proved the perfect weapon: cheap, hard to see coming, hard to trace.

"There shouldn't be any doubt in anybody's mind," Adm. Michael S. Rogers, the director of the National Security Agency and commander of United States Cyber Command, said at a postelection conference. "This was not something that was done casually, this was not something that was done by chance, this was not a target that was selected purely arbitrarily," he said. "This was a conscious effort by a nation-state to attempt to achieve a specific effect."

For the people whose emails were stolen, this new form of political sabotage has left a trail of shock and professional damage. Neera Tanden, president of the Center for American Progress and a key Clinton supporter, recalls walking into the busy Clinton transition offices, humiliated to see her face on television screens as pundits discussed a leaked email in which she had called Mrs. Clinton's instincts "suboptimal."

"It was just a sucker punch to the gut every day," Ms. Tanden said. "It was the worst professional experience of my life."

The United States, too, has carried out cyberattacks, and in decades past the CIA tried to subvert foreign elections. But the Russian attack is increasingly understood across the political spectrum as an ominous historic landmark—with one notable exception: Mr. Trump has rejected the findings of the intelligence agencies he will soon oversee as "ridiculous," insisting that the hacker may be American, or Chinese, but that "they have no idea."

Mr. Trump cited the reported disagreements between the agencies about whether Mr. Putin intended to help elect him. On Tuesday, a Russian government spokesman echoed Mr. Trump's scorn.

"This tale of 'hacks' resembles a banal brawl between American security officials over spheres of influence," Maria Zakharova, the spokeswoman for the Russian Foreign Ministry, wrote on Facebook.

Over the weekend, four prominent senators—two Republicans and two Democrats—joined forces to pledge an investigation while pointedly ignoring Mr. Trump's skeptical claims.

"Democrats and Republicans must work together, and across the jurisdictional lines of the Congress, to examine these recent incidents thoroughly and devise comprehensive solutions to deter and defend against further cyberattacks," said Senators John McCain, Lindsey Graham, Chuck Schumer and Jack Reed.

"This cannot become a partisan issue," they said. "The stakes are too high for our country."

A Target for Break-Ins

Sitting in the basement of the Democratic National Committee headquarters, below a wall-size 2012 portrait of a smiling Barack Obama, is a 1960s-era filing cabinet missing the handle on the bottom drawer. Only a framed newspaper story hanging on the wall hints at the importance of this aged piece of office furniture.

"GOP Security Aide Among 5 Arrested in Bugging Affair," reads the headline from the front page of the *Washington Post* on June 19, 1972, with the bylines of Bob Woodward and Carl Bernstein.

Andrew Brown, 37, the technology director at the D.N.C., was born after that famous break-in. But as he began to plan for this year's election cycle, he was well aware that the D.N.C. could become a break-in target again.

There were aspirations to ensure that the D.N.C. was well protected against cyberintruders—and then there was the reality, Mr. Brown and his bosses at the organization acknowledged: The D.N.C. was a nonprofit group, dependent on donations, with a fraction of the security budget that a corporation its size would have.

"There was never enough money to do everything we needed to do," Mr. Brown said.

The D.N.C. had a standard email spam-filtering service, intended to block phishing attacks and malware created to resemble legitimate email. But when Russian hackers started in on the D.N.C., the committee did not have the most advanced systems in place to track suspicious traffic, internal D.N.C. memos show.

Mr. Tamene, who reports to Mr. Brown and fielded the call from the F.B.I. agent, was not a full-time D.N.C. employee; he works for a Chicago-based contracting firm called The MIS Department. He was left to figure out, largely on his own, how to respond—and even whether the man who had called in to the D.N.C. switchboard was really an F.B.I. agent.

"The F.B.I. thinks the D.N.C. has at least one compromised computer on its network and the F.B.I. wanted to know if the D.N.C. is aware, and if so, what the D.N.C. is doing about it," Mr. Tamene wrote in an internal memo about his contacts with the F.B.I. He added that "the Special Agent told me to look for a specific type of malware dubbed 'Dukes' by the U.S. intelligence community and in cybersecurity circles."

Part of the problem was that Special Agent Hawkins did not show up in person at the D.N.C. Nor could he email anyone there, as that risked alerting the hackers that the F.B.I. knew they were in the system.

Mr. Tamene's initial scan of the D.N.C. system—using his less-than-optimal tools and incomplete targeting information from the F.B.I. —found nothing. So when Special Agent Hawkins called repeatedly in October, leaving voice mail messages for Mr. Tamene, urging him to call back, "I did not return his calls, as I had nothing to report," Mr. Tamene explained in his memo.

In November, Special Agent Hawkins called with more ominous news. A D.N.C. computer was "calling home, where home meant Russia," Mr. Tamene's memo says, referring to software sending information to Moscow. "SA Hawkins added that the F.B.I. thinks that this calling home behavior could be the result of a state-sponsored attack."

Mr. Brown knew that Mr. Tamene, who declined to comment, was fielding calls from the F.B.I. But he was tied up on a different problem: evidence suggesting that the campaign of Senator Bernie Sanders of Vermont, Mrs. Clinton's main Democratic opponent, had improperly gained access to her campaign data.

Ms. Wasserman Schultz, then the D.N.C.'s chairwoman, and Amy Dacey, then its chief executive, said in interviews that neither of them was notified about the early reports that the committee's system had likely been compromised.

Shawn Henry, who once led the F.B.I.'s cyber division and is now president of CrowdStrike Services, the cybersecurity firm retained by the D.N.C. in April, said he was baffled that the F.B.I. did not call a more senior official at the D.N.C. or send an agent in person to the party headquarters to try to force a more vigorous response.

"We are not talking about an office that is in the middle of the woods of Montana," Mr. Henry said. "We are talking about an office that is half a mile from the F.B.I. office that is getting the notification."

"This is not a mom-and-pop delicatessen or a local library. This is a critical piece of the U.S. infrastructure because it relates to our electoral process, our elected officials, our legislative process, our executive process," he added. "To me it is a high-level, serious issue, and if after a couple of months you don't see any results, somebody ought to raise that to a higher level."

The F.B.I. declined to comment on the agency's handling of the hack. "The F.B.I. takes very seriously any compromise of public and private sector systems," it said in a statement, adding that agents "will continue to share information" to help targets "safeguard their systems against the actions of persistent cybercriminals."

What Is phishing?

Phishing uses an innocent-looking email to entice unwary recipients to click on a deceptive link, giving hackers access to their information or a network. In "spear-phishing," the email is tailored to fool a specific person.

By March, Mr. Tamene and his team had met at least twice in person with the F.B.I. and concluded that Agent Hawkins was really a federal employee. But then the situation took a dire turn.

A second team of Russian-affiliated hackers began to target the D.N.C. and other players in the political world, particularly Democrats. Billy Rinehart, a former D.N.C. regional field director who was then working for Mrs. Clinton's campaign, got an odd email warning from Google.

"Someone just used your password to try to sign into your Google account," the March 22 email said, adding that the sign-in attempt had occurred in Ukraine. "Google stopped this sign-in attempt. You should change your password immediately."

Mr. Rinehart was in Hawaii at the time. He remembers checking his email at 4 a.m. for messages from East Coast associates. Without thinking much about the notification, he clicked on the "change password" button and half asleep, as best he can remember, he typed in a new password. What he did not know until months later is that he had just given the Russian hackers access to his email account.

Hundreds of similar phishing emails were being sent to American political targets, including an identical email sent on March 19 to Mr. Podesta, chairman of the Clinton campaign. Given how many emails Mr. Podesta received through this personal email account, several aides also had access to it, and one of them noticed the warning email, sending it to a computer technician to make sure it was legitimate before anyone clicked on the "change password" button.

"This is a legitimate email," Charles Delavan, a Clinton campaign aide, replied to another of Mr. Podesta's aides, who had noticed the alert. "John needs to change his password immediately."

With another click, a decade of emails that Mr. Podesta maintained in his Gmail account —a total of about 60,000—were unlocked for the Russian hackers. Mr. Delavan, in an interview, said that his bad advice was a result of a typo: He knew this was a phishing attack, as the campaign was getting dozens of them. He said he had meant to type that it was an "illegitimate" email, an error that he said has plagued him ever since.

During this second wave, the hackers also gained access to the Democratic Congressional Campaign Committee, and then, through a virtual private network connection, to the main computer network of the D.N.C.

The F.B.I. observed this surge of activity as well, again reaching out to Mr. Tamene to warn him. Yet Mr. Tamene still saw no reason to be alarmed: He found copies of the phishing emails in the D.N.C.'s spam filter. But he had no reason, he said, to believe that the computer systems had been infiltrated.

One bit of progress had finally been made by the middle of April: The D.N.C., seven months after it had first been warned, finally installed a "robust set of monitoring tools," Mr. Tamene's internal memo says.

Honing Stealthy Tactics

The United States had two decades of warning that Russia's intelligence agencies were trying to break into America's most sensitive computer networks. But the Russians have always managed to stay a step ahead.

Their first major attack was detected on Oct. 7, 1996, when a computer operator at the Colorado School of Mines discovered some nighttime computer activity he could not explain. The school had a major contract with the Navy, and the operator warned his contacts there. But as happened two decades later at the D.N.C., at first "everyone was unable to connect the dots," said Thomas Rid, a scholar at King's College in London who has studied the attack.

Investigators gave it a name—Moonlight Maze—and spent two years, often working day and night, tracing how it hopped from the Navy to the Department of Energy to the Air Force and NASA. In the end, they concluded that the total number of files stolen, if printed and stacked, would be taller than the Washington Monument.

Whole weapons designs were flowing out the door, and it was a first taste of what was to come: an escalating campaign of cyberattacks around the world.

But for years, the Russians stayed largely out of the headlines, thanks to the Chinese—who took bigger risks, and often got caught. They stole the designs for the F-35 fighter jet, corporate secrets for rolling steel, even the blueprints for gas pipelines that supply much of the United States. And during the 2008 presidential election cycle, Chinese intelligence hacked into the campaigns of Mr. Obama and Mr. McCain, making off with internal position papers and communications. But they didn't publish any of it.

The Russians had not gone away, of course. "They were just a lot more stealthy," said Kevin Mandia, a former Air Force intelligence officer who spent most of his days fighting off Russian cyberattacks before founding Mandiant, a cybersecurity firm that is now a division of FireEye—and the company the Clinton campaign brought in to secure its own systems.

The Russians were also quicker to turn their attacks to political purposes. A 2007 cyberattack on Estonia, a former Soviet republic that had joined NATO, sent a message that Russia could paralyze the country without invading it. The next year cyberattacks were used during Russia's war with Georgia.

But American officials did not imagine that the Russians would dare try those techniques inside the United States. They were largely focused on preventing what former Defense Secretary Leon E. Panetta warned was an approaching "cyber Pearl Harbor" —a shutdown of the power grid or cellphone networks.

But in 2014 and 2015, a Russian hacking group began systematically targeting the State Department, the White House and the Joint Chiefs of Staff. "Each time, they eventually met with some form of success," Michael Sulmeyer, a former cyberexpert for the secretary of defense, and Ben Buchanan, now both of the Harvard Cyber Security Project, wrote recently in a soon-to-be published paper for the Carnegie Endowment.

The Russians grew stealthier and stealthier, tricking government computers into sending out data while disguising the electronic "command and control" messages that set off alarms for anyone looking for malicious actions. The State Department was so crippled that it repeatedly closed its systems to throw out the intruders. At one point, officials traveling to Vienna with Secretary of State John Kerry for the Iran nuclear negotiations had to set up commercial Gmail accounts just to communicate with one another and with reporters traveling with them.

Mr. Obama was briefed regularly on all this, but he made a decision that many in the White House now regret: He did not name Russians publicly, or issue sanctions. There was always a reason: fear of escalating a cyberwar, and concern that the United States needed Russia's cooperation in negotiations over Syria.

"We'd have all these circular meetings," one senior State Department official said, "in which everyone agreed you had to push back at the Russians and push back hard. But it didn't happen."

So the Russians escalated again—breaking into systems not just for espionage, but to publish or broadcast what they found, known as "doxing" in the cyberworld. It was a brazen change in tactics, moving the Russians from espionage to influence operations. In February 2014, they broadcast an intercepted phone call between

> **There's no plausible actor that has an interest in all those victims other than Russia.'**
> *Dmitri Alperovitch, co-founder of CrowdStrike, a cybersecurity firm retained by the DNC*

Victoria Nuland, the assistant secretary of state who handles Russian affairs and has a contentious relationship with Mr. Putin, and Geoffrey Pyatt, the United States ambassador to Ukraine. Ms. Nuland was heard describing a little-known American effort to broker a deal in Ukraine, then in political turmoil.

They were not the only ones on whom the Russians used the steal-and-leak strategy. The Open Society Foundation, run by George Soros, was a major target, and when its documents were released, some turned out to have been altered to make it appear as if the foundation was financing Russian opposition members.

Last year, the attacks became more aggressive. Russia hacked a major French television station, frying critical hardware. Around Christmas, it attacked part of the power grid in Ukraine, dropping a portion of the country into darkness, killing back-up generators and taking control of generators. In retrospect, it was a warning shot.

The attacks "were not fully integrated military operations," Mr. Sulmeyer said. But they showed an increasing boldness.

Cozy Bear and Fancy Bear

The day before the White House Correspondents' Association dinner in April, Ms. Dacey, the D.N.C.'s chief executive, was preparing for a night of parties when she got an urgent phone call.

With the new monitoring system in place, Mr. Tamene had examined administrative logs of the D.N.C.'s computer system and found something very suspicious: An unauthorized person, with administrator-level security status, had gained access to the D.N.C.'s computers.

"Not sure it is related to what the F.B.I. has been noticing," said one internal D.N.C. email sent on April 29. "The D.N.C. may have been hacked in a serious way this week, with password theft, etc."

No one knew just how bad the breach was—but it was clear that a lot more than a single filing cabinet worth of materials might have been taken. A secret committee was immediately created, including Ms. Dacey, Ms. Wasserman Schultz, Mr. Brown and Michael Sussmann, a former cybercrimes prosecutor at the Department of Justice who now works at Perkins Coie, the Washington law firm that handles D.N.C. political matters.

"Three most important questions," Mr. Sussmann wrote to his clients the night the break-in was confirmed. "(1) What data was accessed? (2) How was it done? (3) How do we stop it?"

Mr. Sussmann instructed his clients not to use D.N.C. email because they had just one opportunity to lock the hackers out—an effort that could be foiled if the hackers knew that the D.N.C. was on to them.

"You only get one chance to raise the drawbridge," Mr. Sussmann said. "If the adversaries know you are aware of their presence, they will take steps to burrow in, or erase the logs that show they were present."

The D.N.C. immediately hired CrowdStrike, a cybersecurity firm, to scan its computers, identify the intruders and build a new computer and telephone system from scratch. Within a day, CrowdStrike confirmed that the intrusion had originated in Russia, Mr. Sussmann said.

The work that such companies do is a computer version of old-fashioned crime scene investigation, with fingerprints, bullet casings and DNA swabs replaced by an electronic trail that can be just as incriminating. And just as police detectives learn to identify the telltale methods of a veteran burglar, so CrowdStrike investigators recognized the distinctive handiwork of Cozy Bear and Fancy Bear.

Those are CrowdStrike's nicknames for the two Russian hacking groups that the firm found at work inside the D.N.C. network. Cozy Bear—the group also known as the Dukes or A.P.T. 29, for "advanced persistent threat" —may or may not be associated with the F.S.B., the main successor to the Soviet-era KGB, but it is widely believed to be a Russian government operation. It made its first appearance in 2014, said Dmitri Alperovitch, CrowdStrike's co-founder and chief technology officer.

It was Cozy Bear, CrowdStrike concluded, that first penetrated the D.N.C. in the summer of 2015, by sending spear-phishing emails to a long list of American government agencies, Washington nonprofits and government contractors. Whenever someone clicked on a phishing message, the Russians would enter the network, "exfiltrate" documents of interest and stockpile them for intelligence purposes.

"Once they got into the D.N.C., they found the data valuable and decided to continue the operation," said Mr. Alperovitch, who was born in Russia and moved to the United States as a teenager.

Only in March 2016 did Fancy Bear show up—first penetrating the computers of the Democratic Congressional Campaign Committee, and then jumping to the D.N.C., investigators believe. Fancy Bear, sometimes called A.P.T. 28 and believed to be directed by the GRU, Russia's military intelligence agency, is an older outfit, tracked by Western investigators for nearly a decade. It was Fancy Bear that got hold of Mr. Podesta's email.

Attribution, as the skill of identifying a cyberattacker is known, is more art than science. It is often impossible to name an attacker with absolute certainty. But over time, by accumulating a reference library of hacking techniques and targets, it is possible to spot repeat offenders. Fancy Bear, for instance, has gone after military and political targets in Ukraine and Georgia, and at NATO installations.

That largely rules out cybercriminals and most countries, Mr. Alperovitch said. "There's no plausible actor that has an interest in all those victims other than Russia," he said. Another clue: The Russian hacking groups tended to be active during working hours in the Moscow time zone.

To their astonishment, Mr. Alperovitch said, CrowdStrike experts found signs that the two Russian hacking groups had not coordinated their attacks. Fancy Bear, apparently not knowing that Cozy Bear had been rummaging in D.N.C. files for months, took many of the same documents.

In the six weeks after CrowdStrike's arrival, in total secrecy, the computer system at the D.N.C. was replaced. For a weekend, email and phones were shut off; employees were told it was a system upgrade. All laptops were turned in and the hard drives wiped clean, with the uninfected information on them imaged to new drives.

Though D.N.C. officials had learned that the Democratic Congressional Campaign Committee had been infected, too, they did not notify their sister organization, which was in the same building, because they were afraid that it would leak.

All of this work took place as the bitter contest for the Democratic nomination continued to play out between Mrs. Clinton and Mr. Sanders, and it was already causing a major distraction for Ms. Wasserman Schultz and the D.N.C.'s chief executive.

"This was not a bump in the road—bumps in the road happen all the time," she said in an interview. "Two different Russian spy agencies had hacked into our network and stolen our property. And we did not yet know what they had taken. But we knew they had very broad access to our network. There was a tremendous amount of uncertainty. And it was chilling."

The D.N.C. executives and their lawyer had their first formal meeting with senior F.B.I. officials in mid-June, nine months after the bureau's first call to the tech-support contractor. Among the early requests at that meeting, according to participants: that the federal government make a quick "attribution" formally blaming actors with ties to Russian government for the attack to make clear that it was not routine hacking but foreign espionage.

"You have a presidential election underway here and you know that the Russians have hacked into the D.N.C.," Mr. Sussmann said, recalling the message to the F.B.I. "We need to tell the American public that. And soon."

The Media's Role

In mid-June, on Mr. Sussmann's advice, D.N.C. leaders decided to take a bold step. Concerned that word of the hacking might leak, they decided to go public in the *Washington Post* with the news that the committee had been attacked. That way, they figured, they could get ahead of the story, win a little sympathy from voters for being victimized by Russian hackers and refocus on the campaign.

But the very next day, a new, deeply unsettling shock awaited them. Someone calling himself Guccifer 2.0 appeared on the web, claiming to be the D.N.C. hacker—and he posted a confidential committee document detailing Mr. Trump's record and half a dozen other documents to prove his bona fides.

"And it's just a tiny part of all docs I downloaded from the Democrats networks," he wrote. Then something more ominous: "The main part of the papers, thousands of files and mails, I gave to WikiLeaks. They will publish them soon."

It was bad enough that Russian hackers had been spying inside the committee's network for months. Now the public release of documents had turned a conventional espionage operation into something far more menacing: political sabotage, an unpredictable, uncontrollable menace for Democratic campaigns.

Guccifer 2.0 borrowed the moniker of an earlier hacker, a Romanian who called himself Guccifer and was jailed for breaking into the personal computers of former President George W. Bush, former Secretary of State Colin L. Powell and other notables. This new attacker seemed intent on showing that the D.N.C.'s cyberexperts at CrowdStrike were wrong to blame Russia. Guccifer 2.0 called himself a "lone hacker" and mocked CrowdStrike for calling the attackers "sophisticated."

But online investigators quickly undercut his story. On a whim, Lorenzo Franceschi-Bicchierai, a writer for *Motherboard*, the tech and culture site of Vice, tried to contact Guccifer 2.0 by direct message on Twitter.

"Surprisingly, he answered right away," Mr. Franceschi-Bicchierai said. But whoever was on the other end seemed to be mocking him. "I asked him why he did it, and he said he wanted to expose the Illuminati. He called himself a Gucci lover. And he said he was Romanian."

That gave Mr. Franceschi-Bicchierai an idea. Using Google Translate, he sent the purported hacker some questions in Romanian. The answers came back in Romanian. But when he was offline, Mr. Franceschi-Bicchierai checked with a couple of native speakers, who told him Guccifer 2.0 had apparently been using Google Translate as well—and was clearly not the Romanian he claimed to be.

Cyberresearchers found other clues pointing to Russia. Microsoft Word documents posted by Guccifer 2.0 had been edited by someone calling himself, in Russian, Felix Edmundovich—an obvious nom de guerre honoring the founder of the Soviet secret police, Felix Edmundovich Dzerzhinsky. Bad links in the texts were marked by warnings in Russian, generated by what was clearly a Russian-language version of Word.

When Mr. Franceschi-Bicchierai managed to engage Guccifer 2.0 over a period of weeks, he found that his interlocutor's tone and manner changed. "At first he was careless and colloquial. Weeks later, he was curt and more calculating," he said. "It seemed like a group of people, and a very sloppy attempt to cover up."

Computer experts drew the same conclusion about *DCLeaks.com*, a site that sprang up in June, claiming to be the work of "hacktivists" but posting more stolen documents. It, too, seemed to be a clumsy front for the same Russians who had stolen the documents. Notably, the website was registered in April, suggesting that the Russian hacking team planned well in advance to make public what it stole.

In addition to what Guccifer 2.0 published on his site, he provided material directly on request to some bloggers and publications. The steady flow of Guccifer 2.0 documents constantly undercut Democratic messaging efforts. On July 6, 12 days before the Republican National Convention began in Cleveland, Guccifer released the D.N.C.'s battle plan and budget for countering it. For Republican operatives, it was insider gold.

Then WikiLeaks, a far more established outlet, began to publish the hacked material—just as Guccifer 2.0 had promised. On July 22, three days before the start of the Democratic National Convention in Philadelphia, WikiLeaks dumped out 44,053 D.N.C. emails with 17,761 attachments. Some of the messages made clear that some D.N.C. officials favored Mrs. Clinton over her progressive challenger, Mr. Sanders.

That was no shock; Mr. Sanders, after all, had been an independent socialist, not a Democrat, during his long career in Congress, while Mrs. Clinton had been one of the party's stars for decades. But the emails, some of them crude or insulting, infuriated Sanders delegates as they arrived in Philadelphia. Ms. Wasserman Schultz resigned under pressure on the eve of the convention where she had planned to preside.

Mr. Trump, by now the Republican nominee, expressed delight at the continuing jolts to his opponent, and he began to use Twitter and his stump speeches to highlight the WikiLeaks releases. On July 25, he sent out a lighthearted tweet: "The new joke in town," he wrote, "is that Russia leaked the disastrous D.N.C. e-mails, which should never have been written (stupid), because Putin likes me."

But WikiLeaks was far from finished. On Oct. 7, a month before the election, the site began the serial publication of thousands of private emails to and from Mr. Podesta, Mrs. Clinton's campaign manager.

The same day, the United States formally accused the Russian government of being behind the hackings, in a joint statement by the director of national intelligence and the Department of Homeland Security, and Mr. Trump suffered his worst blow to date, with the release of a recording in which he bragged about sexually assaulting women.

The Podesta emails were nowhere near as sensational as the Trump video. But, released by WikiLeaks day after day over the last month of the campaign, they provided material for countless news reports. They disclosed the contents of Mrs. Clinton's speeches to large banks, which she had refused to release. They exposed tensions inside the campaign, including disagreements over donations to the Clinton Foundation that staff members thought might look bad for the candidate and Ms. Tanden's complaint that Mrs. Clinton's instincts were "suboptimal."

"I was just mortified," Ms. Tanden said in an interview. Her emails were released on the eve of one of the presidential debates, she recalled. "I put my hands over my head and said, 'I can't believe this is happening to me.'" Though she had regularly appeared on television to support Mrs. Clinton, she canceled her appearances because all the questions were about what she had said in the emails.

Ms. Tanden, like other Democrats whose messages became public, said it was obvious to her that WikiLeaks was trying its best to damage the Clinton campaign. "If you care about transparency, you put all the emails out at once," she said. "But they wanted to hurt her. So they put them out 1,800 to 3,000 a day."

The Trump campaign knew in advance about WikiLeaks' plans. Days before the Podesta email release began, Roger Stone, a Republican operative working with the Trump campaign, sent out an excited tweet about what was coming.

But in an interview, Mr. Stone said he had no role in the leaks; he had just heard from an American with ties to WikiLeaks that damning emails were coming.

Julian Assange, the WikiLeaks founder and editor, has resisted the conclusion that his site became a pass-through for

> **An American counterstrike has 'got to be overt. It needs to be seen.'**
> *Michael Morell, Former Deputy Director of the CIA*

Russian hackers working for Mr. Putin's government or that he was deliberately trying to undermine Mrs. Clinton's candidacy. But the evidence on both counts appears compelling.

In a series of email exchanges, Mr. Assange refused to say anything about WikiLeaks' source for the hacked material. He denied that he had made his animus toward Mrs. Clinton clear in public statements ("False. But what is this? Junior high?") or that the site had timed the releases for maximum negative effect on her campaign. "WikiLeaks makes its decisions based on newsworthiness, including for its recent epic scoops," he wrote.

Mr. Assange disputed the conclusion of the Oct. 7 statement from the intelligence agencies that the leaks were "intended to interfere with the U.S. election process."

"This is false," he wrote. "As the disclosing party we know that this was not the intent. Publishers publishing newsworthy information during an election is part of a free election."

But asked whether he believed the leaks were one reason for Mr. Trump's election, Mr. Assange seemed happy to take credit. "Americans extensively engaged with our publications," he wrote. "According to Facebook statistics WikiLeaks was the most referenced political topic during October."

Though Mr. Assange did not say so, WikiLeaks' best defense may be the conduct of the mainstream American media. Every major publication, including the *Times*, published multiple stories citing the D.N.C. and Podesta emails posted by WikiLeaks, becoming a de facto instrument of Russian intelligence.

Mr. Putin, a student of martial arts, had turned two institutions at the core of American democracy—political campaigns and independent media—to his own ends. The media's appetite for the hacked material, and its focus on the gossipy content instead of the Russian source, disturbed some of those whose personal emails were being reposted across the web.

"What was really surprising to me?" Ms. Tanden said. "I could not believe that reporters were covering it."

Devising a Government Response

Inside the White House, as Mr. Obama's advisers debated their response, their conversation turned to North Korea.

In late 2014, hackers working for Kim Jong-un, the North's young and unpredictable leader, had carried out a well-planned attack on Sony Pictures Entertainment intended to stop the Christmastime release of a comedy about a C.I.A. plot to kill Mr. Kim.

In that case, embarrassing emails had also been released. But the real damage was done to Sony's own systems: More than 70 percent of its computers melted down when a particularly virulent form of malware was released. Within weeks, intelligence agencies traced the attack back to the North and its leadership. Mr. Obama called North Korea out in public, and issued some not-very-effective sanctions. The Chinese even cooperated, briefly cutting off the North's internet connections.

As the first Situation Room meetings on the Russian hacking began in July, "it was clear that Russia was going to be a much more complicated case," said one participant. The Russians clearly had a more sophisticated understanding of American politics, and they were masters of "kompromat," their term for compromising information.

But a formal "attribution report" still had not been forwarded to the president.

"It took forever," one senior administration official said, complaining about the pace at which the intelligence assessments moved through the system.

In August a group that called itself the "Shadow Brokers" published a set of software tools that looked like what the NSA uses to break into foreign computer networks and install "implants," malware that can be used for surveillance or attack. The code came from the Tailored Access Operations unit of the NSA, a secretive group that mastered the arts of surveillance and cyberwar.

The assumption—still unproved—was that the code was put out in the open by the Russians as a warning: Retaliate for the D.N.C., and there are a lot more secrets, from the hackings of the State Department, the White House and the Pentagon, that might be spilled as well. One senior official compared it to the scene in "The Godfather" where the head of a favorite horse is left in a bed, as a warning.

The NSA said nothing. But by late August, Admiral Rogers, its director, was pressing for a more muscular response to the Russians. In his role as director of the Pentagon's Cyber Command, he proposed a series of potential counter-cyberstrikes.

While officials will not discuss them in detail, the possible counterstrikes reportedly included operations that would turn the tables on Mr. Putin, exposing his financial links to Russia's oligarchs, and punching holes in the Russian internet to allow dissidents to get their message out. Pentagon officials judged the measures too unsubtle and ordered up their own set of options.

But in the end, none of those were formally presented to the president.

In a series of "deputies meetings" run by Avril Haines, the deputy national security adviser and a former deputy director of the CIA, several officials warned that an overreaction by the administration would play into Mr. Putin's hands.

"If we went to Defcon 4," one frequent participant in Ms. Haines's meetings said, using a phrase from the Cold War days of warnings of war, "we would be saying to the public that we didn't have confidence in the integrity of our voting system."

Even something seemingly straightforward—using the president's executive powers, bolstered after the Sony incident, to place economic and travel sanctions on cyberattackers—seemed too risky.

"No one was all that eager to impose costs before Election Day," said another participant in the classified meeting. "Any retaliatory measures were seen through the prism of what would happen on Election Day."

Instead, when Mr. Obama's national security team reconvened after summer vacation, the focus turned to a crash effort to secure the nation's voting machines and voter-registration rolls from hacking. The scenario they discussed most frequently—one that turned out not to be an issue—was a narrow vote in favor of Mrs. Clinton, followed by a declaration by Mr. Trump that the vote was "rigged" and more leaks intended to undercut her legitimacy.

Donna Brazile, the interim chairwoman of the DNC, became increasingly frustrated as the clock continued to run down on the presidential election—and still there was no broad public condemnation by the White House, or Republican Party leaders, of the attack as an act of foreign espionage.

Ms. Brazile even reached out to Reince Priebus, the chairman of the Republican National Committee, urging him twice in private conversations and in a letter to join her in condemning the attacks—an offer he declined to take up.

"We just kept hearing the government would respond, the government would respond," she said. "Once upon a time, if a foreign government interfered with our election we would respond as a nation, not as a political party."

But Mr. Obama did decide that he would deliver a warning to Mr. Putin in person at a Group of 20 summit meeting in Hangzhou, China, the last time they would be in the same place while Mr. Obama was still in office. When the two men met for a tense pull-aside, Mr. Obama explicitly warned Mr. Putin of a strong American response if there was continued effort to influence the election or manipulate the vote, according to White House officials who were not present for the one-on-one meeting.

Later that day, Mr. Obama made a rare reference to America's own offensive cybercapacity, which he has almost never talked about. "Frankly, both offensively and defensively, we have more capacity," he told reporters.

But when it came time to make a public assertion of Russia's role in early October, it was made in a written statement from the director of national intelligence and the secretary of homeland security. It was far less dramatic than the president's appearance in the press room two years before to directly accuse the North Koreans of attacking Sony.

The reference in the statement to hackings on "political organizations," officials now say, encompassed a hacking on data stored by the Republicans as well. Two senior officials say the forensic evidence was accompanied by "human and technical" sources in Russia, which appears to mean that the United States' implants or taps in Russian computer and phone networks helped confirm the country's role.

But that may not be known for decades, until the secrets are declassified.

A week later Vice President Joseph R. Biden Jr. was sent out to transmit a public warning to Mr. Putin: The United States will retaliate "at the time of our choosing. And under the circumstances that have the greatest impact."

Later, after Mr. Biden said he was not concerned that Russia could "fundamentally alter the election," he was asked whether the American public would know if the message to Mr. Putin had been sent.

"Hope not," Mr. Biden responded.

Some of his former colleagues think that was the wrong answer. An American counterstrike, said Michael Morell, the former deputy director of the CIA under Mr. Obama, has "got to be overt. It needs to be seen."

A covert response would significantly limit the deterrence effect, he added. "If you can't see it, it's not going to deter the Chinese and North Koreans and Iranians and others." The Obama administration says it still has more than 30 days to do exactly that.

The Next Target

As the year draws to a close, it now seems possible that there will be multiple investigations of the Russian hacking—the intelligence review Mr. Obama has ordered completed by Jan. 20, the day he leaves office, and one or more congressional inquiries. They will wrestle with, among other things, Mr. Putin's motive.

Did he seek to mar the brand of American democracy, to forestall anti-Russian activism for both Russians and their neighbors? Or to weaken the next American president, since presumably Mr. Putin had no reason to doubt American forecasts that Mrs. Clinton would win easily? Or was it, as the CIA concluded last month, a deliberate attempt to elect Mr. Trump?

In fact, the Russian hack-and-dox scheme accomplished all three goals.

What seems clear is that Russian hacking, given its success, is not going to stop. Two weeks ago, the German intelligence chief, Bruno Kahl, warned that Russia might target elections in Germany next year. "The perpetrators have an interest to delegitimize the democratic process as such," Mr. Kahl said. Now, he added, "Europe is in the focus of these attempts of disturbance, and Germany to a particularly great extent."

But Russia has by no means forgotten its American target. On the day after the presidential election, the cybersecurity company Volexity reported five new waves of phishing emails, evidently from Cozy Bear, aimed at think tanks and nonprofits in the United States.

One of them purported to be from Harvard University, attaching a fake paper. Its title: "Why American Elections Are Flawed."

Print Citations

CMS: Lipton, Eric, David E. Sanger, and Scott Shane. "The Perfect Weapon: How Russian Cyberpower Invaded the U.S." In *The Reference Shelf: Internet Abuses and Privacy Rights*, edited by Betsy Maury, 161-177. Ipswich, MA: H.W. Wilson, 2017.

MLA: Lipton, Eric, David E. Sanger, and Scott Shane. "The Perfect Weapon: How Russian Cyberpower Invaded the U.S." *The Reference Shelf: Internet Abuses and Privacy Rights*. Ed. Betsy Maury. Ipswich: H.W. Wilson, 2017. 161-177. Print.

APA: Lipton, E., D. Sanger, & S. Shane. (2017). The perfect weapon: How Russian cyberpower invaded the U.S. In Betsy Maury (Ed.), *The Reference Shelf: Internet Abuses and Privacy Rights* (pp. 161-177). Ipswich, MA: H.W. Wilson. (Original work published 2016)

Hacking the Attention Economy

By Danah Boyd

Points: Data + Society, January 5, 2017

For most non-technical folks, "hacking" evokes the notion of using sophisticated technical skills to break through the security of a corporate or government system for illicit purposes. Of course, most folks who were engaged in cracking security systems weren't necessarily in it for espionage and cruelty. In the 1990s, I grew up among teenage hackers who wanted to break into the computer systems of major institutions that were part of the security establishment, just to show that they could. The goal here was to feel a sense of power in a world where they felt pretty powerless. The rush was in being able to do something and feel smarter than the so-called powerful. It was fun and games. At least until they started getting arrested.

Hacking has always been about leveraging skills to push the boundaries of systems. Keep in mind that one early definition of a hacker (from the *Jargon File* by Eric Raymond) was "A person who enjoys learning the details of programming systems and how to stretch their capabilities, as opposed to most users who prefer to learn only the minimum necessary." In another early definition (RFC:1392 from the *Internet User's Glossary*), a hacker is defined as "A person who delights in having an intimate understanding of the internal workings of a system, computers and computer networks in particular." Both of these definitions highlight something important: violating the security of a technical system isn't necessarily the primary objective.

Indeed, over the last 15 years, I've watched as countless hacker-minded folks have started leveraging a mix of technical and social engineering skills to reconfigure networks of power. Some are in it for the fun. Some see dollar signs. Some have a much more ideological agenda. But above all, what's fascinating is how many people have learned to play the game. And in some worlds, those skills are coming home to roost in unexpected ways, especially as groups are seeking to mess with information intermediaries in an effort to hack the attention economy.

It All Began with Memes... (and Porn...)

In 2003, a 15-year-old named Chris Poole started an image board site based on a Japanese trend called 4chan. His goal was not political. Rather, like many of his male teenage peers, he simply wanted a place to share pornography and anime. But as his site's popularity grew, he ran into a different problem—he couldn't manage the traffic while storing all of the content. So he decided to delete older content as newer content came in. Users were frustrated that their favorite images disappeared so they reposted them, often with slight modifications. This gave birth to a phenomenon now understood as "meme culture." Lolcats are an example. These are images of cats captioned with a specific font and a consistent grammar for entertainment.

Those who produced meme-like images quickly realized that they could spread like wildfire thanks to new types of social media (as well as older tools like blogging). People began producing memes just for fun. But for a group of hacker-minded teenagers who were born a decade after I was, a new practice emerged. Rather than trying to hack the security infrastructure, they wanted to attack the emergent attention economy. They wanted to show that they could manipulate the media narrative, just to show that they could. This was happening at a moment when social media sites were skyrocketing, YouTube and blogs were challenging mainstream media, and pundits were pushing the idea that anyone could control the narrative by being their own media channel. Hell, "You" was *Time* magazine's person of the year in 2006.

Taking a humorist approach, campaigns emerged within 4chan to "hack" mainstream media. For example, many inside 4chan felt that widespread anxieties about pedophilia were exaggerated and sensationalized. They decided to target Oprah Winfrey, who, they felt, was amplifying this fear-mongering. Trolling her online message board, they got her to talk on live TV about how "over 9,000 penises" were raping children. Humored by this success, they then created a broader campaign around a fake character known as Pedobear. In a different campaign, 4chan "b-tards" focused on gaming the *Time* 100 list of "the world's most influential people" by arranging it such that the first letter of each name on the list spelled out "Marblecake also the game," which is a known in-joke in this community. Many other campaigns emerged to troll major media and other cultural leaders. And frankly, it was hard not to laugh when everyone started scratching their heads about why Rick Astley's 1987 song "Never Gonna Give You Up" suddenly became a phenomenon again.

By engaging in these campaigns, participants learned how to shape information within a networked ecosystem. They learned how to design information for it to spread across social media.

They also learned how to game social media, manipulate its algorithms, and mess with the incentive structure of both old and new media enterprises. They weren't alone. I watched teenagers throw brand names and *Buzzfeed* links into their Facebook posts to increase the likelihood that their friends would see their posts in their News Feed. Consultants started working for companies to produce catchy content that would get traction and clicks. Justin Bieber fans ran campaign after campaign to keep Bieber-related topics in Twitter Trending Topics. And the activist group Invisible Children leveraged knowledge of how social media worked to architect the #Kony2012 campaign. All of this was seen as legitimate "social media marketing," making it hard to detect where the boundaries were between those who were hacking for fun and those who were hacking for profit or other "serious" ends.

Running campaigns to shape what the public could see was nothing new, but social media created new pathways for people and organizations to get information out to wide audiences. Marketers discussed it as the future of marketing. Activists talked about it as the next frontier for activism. Political consultants talked about it as the future of political campaigns. And a new form of propaganda emerged.

The Political Side to the lulz

In her phenomenal account of Anonymous—"Hacker, Hoaxer, Whistleblower, Spy" —Gabriella Coleman describes the interplay between different networks of people playing similar hackeresque games for different motivations. She describes the goofy nature of those "Anons" who created a campaign to expose Scientology, which many believed to be a farcical religion with too much power and political sway. But she also highlights how the issues became more political and serious as WikiLeaks emerged, law enforcement started going after hackers, and the Arab Spring began.

Anonymous was birthed out of 4chan, but because of the emergent ideological agendas of many Anons, the norms and tactics started shifting. Some folks were in it for fun and games, but the "lulz" started getting darker and those seeking vigilante justice started using techniques like "doxing" to expose people who were seen as deserving of punishment. Targets changed over time, showcasing the divergent political agendas in play.

Perhaps the most notable turn involved "#GamerGate" when issues of sexism in the gaming industry emerged into a campaign of harassment targeted at a group of women. Doxing began being used to enable "swatting" —in which false reports called in by perpetrators would result in SWAT teams sent to targets' homes. The strategies and tactics that had been used to enable decentralized but coordinated campaigns were now being used by those seeking to use the tools of media and attention to do serious reputational, psychological, economic, and social harm to targets. Although 4chan had long been an "anything goes" environment (with notable exceptions), #GamerGate became taboo there for stepping over the lines.

As #GamerGate unfolded, men's rights activists began using the situation to push forward a long-standing political agenda to counter feminist ideology, pushing for #GamerGate to be framed as a serious debate as opposed to being seen as a campaign of hate and harassment. In some ways, the resultant media campaign was quite successful: major conferences and journalistic enterprises felt the need to "hear both sides" as though there was a debate unfolding. Watching this, I couldn't help but think of the work of Frank Luntz, a remarkably effective conservative political consultant known for reframing issues using politicized language.

As doxing and swatting have become more commonplace, another type of harassment also started to emerge en masse: gaslighting. This term refers to a 1944 Ingrid Bergman film called *Gas Light* (which was based on a 1938 play). The film depicts psychological abuse in a domestic violence context, where the victim starts to doubt reality because of the various actions of the abuser. It is a form of psychological warfare that can work tremendously well in an information ecosystem, especially one where it's possible to put up information in a distributed way to make it very unclear what is legitimate, what is fake, and what is propaganda. More importantly, as many autocratic regimes have learned, this tactic is fantastic for seeding the public's doubt in institutions and information intermediaries.

The Democratization of Manipulation

In the early days of blogging, many of my fellow bloggers imagined that our practice could disrupt mainstream media. For many progressive activists, social media could be a tool that could circumvent institutionalized censorship and enable a plethora of diverse voices to speak out and have their say. Civic minded scholars were excited by "smart mobs" who leveraged new communications platforms to coordinate in a decentralized way to speak truth to power. Arab Spring. Occupy Wall Street. Black Lives Matter. These energized progressives as "proof" that social technologies could make a new form of civil life possible.

Hacking has always been about leveraging skills to push the boundaries of systems.

I spent 15 years watching teenagers play games with powerful media outlets and attempt to achieve control over their own ecosystem. They messed with algorithms, coordinated information campaigns, and resisted attempts to curtail their speech. Like Chinese activists, they learned to hide their traces when it was to their advantage to do so. They encoded their ideas such that access to content didn't mean access to meaning.

Of course, it wasn't just progressive activists and teenagers who were learning how to mess with the media ecosystem that has emerged since social media unfolded. We've also seen the political establishment, law enforcement, marketers, and hate groups build capacity at manipulating the media landscape. Very little of what's happening is truly illegal, but there's no widespread agreement about which of these practices are socially and morally acceptable or not.

The techniques that are unfolding are hard to manage and combat. Some of them look like harassment, prompting people to self-censor out of fear. Others look like "fake news," highlighting the messiness surrounding bias, misinformation, disinformation, and propaganda. There is hate speech that is explicit, but there's also suggestive content that prompts people to frame the world in particular ways. Dog whistle politics have emerged in a new form of encoded content, where you have to be in the know to understand what's happening. Companies who built tools to help people communicate are finding it hard to combat the ways their tools are being used by networks looking to skirt the edges of the law and content policies. Institutions and legal instruments designed to stop abuse are finding themselves ill-equipped to function in light of networked dynamics.

The Internet has long been used for gaslighting, and trolls have long targeted adversaries. What has shifted recently is the scale of the operation, the coordination of the attacks, and the strategic agenda of some of the players.

For many who are learning these techniques, it's no longer simply about fun, nor is it even about the lulz. It has now become about acquiring power.

A new form of information manipulation is unfolding in front of our eyes. It is political. It is global. And it is populist in nature. The news media is being played like a fiddle, while decentralized networks of people are leveraging the ever-evolving networked tools around them to hack the attention economy.

I only wish I knew what happens next.

Print Citations

CMS: Boyd, Danah. "Hacking the Attention Economy." In *The Reference Shelf: Internet Abuses and Privacy Rights*, edited by Betsy Maury, 178-182. Ipswich, MA: H.W. Wilson, 2017.

MLA: Boyd, Danah. "Hacking the Attention Economy." *The Reference Shelf: Guns in America The Reference Shelf: Internet Abuses and Privacy Rights*. Ed. Betsy Maury. Ipswich: H.W. Wilson, 2017. 178-182. Print.

APA: Boyd, D. (2017). Hacking the attention economy. In Betsy Maury (Ed.), *The Reference Shelf: Internet Abuses and Privacy Rights* (pp. 178-182). Ipswich, MA: H.W. Wilson. (Original work published 2017)

Partisan Politics and the Russian Hacking Imbroglio

By Jonah Goldberg
The National Review, **January 6, 2017**

It is a natural human tendency to want all good things to go together and all bad things to go together. That's why we don't like hearing that Hitler built great roads and was kind to animals, or that Mahatma Gandhi could be petty and nasty. In other words, we hate hearing good things about our villains and bad things about our heroes. This sort of thinking is downstream of tribalism. The essence of tribal thinking boils down to: "The enemy of my enemy is my friend, and the friend of my enemy is my enemy."

Politics has its own kind of tribalism as well, bending facts and principles to partisan loyalties. The clearest sign that one has given over to a kind of tribal partisanship is when someone—or whole groups of people—cannot countenance inconvenient truths.

In the 1990s, for example, feminists had laid down a series of arguments about sexual harassment. Then Bill Clinton got in trouble. Rather than maintain the principles they'd been asserting or acknowledge the facts they found regrettable, they rallied to Clinton's defense. In their rush to help him, they left behind the baggage of their credibility.

Which brings me to Julian Assange and the issue of Russian hacking. Donald Trump and many of his supporters are having a hard time acknowledging the following: Assange, the founder of WikiLeaks, is an avowed enemy of the United States who has openly admitted—and acted on—his animosity toward America. A onetime TV host for Russia Today, a Vladimir Putin–directed propaganda network, he is, if not in the employ of Russia, then objectively in service to it.

The government of Russia, through surrogates and proxies, meddled in the 2016 U.S. presidential election, much as it has done in numerous other countries. The Russians used WikiLeaks as a very effective tool for their mischief. That mischief probably had some effect on how the election played out. Russia, under Putin's authoritarian rule, seeks to undermine the legitimacy of American and Western democracy and to weaken NATO. Democrats and many people in the media are having a hard time admitting the following: All of the election-related documents leaked to and by WikiLeaks have been authentic and pertain to legitimate issues for news organizations to explore. Much of the evidence for Russia's meddling may

> The government of Russia, through surrogates and proxies, meddled in the 2016 U.S. presidential election, much as it has done in numerous other countries.

in fact be circumstantial or hard to prove unequivocally.

The appointed leadership of the U.S. intelligence community, under Barack Obama in particular, has been politicizing intelligence (downplaying ISIS and Islamic terrorism generally, hyping the extent of al-Qaeda's degradation, soft-peddling Iran's intentions, etc.). Skepticism toward what they say on the way out the door is warranted (though perhaps not in the way Trump has expressed it). Even if Russia meddled in the election, Trump was legitimately elected.

Now, I consider all of these things to be true. But that leaves me—and many like me—in the middle of a partisan shooting war. Trump and his subalterns have found themselves in the position of rehabilitating Assange as some kind of heroic truth-teller, because they feel it necessary for political reasons. In 2010, Sarah Palin rightly described Assange as "an anti-American operative with blood on his hands." This week, she apologized.

In 2010, with a bit of hyperbole, Newt Gingrich declared: "Julian Assange is engaged in terrorism. He should be treated as an enemy combatant." This week, Gingrich told Sean Hannity (one of Assange's most prominent fans these days) that Assange is a "down-to-earth, straightforward interviewee."

In 2010, Michael Moore put up $20,000 for Assange's bail—he'd been charged with rape in Sweden—because "there is a concerted attempt to stop . . . anybody that is trying to do the job of telling us the truth." Now, Moore says Trump has no right to be president because of Russia's use of WikiLeaks's truth-telling. The Huffington Post was initially enthralled by WikiLeaks, running pieces with such headlines as "Let Us Now Praise WikiLeaks." Now, the Huffington Post's hyperventilating threatens to suck the oxygen out of the atmosphere.

Of course, people are allowed to change their minds when new facts present themselves. But those facts should be relevant. The problem is that the most pertinent facts—about Assange, Russia, etc.—have not changed. The only truly relevant new fact is that Assange is a useful tool for Republicans, and all other facts must be bent—on the left and right—to fit that new reality.

Print Citations

CMS: Goldberg, Jonah. "Partisan Politics and the Russian Hacking Imbroglio." In *The Reference Shelf: Internet Abuses and Privacy Rights,* edited by Betsy Maury, 183-185. Ipswich, MA: H.W. Wilson, 2017.

MLA: Goldberg, Jonah. "Partisan Politics and the Russian Hacking Imbroglio." *The Reference Shelf: Internet Abuses and Privacy Rights.* Ed. Betsy Maury. Ipswich: H.W. Wilson, 2017. 183-185. Print.

APA: Goldberg, J. (2017). Partisan politics and the Russian Hacking imbroglio. In Betsy Maury (Ed.), *The Reference Shelf: Internet Abuses and Privacy Rights* (pp. 183-185). Ipswich, MA: H.W. Wilson. (Original work published 2017)

Feds: We Can Read All Your Email, and You'll Never Know

By Clark D. Cunningham
The Conversation, September 21, 2016

Fear of hackers reading private emails in cloudbased systems like Microsoft Outlook, Gmail or Yahoo! has recently sent regular people and public officials scrambling to delete entire accounts full of messages dating back years. What we don't expect is our own government to hack our email—but it's happening. Federal court cases going on right now are revealing that federal officials can read all your email without your knowledge.

As a scholar and lawyer who started researching and writing about the history and meaning of the Fourth Amendment to the Constitution more than 30 years ago, I immediately saw how the FBI versus Apple controversy earlier this year was bringing the founders' fight for liberty into the 21st century. My study of that legal battle caused me to dig into the federal government's actual practices for getting email from cloud accounts and cellphones, causing me to worry that our basic liberties are threatened.

A New Type of Government Search

The federal government is getting access to the contents of entire email accounts by using an ancient procedure—the search warrant—with a new, sinister twist: secret court proceedings.

The earliest search warrants had a very limited purpose—authorizing entry to private premises to find and recover stolen goods. During the era of the American Revolution, British authorities abused this power to conduct dragnet searches of colonial homes and to seize people's private papers looking for evidence of political resistance.

To prevent the new federal government from engaging in that sort of tyranny, special controls over search warrants were written into the Fourth Amendment to the Constitution. But these constitutional provisions are failing to protect our personal documents if they are stored in the cloud or on our smartphones.

Fortunately, the government's efforts are finally being made public, thanks to legal battles taken up by Apple, Microsoft and other major companies. But the feds are fighting back, using even more subversive legal tactics.

Searching in Secret

To get these warrants in the first place, the feds are using the Electronic Communications Privacy Act, passed in 1986—long before widespread use of cloudbased email and smartphones. That law allows the government to use a warrant to get electronic communications from the company providing the service—rather than the true owner of the email account, the person who uses it.

> If the government were serious about obeying the Constitution, when it asks for an entire email account, at least it would write into the warrant limits on its forensic analysis so only emails that are evidence of a crime could be viewed.

And the government then usually asks that the warrant be "sealed," which means it won't appear in public court records and will be hidden from you. Even worse, the law lets the government get what is called a "gag order," a court ruling preventing the company from telling you it got a warrant for your email.

You might never know that the government has been reading all of your email—or you might find out when you get charged with a crime based on your messages.

Microsoft Steps Up

Much was written about Apple's successful fight earlier this year to prevent the FBI from forcing the company to break the iPhone's security system.

But relatively little notice has come to a similar Microsoft effort on behalf of customers that began in April 2016. The company's suit argued that search warrants delivered to Microsoft for customers' emails are violating regular people's constitutional rights. (It also argued that being gagged violates Microsoft's own First Amendment rights.)

Microsoft's suit, filed in Seattle, says that over the course of 20 months in 2015 and 2016, it received more than 3,000 gag orders—and that more than twothirds of the gag orders were effectively permanent, because they did not include end dates. Court documents supporting Microsoft describe thousands more gag orders issued against Google, Yahoo!, Twitter and other companies. Remarkably, three former chief federal prosecutors, who collectively had authority for the Seattle region for every year from 1989 to 2009, and the retired head of the FBI's Seattle office have also joined forces to support Microsoft's position.

The Feds Get Everything

It's very difficult to get a copy of one of these search warrants, thanks to orders sealing files and gagging companies. But in another Microsoft lawsuit against the government a redacted warrant was made part of the court record. It shows how the government asks for—and receives—the power to look at all of a person's email.

On the first page of the warrant, the cloudbased email account is clearly treated as "premises" controlled by Microsoft, not by the email account's owner:

> "An application by a federal law enforcement officer or an attorney for the government requests the search of the following ... property located in the Western District of Washington, the premises known and described as the email account [REDACTED]@ MSN.COM, which is controlled by Microsoft Corporation."

The Fourth Amendment requires that a search warrant must "particularly describe the things to be seized" and there must be "probable cause" based on sworn testimony that those particular things are evidence of a crime. But this warrant orders Microsoft to turn over "the contents of all emails stored in the account, including copies of emails sent from the account." From the day the account was opened to the date of the warrant, everything must be handed over to the feds.

Reading All of It

In warrants like this, the government is deliberately not limiting itself to the constitutionally required "particular description" of the messages it's looking for. To get away with this, it tells judges that incriminating emails can be hard to find—maybe even hidden with misleading names, dates and file attachments—so their computer forensic experts need access to the whole data base to work their magic.

If the government were serious about obeying the Constitution, when it asks for an entire email account, at least it would write into the warrant limits on its forensic analysis so only emails that are evidence of a crime could be viewed. But this Microsoft warrant says an unspecified "variety of techniques may be employed to search the seized emails," including "email by email review."

As I explain in a forthcoming paper, there is good reason to suspect this type of warrant is the government's usual approach, not an exception.

Former federal computercrimes prosecutor Paul Ohm says almost every federal computer search warrant lacks the required particularity.

Another former prosecutor, Orin Kerr, who wrote the first edition of the federal manual on searching computers, agrees: "Everything can be seized. Everything can be searched." Even some federal judges are calling attention to the problem, putting into print their objections to signing such warrants—but unfortunately most judges seem all too willing to go along.

What Happens Next

If Microsoft wins, then citizens will have the chance to see these search warrants and challenge the ways they violate the Constitution. But the government has come up with a clever—and sinister—argument for throwing the case out of court before it even gets started.

The government has asked the judge in the case to rule that Microsoft has no legal right to raise the Constitutional rights of its customers. Anticipating this move, the American Civil Liberties Union asked to join the lawsuit, saying it uses Outlook and wants notice if Microsoft were served with a warrant for its email.

The government's response? The ACLU has no right to sue because it can't prove that there has been or will be a search warrant for its email. Of course the point of the lawsuit is to protect citizens who can't prove they are subject to a search warrant because of the secrecy of the whole process. The government's position is that no one in America has the legal right to challenge the way prosecutors are using this law.

Far from the Only Risk

The government is taking a similar approach to smartphone data.

For example, in the case of U.S. v. Ravelo, pending in Newark, New Jersey, the government used a search warrant to download the entire contents of a lawyer's personal cellphone—more than 90,000 items including text messages, emails, contact lists and photos. When the phone's owner complained to a judge, the government argued it could look at everything (except for privileged lawyerclient communications) before the court even issued a ruling.

The federal prosecutor for New Jersey, Paul Fishman, has gone even farther, telling the judge that once the government has cloned the cellphone it gets to keep the copies it has of all 90,000 items even if the judge rules that the cellphone search violated the Constitution.

Where does this all leave us now? The judge in Ravelo is expected to issue a preliminary ruling on the feds' arguments sometime in October. The government will be filing a final brief on its motion to dismiss the Microsoft case September 23. All Americans should be watching carefully to what happens next in these cases—the government may be already watching you without your knowledge.

Print Citations

CMS: Cunningham, Clark D. "Feds: We Can Read All Your Email, and You'll Never Know." In *The Reference Shelf: Internet Abuses and Privacy Rights*, edited by Betsy Maury, 186-189. Ipswich, MA: H.W. Wilson, 2017.

MLA: Cunningham, Clark D. "Feds: We Can Read All Your Email, and You'll Never Know." *The Reference Shelf: Internet Abuses and Privacy Rights*. Ed. Betsy Maury. Ipswich: H.W. Wilson, 2017. 186-189. Print.

APA: Cunningham, C.D. (2017). Feds: We can read all your email and you'll never know. In Betsy Maury (Ed.), *The Reference Shelf: Internet Abuses and Privacy Rights* (pp. 186-189). Ipswich, MA: H.W. Wilson. (Original work published 2016)

Lobbying Muscle May Help Tech Titans "Trump" Trump

By Allan Holmes and Jared Bennett
The Center for Public Integrity, December 13, 2016

The conventional wisdom in the nation's capital is that President-elect Donald Trump is bad news for Silicon Valley technology giants and their policy agendas. And it's easy to see why that's the script.

Throughout his campaign, Trump teed off on internet companies. He theorized that Amazon.com founder Jeff Bezos bought the *Washington Post* in 2013 to influence federal policies and warned the largest online commerce retailer it would "have … problems" if he became president. Trump ridiculed Facebook Inc. founder Mark Zuckerberg's pro-immigration stance. And Trump charged Google Inc. with favoring Hillary Clinton by prioritizing positive news stories about her in search results.

Even Trump's invitation to tech's biggest executives to meet him in New York this week could result in a frosty encounter.

But dig a little deeper and a more complex tale emerges. In recent years, internet firms and their trade associations have spent lavishly to become some of the most powerful influencers in Washington, shaping a range of policies that extend from immigration to privacy to taxes. And that may be difficult to change. Companies such as Alphabet Inc. (Google's parent), Facebook Inc., Amazon.com Inc., and their trade groups such as the Internet Association spent $50.9 million on lobbying in 2015, more than four times what they spent in 2009, according to data compiled by the Center for Responsive Politics and the Center for Public Integrity. Campaign contributions from these technology companies, many less than 10 years old, quintupled between 2009 and 2016.

The investments reflect lessons sometimes painfully learned. Just a few years ago, America's technology companies held a bemused disdain for Washington, which they saw as an anachronism in the emerging digital culture. But times have changed, and so have the stakes—as digital devices and apps have advanced to collect more of consumers' personal information. So internet companies have turned their sights and pocketbooks on Congress and additionally have involved themselves on boards and committees that inform the agencies writing oversight rules.

In 2003, at the tender age of 5, Google hired its first two lobbyists, and spent a comparatively paltry $80,000. In retrospect, it almost seems quaint. In 2015 the company had 84 lobbyists, spending $16.7 million, coming in just short of the top 10 biggest spenders, according to the Center for Responsive Politics. Facebook, a relative newcomer in Washington, has ramped up its spending from a scant $208,000 in 2009 to nearly $10 million last year, with 31 lobbyists, according to CRP. More recently, Twitter and Uber have come to Washington spending millions more. Overall, internet companies, as the Center for Public Integrity defined them, now employ nearly 500 lobbyists in Washington—almost three times the number just five years ago—to weigh in on everything from privacy to patents to antitrust to security.

The digital companies, which additionally include Yahoo! Inc., eBay Inc. and Netflix Inc., have also grown more comfortable in recent years with their newfound power, showing willingness to push back hard on bills or take other actions that may affect them, said a senior Senate staffer who works on consumer privacy issues.

The result: a veritable freeze for the past seven years in new laws or regulations covering such issues as consumer privacy, which for decades was an annual rite of passage in Congress. Same for securing data. Meanwhile, the emergent giants have succeeded in holding on to controversial policies they favor, like specialized immigration visas for programmers and other tech positions.

"This is an historic shift and it has consequences," said Alvaro Bedoya, executive director of the Center on Privacy & Technology at Georgetown University, describing the growing influence of these firms. "Internet companies wield an outsized influence, but it's not so much the power to pass new laws as it is the power to say 'no.'"

Even for recent rulings that Republicans opposed—such as net neutrality, which blocked internet providers from creating faster lanes for those who can pay—internet companies may not lose all the hard-won ground they gained.

"Deals will be cut," said Jeff Chester, executive director of the Center for Digital Democracy, a digital rights group in Washington, D.C, "This is a new political battleground here. In the initial start of the Trump administration, it's going to be all about wheeling and dealing."

Despite Trump's animosity towards an industry that has favored Democrats, the digital titans are well placed to negotiate some compromises, even on immigrant visas for technology jobs, which Trump has both supported and opposed, and on net neutrality, in which internet providers and the online content producers are likely to work out some kind of compromise. And just three weeks after the election, Financial Innovation Now, a group formed by Google, Amazon, Apple Inc., Intuit Inc. and PayPal that's pushing financial reforms for digital commerce, sent Trump a *letter* laying out possible changes to support online commerce.

"Your business experience, unique for any incoming President in history, offers a rare leadership opportunity that we believe sets the stage for modernizing some of our most antiquated financial rules," wrote Brian Peters, executive director of Financial Innovation Now.

New Lineup

No internet company has ramped up its Washington presence more than Google, which moved into a new office just a few blocks from the Capitol in 2014, where employees have access to a video game room and nap capsules. Shortly after the office opened, Google held a party featuring peach cobbler milkshakes, meatball stations and "molecular" gin and tonics. In attendance were numerous politicians including Rep. Darrell Issa, R-Calif., who was a member of the House Judiciary's subcommittee that oversees intellectual property and the internet, and Sen. Chuck Grassley, R-Iowa, who was a member of that chamber's Judiciary Committee and sat on the panel governing antitrust, competition policy and consumer rights, all hot topics for the technology industry.

Since 2009, when President Barack Obama took office, Google has spent more than $90.7 million on lobbying, more than twice any of its closest rivals Facebook, Amazon.com and Yahoo!. The company has retained 85 lobbyists this year, 10 of whom are in house, headed by Susan Molinari, a former GOP member of Congress from New York City. Among its outside lobbyists: two-time presidential candidate and former House Majority Leader Richard Gephardt and Tony Podesta, brother of Hillary Clinton campaign chairman John Podesta. Podesta's bio boasts that he is "one of Washington's 'super lobbyists.'" Nearly three out of four of Google's lobbyists have previously worked in Congress, the White House or in a government agency. Because Google's business operations touch on almost every aspect of American lives, it lobbies on an array of issues, from patent and copyright law to taxes to immigration to driverless cars.

Google, along with other internet companies, has also learned that giving money to trade groups pays off in influencing policy, or stopping it. Google, Facebook and Amazon, along with 37 other internet companies that include the likes of eBay, Netflix and LinkedIn, fund the Internet Association, the self-proclaimed "voice of the internet economy" that was created in 2012 and already ranks among the largest internet lobby spenders. Other trade groups that lobby on the companies' behalf: the Internet Commerce Coalition and the Interactive Advertising Bureau.

Internet firms have also joined the more established and influential trade groups in Washington. Google alone belongs to 43 trade groups and associations that lobby lawmakers and regulators on policies that include not only digital advertising, but wireless technology, cybersecurity and unmanned aerial vehicles. Among the 43 is the U.S. Chamber of Commerce, which perennially ranks as the biggest lobby spender in Washington.

It doesn't stop there. Google lists on its website nearly 100—just "some examples," Google says— "third-party organizations" that it supports because their "work intersects in some way with technology and Internet policy." These groups publish academic research (the left-leaning Brookings Institute, the conservative Heritage Foundation), are involved in advocacy (the Consumer Federation of America) and are powerful lobbyists in their own right (the AARP).

Google didn't respond to repeated requests for comment. Facebook and Amazon declined to comment.

Flexing Muscle

Internet companies' rapid buildup of spending in Washington has affected a wide range of policies, including cybersecurity, taxes, immigration, transportation and, perhaps most dramatically, consumer privacy.

For literally four decades, lawmakers regularly passed bills that expanded privacy protections for consumers—about a law every two years on average. In 2009, as part of a massive economic recovery bill, lawmakers expanded the scope of who must protect Americans' health information from disclosure, to include just about anyone who has access to the data, such as a claims processor or accounting firm hired by an insurance company.

> **Not one major privacy bill has cleared Capitol Hill—this despite unprecedented growth in social networks, advanced technology such as wearable devices and in-home monitoring tools, as well as apps that collect ever-more personal information that companies could use to discriminate against Americans.**

But in the seven years since that 2009 measure, nothing. Not one major privacy bill has cleared Capitol Hill—this despite unprecedented growth in social networks, advanced technology such as wearable devices and in-home monitoring tools, as well as apps that collect ever-more personal information that companies could use to discriminate against Americans. Only two measures have passed and were signed into law: one that arguably weakens privacy protections governing video downloads and another that affirms the data collected by a car's "black box" is the property of the vehicle's owner—but provides no penalties for violating the law.

The post-2009 void has not been due to a lack of effort; some 92 consumer privacy bills have been proposed during the seven-year period since, according to the Center. But that period coincides with internet firms' cascading investment in lobbying spending, along with a quintupling of campaign contributions from top internet executives and company PACs.

One bill that was no match for the internet lobby: the Location Privacy Protection Act, which Sen. Al Franken, D-Minn., one of Congress' leading consumer-privacy proponents, first introduced in 2011 when he was chairman of the Judiciary Subcommittee on Privacy, Technology, and the Law. The bill's aim seemed unobjectionable: outlaw so-called stalking apps, which allow someone, such as an abusive husband, to track the location of his estranged wife using the GPS coordinates emitted by her smartphone. But the bill also would have required internet companies to obtain permission from smartphone and tablet users to collect their location data and to share it with third parties, such as advertisers. Something consumers want, but internet companies and their trade groups didn't like at all.

Lobbyists representing 54 companies and trade groups—including Google, Facebook, Yahoo!, as well as trade groups such as the Interactive Advertising Bureau and the U.S. Chamber of Commerce—descended on the Hill. Calls were made, letters written, emails sent and meetings scheduled. To encourage members of Congress to answer phone calls and emails, corporations contribute to lawmakers' campaigns, current and former Hill staffers said. And internet companies have learned the game. The senator with by far the most campaign contributions from internet firms' employees and their related political action committees is Charles Schumer, D-N.Y., who has been a member of the Judiciary Committee since he was first elected to the Senate in 1998. Schumer and his leadership PAC has received $278, 668 from contributions from employees with internet companies and their PACs since 2000, the second most among members of Congress. Rep. Zoe Lofgren, a Democrat who represents much of Silicon Valley, received more—$332,553—as did just-elected Ro Khanna, who also hails from Silicon Valley. The contributions include those from affiliated leadership PACs, which are associated with a single member of Congress but make contributions to candidates.

When the bill was considered by the full committee in December 2012, Schumer, who eventually voted in favor of the bill, nevertheless echoed concerns of the tech companies, saying it "still needs a lot of work to assuage the concerns of tech innovators." Sen. Grassley, who also voted for the measure, said he had the same worries, saying the bill needed to address industry concerns that it would hurt the internet companies' business model of collecting personal data. Grassley and his leadership PAC have received $60,950 in campaign contributions since 2000 from Silicon Valley employees, their PACs. The committee voted to advance the bill, but it never came up for a vote on the floor.

Two years later, when Franken reintroduced the bill and it was back in the Judiciary's Subcommittee on Privacy, Technology, and the Law, first-term Sen. Jeff Flake, an Arizona Republican who had also represented the state in the House of Representatives, echoed the same concerns about harming the business model of collecting personal information.

"In our efforts to protect the privacy of Americans, which is extremely important, we got to be careful not to stifle innovation and dynamic sectors of the economy," Flake said.

Flake has received $29,000 in contributions from the internet companies' PACs, with most of it coming since he was elected senator and placed on the Judiciary Committee. Google, Facebook, Yahoo!, eBay and Yelp Inc., which offers crowdsourced online reviews of local businesses, have all given to Flake.

The bill never came up for a vote.

All that money buys access. Typically, internet companies are relatively cordial in their opposition to a bill, say several current and former Capitol Hill staffers. Often it's the related trade groups, which many of them belong to, that provide the muscle, they say. One of the most effective is the U.S. Chamber of Commerce, which counts Google and other internet companies as members. In 2012, R. Bruce Josten, the chamber's top lobbyist, sent a letter to then-Judiciary Committee Chairman Patrick Leahy, D-Vt., and then-ranking member Grassley opposing the location bill. Josten said Franken's bill would derail "the tremendous growth in wireless applications, services, and devices that has benefited both businesses and consumers."

Large companies that typically are not considered digital enterprises also weighed in, using their associations. The National Business Coalition on E-Commerce and Privacy, which counts as members' credit-tracker Experian as well as Bank of America and Charles Schwab & Co., came out hard against the legislation. In a letter sent to Leahy and Grassley two days before the location bill was reported out of subcommittee, the coalition called the measure "defective" and "counterproductive," warning that it would threaten what was at the time "a very fragile economy."

The Interactive Advertising Bureau, which counts Google and Facebook as members, as well as the Direct Marketing Association, which Facebook also belongs to, lobbied against the bill. About 10 consumer and trade groups, including the Center for Democracy and Technology, and the National Consumers League, supported the bill, but they didn't or couldn't lobby on behalf of the measure. The Location Privacy Protection Act didn't stall because it lacked support, it got out lobbied.

"That's how privacy bills die," a former Hill staffer said.

In the end, proponents of the bill could count only two lobby groups that supported the legislation—the Consumers Union and the National Women's Law Center. The two organizations, reported spending just $250,000 in their quarterly lobbying reports that mentioned the location privacy legislation. Of those identified as opposing the bill, 10 at least—including online advertising associations, internet trade groups such as NetChoice, the loyalty program marketer Affinion Group, and nontech organizations like the National Retail Federation and Bank of America—reported collectively spending nearly $155 million in quarterly reports that mentioned the bill, according to the Center's analysis. Franken has introduced the location bill in every Congress since then.

Franken likely will try again in the new Congress.

Steady as She Goes

Trump's campaign saber-rattling aside, veteran Capitol Hill observers believe Internet companies will likely continue to have their way.

Trump sees himself first and foremost a businessman, they say, having repeatedly boasted about his executive acumen on the campaign trail. Both Trump and Congress understand internet companies have been powering the U.S. economy for years. At one point this year, the five largest companies measured by market capitalization were all technology companies, for the first time, replacing big oil, which held three of the top five spots as recently as 2011.

So information is now the economy's hottest commodity. And Trump, who incessantly talked about jobs, jobs and jobs on the stump, is unlikely to take actions that might retard the growth of an industry that has expanded at breakneck pace, privacy concerns aside, experts say. Revenue from selling targeted ads, for instance, is estimated to reach $33 billion by 2020, with advertising accounting for 90 percent plus of Google's and Facebook's revenue.

"Unfortunately, it feels like Congress and the incoming policymakers have prioritized businesses' ability to make money and profits over consumers' right to protect their own privacy," said Claire Gartland, consumer protection counsel at the

> **Internet companies such as Google are now evaluating their approach to the Trump administration and the Republican party, which includes possibly funneling more money to conservative groups and causes, according to a long-time tech lobbyist who requested anonymity.**

Electronic Privacy Information Center, which advocates for privacy and civil liberties protections.

During the Obama administration, a revolving door spun between Google and the federal government, with Google employees moving into top positions within the federal government or national political campaigns, and federal or campaign employees leaving to work for Google—with a total of 251 individuals moving one way or the other, according to the Campaign for Accountability, a government watchdog group. Google veteran Alan Davidson works as the director of digital economy at the Commerce Department and Megan Smith is the U.S. chief technology officer in the White House. Austin Schlick, general counsel at the FCC, joined Google as the company's head of communications law, and Suzanne Michel left the FTC where she served as deputy director of the Office of Policy Planning to be a senior patent counsel at Google.

Internet companies such as Google are now evaluating their approach to the Trump administration and the Republican party, which includes possibly funneling more money to conservative groups and causes, according to a long-time tech lobbyist who requested anonymity. Just days after the election, Google posted a help-wanted ad for a "Manager for Conservative Outreach and Public Policy Partnerships," who would act "as Google's liaison to conservative, libertarian and free market groups," *Bloomberg* reported. The new hire would also "work with partner organizations on shared projects to advance Google's public policy goals," according to the post.

Policy experts with Google ties are also working with Trump's transition team. Joshua Wright, who conducted Google-supported research while a professor at George Mason University just outside Washington, D.C., is leading the team looking at the Federal Trade Commission, which oversees consumer protection and anti-competitive practices. Even top government executives with Google experience wouldn't rule out working with Trump. Former 12-year Google veteran Smith and Michelle Lee, head of the U.S. Patent and Trademark Office and formerly in charge of Google's patent strategy, both told *Politico* that they were open to a position in a Trump administration. And even tech startups that have lobbied the government over workplace issues such as benefits might find a friend in Trump's nomination for Labor Department secretary, anti-regulation crusader Andrew Puzder, who is a big fan of startups.

"Whatever kinship individuals at Google may have felt with this president and this administration, that will not stop them to build up a sphere of influence in the incoming administration," said Anne Weismann, executive director of the Campaign for Accountability. "They have money and enormous power."

Which is not to say there aren't some nasty policy fights in the offing. There are. Republicans have been looking to kill the net neutrality rules the FCC passed in 2015 and defended successfully in court this year. Trump named to oversee the FCC transition net-neutrality-foes Jeffrey Eisenach, a visiting scholar at the American Enterprise Institute, and Mark Jamison, head of the Public Utility Research Center at the University of Florida, who wrote, "Net neutrality in the U.S. is back-firing."

Trump also met in late November with Rep. Marsha Blackburn, R-Tenn., who is vice chair of the Energy and Commerce Committee and a Trump surrogate during the campaign, to discuss numerous issues. Blackburn has led the charge against the FCC's rules, calling them "a Trojan horse for government takeover of the Internet."

But on issues internet firms care about writ large, Trump remains an enigma, just as he is on other policy fronts—changing positions and making it difficult to discern his intentions. For example, on so-called H-1B immigrant visas, which technology companies heavily rely on to hire programmers, engineers and other technologists—and the subject over which he took Zuckerberg to task—Trump has waffled. He said he would "end forever the use of H-1B as a cheap labor program" after he said "as far as the visas are concerned, if we need people, it's fine."

Like other policy issues, it's likely the tech giants can carve out a compromise on the visas to their liking, said digital-rights advocate Chester.

That leaves lobbyists, government officials and privacy and security advocates confused—and apprehensive. But almost everyone comes back to this: Trump is a capitalist. And so he will aim to do what is right for corporations, whether they make widgets or search engines.

"I think the consumer is going to be the loser," said Weismann of the Campaign for Accountability. "At his heart, Trump is a businessman, which will make it easier for corporations like Google and others to appeal to the bottom line as something to protect. That, he understands."

Print Citations

CMS: Holmes, Allan, and Jared Bennett. "Lobbying Muscle May Help Tech Titans "Trump" Trump." In *The Reference Shelf: Internet Abuses and Privacy Rights*, edited by Betsy Maury, 190-197. Ipswich, MA: H.W. Wilson, 2017.

MLA: Holmes, Allan, and Jared Bennett. "Lobbying Muscle May Help Tech Titans "Trump" Trump." *The Reference Shelf: Internet Abuses and Privacy Rights*. Ed. Betsy Maury. Ipswich: H.W. Wilson, 2017. 190-197. Print.

APA: Holmes, A., & J. Bennett. (2017). Lobbying muscle may help tech titans "trump" Trump. In Betsy Maury (Ed.), *The Reference Shelf: Internet Abuses and Privacy Rights* (pp. 190-197). Ipswich, MA: H.W. Wilson. (Original work published 2016)

Reboot the World

By Paul Ford
The New Republic, June 22, 2016

"Some buddies of mine need your help with a database," my friend said.

"I'm good at databases," I replied. "And I like to help."

So I found myself in a large conference room with two nervous men who wanted to know exactly how exposed they were by the Ashley Madison leak. They wanted me to look inside the leaked data to see if I could find any traces of their exploits.

"I can do this," I said.

Ashley Madison

This was several leaks ago, so a refresher: Ashley Madison is a web site that helps you have affairs. You enter your personal information and the site lets you look at other people who have also entered their information. Then you can make arrangements to have sex with these other people.

And because it is digital, it felt anonymous, which meant you could structure the social interactions so that no one in your immediate vicinity (spouse, children) would ever know.

Ashley Madison is a heavily advertised digital product, and until the leak it was doing pretty well. Roughly 35 million people had signed up, and presumably more than one of them had sexual intercourse without the knowledge of their spouses. By which I mean wives—the users were overwhelmingly men.

Then it all went pear-shaped. One day last summer, an individual or individuals known as "The Impact Team" determined that all of the information in the Ashley Madison database should be made public. This was a lot of data: tens of millions of names, addresses, profiles, and credit card transactions. The database, in essence, was Ashley Madison.

It felt as if a nuclear bomb had gone off in the datasphere. The files were spread through the BitTorrent network, which meant that lots of people could easily download them; it also meant that the files were difficult to suppress, because they were so widely distributed.

I downloaded the database in anticipation of my new friends' arrival. And while I was unimpressed by the database itself—the typical mess of MySQL fields, with functional but hardly exemplary data modeling—I was staggered by its scope, the fact that one big database could serve all these people looking for affairs. It was the encapsulation of so much human desire. I poked around. Then, seeing a name I recognized, I stopped poking around. It wasn't worth knowing.

One of the visitors was sweating as he handed me a list of names written in pencil on the back of an envelope. I'd never seen that before: a man in a cold, air-conditioned room sweating, slightly wild-eyed.

"I just need to know," he said. "How bad is it?" I started with last names.

"That's not me," said the other man. "That's my brother. I'll have to talk with him."

We found some profiles, and I read them. Walks on the beach. Long nights, fine wines. Nothing cruel or strange. We also found records of credit card transactions. They'd signed up, left a trail, and it was still there. One of them had a credit card connected to his home address. His friend shook his head. Poor bastard.

"OK," the man said. "It's better to know."

Once there was a time when if you wanted to have an affair, you had to take charge of keeping it a secret. Wink slyly at a prospective lover and receive a subtle nod in return. Leave a scented note in a mailbox. Meet at a motel off the main route. Pay the bill in cash; never call your lover's house. Ashley Madison's innovation was that it took care of all that for you. The entire come-on of the site was that it would make seamless—frictionless—something that had previously been difficult and time-consuming. All while reducing the risk.

> **The internet was supposed to be democratic and open to all. Then Facebook and the NSA got their hands on it. Is it too late to reclaim our digital future?**

It seemed safe and secure, but it wasn't. Ashley Madison knew what you told it: name, email address, sometimes a home address. It knew your credit card information, provided so that you could pursue conversations and thus sex. It promised anonymity, but the service it delivered was sitting right in the middle of a world of transactional processing. Thirty-five million individuals had placed responsibility for the continuance of their marriages and relationships in the hands of a single company. Ashley Madison was a massive, centralized agglomeration of indiscretion.

Early Days of the Internet

The internet was once a highly decentralized system. In the earliest days, there were no large corporations or service providers like Ashley Madison or Facebook or Twitter, or behemoth databases to house your information. If you wanted to join up, you plugged in a computer and found a connection through a service provider, and that was basically it. You were online. Your computer was a "peer" of the other computers. It was a computocracy.

When the web came along, it was the same. You wanted to say something, so you ran a web server on a computer. You put some web pages in a folder. Your web server waited, night and day, for other computers to ask it for pages and files, and then sent those files back over the network. The servers were still off on their own, but now they could talk to each other.

That's really all there is to it. It is, at its core, a wonderfully autonomous, independent, and decentralized arrangement. Anyone can set up a web site and point to all the other web pages. Everyone is a publisher. Everyone is a peer. That's why it's called a web. Individuals knit themselves together by linking to one another. Everyone tends his or her own little epistemological garden, growing ideas from seed and sharing them with anyone who comes by.

Yet as the web grew, the problem of finding information arose. Search engines were needed that could crawl across the web, indexing the words in web pages; this way someone could type a word in a box and the machine could consult its index and list the pages that matched. But once you do that successfully, you have created something that appeals to larger forces. The search engine has power over other pages—you're no longer a peer.

Imagine you had a huge bread machine and an enormous bag of flour. You made so much bread that you gave some away. And people came to eat the free bread, and they liked it and wanted more. They told their friends. Free bread! People just kept coming—ten people; 100; 100,000; 100,000 million. A googol. To keep up with demand, you find yourself in need of not just more flour, but more bread machines. Fortunately, there are companies that are willing to pay you—not for your bread, but for the right to say, "This bread was brought to you by…" All because you've done the work of getting a lot of people in one place to eat free bread. Eventually you turn out enough loaves that you're designing wearable technology and self-driving cars.

There were other technical demands that chipped away at the decentralized nature of the internet. All those files spread across the web, it turned out, are a chore to manage. You need to update the copyright statement at the bottom of every page you've published, because you're in a new year. Or you need to wipe the CEO's name from all the pages after he resigned in the wake of a sexual harassment scandal. Doing that one page at a time would be a real pain. At the same time, it became possible to rent access to a database on a server somewhere. To solve this too-many-pages problem, people began to put their "content" into databases, and then publish everything through consistent, replicable "templates." As a result, every page on your web site—and everyone else's—eventually came to look roughly the same. Data went into the database via forms and came out via templates. Content was thusly managed. To change the copyright notice across all 100,000 pages of your retro sneaker site, you only needed to change a single line of one template. The CEO's photo could be briskly removed and replaced by the photo of the new, interim CEO. This was obviously a better state of affairs.

Soon the home page, which had enabled individual expressions of interest in mycology or Star Trek or bondage, was subsumed by the blog, which brought form and chronological order to the universe of web content. Tools like Movable Type, Blogger, and Typepad emerged, which "hosted" your content in their databases. No longer did people tend their own digital gardens. The gardens were tended for them.

Freed from the need to build and manage their own web sites, people could do more social things with their computers. They could talk to each other, start conversations, argue endlessly. They could leave private messages. Many found a community. And the companies that hosted the databases found a business model. Make the messages short, and adapt the database to manage millions of "friends" and "followers" (Friendster, then Twitter). Make a blogging engine that allows you to post short updates and keep track of your friends (MySpace, then Facebook). The computocracy was now something else—a Googlopoly.

The technology that let people make web sites never went away. You can still set up a site as if it were 1995. But culture changes, as do expectations. It takes a certain set of skills to create your own web site, populate it with cool stuff, set up a web server, and publish your own cool-stuff web pages. I would argue that those skills should be a basic part of living in a transparent and open culture where individuals are able to communicate on an equal field of play. Some fellow nerds would argue the same. But most everyone else, statistically, just uses Facebook and plays along.

Sensitive Information

There's an obvious connection between a decentralized internet, in which individuals create and oversee their own digital identities, and a functioning democracy, in which we make informed choices about who rules us and how we are ruled. Yet too few people make that link. We live in a world in which sensitive information of every conceivable sort—financial, sexual, medical, legal, familial, governmental—is now kept, and presumably guarded, online. It's guarded in gigantic treasure chests labeled "important data here." So many plums for hackers to pluck.

> **If you don't take care of yourself online, someone else will. That someone is likely a megacorporation.**

If you don't take care of yourself online, someone else will. That someone is likely not a peer but a megacorporation that is tracking and selling your preferences in a silent auction, a government surveilling your movements and religious affiliations, or a hacker collective that feels entitled to publish your sexual indelicacies. That someone probably already is.

So what is the alternative? For starters: In a utopian vision of a better, devolved-but-more-human internet, I would never post to your database. There'd be zillions of personal data sets, and every individual would have the technical capacity and social resolve to share only what they wanted, plus the power to revoke information from the commons. It's much easier to load my thoughts into someone else's little box and hit "Submit" (perhaps the most well-chosen interface word of all time). But submission comes at a price. My personal information, my finances, my family connections, my ideas—all are now in the hands of those to whom I have submitted.

The temptations of centralization are powerful. With a few employees you can make something worth a billion dollars, as Instagram did. You don't need to worry about advertising. You just create a situation where a larger company sees an opportunity to insert lots of ads. People are desperate to buy places to insert lots of ads so they can resell those places, which is what Facebook did when it bought Instagram. It bought future ad inventory. No one is paying attention to individuals online, at least not any more. There's no money in it. What they are looking for is tens of millions of people all in one place, moving in one direction. If you're Facebook, you need to get in front of that mass of humanity; you need to define their destiny. You need centralization.

Standing against this tide of centralization is the indie web movement. (And hackers, the black hat kind and otherwise.) Perhaps "movement" is too strong—it's more an aesthetic of independence and decentralization. The IndieWebCamp web page states: "When you post something on the web, it should belong to you, not a corporation." You should own your information and profit from it. You should have your own servers. Your destiny, which you signed over to Facebook in order to avoid learning a few lines of code, would once again be your own.

But an affair? That's trickier. A decentralized dating system would end up being a lot like Bitcoin—confusing, briefly exciting, and overpopulated by desperate, libertarian men. And the sites would be vulnerable, hackable. But big decentralized systems have many points of failure, rather than just one. The government could still spy on you, but the damage would be limited. The data wouldn't be in one place.

I'm not proposing some sort of digital back-to-the-land, communal-living, anti-regulation paradise that does away with food-delivery apps and secure online banking. I am an avid self-publisher and web site geek, but I also make a living as a paid client of centralizers.

Oddly, the people most excited about peer-to-peer technologies are not hackers but bankers. "Decentralized applications will someday surpass the world's largest software corporations in utility, user-base, and network valuation," writes David Johnston, managing director of the Dapps Fund, which helps bankroll decentralized consumer apps. There will always be money to be made in big and few. But there is also money—lots of it—in small and many.

Think of Bitcoin, which pioneered a block chain model of financial transactions that has been used by millions. Or Ethereum, which raised $18 million in a single crowd-funding campaign for its secure, peer-to-peer platform for consumer transactions. Or all those little apps on our phones—those incredible pocket supercomputers—talking to billions of other little apps. This is how file-sharing networks already work. BitTorrent uses "trackers" to keep, well, track of the files that people are sharing; the software functions as a tiny server. "I am here," it says. "I have these files, some in completeness and others in parts. I seek parts of some files as well." And that signal goes out to one or more trackers, and then to other clients, and in this way files are distributed.

This was how the centralized Ashley Madison database was ultimately decentralized, by force. Someone took the pirated data, zipped it up, and made it available as one big torrent. An older, smaller internet protocol brought down a newer, larger, corporatized database.

The Future

Making a shift to a more democratized internet won't be easy. Once you start to rally your energies toward a more open future, you will be shocked by the forces arrayed against you; the intransigence of the people who want to buy and sell your information; the amorality of the hackers who play with millions of people for sport; the cold, endemic corruption of intellectual property and patent law; the infinite protections for copyright. It can get a person down.

We could still live in that decentralized world, if we wanted to. Despite the rise of the all-seeing database, the core of the internet remains profoundly open. I can host it from my apartment, on a machine that costs $35. You can link to me from your site. Just the two of us. This is an age of great enterprise, no time to think small. Yet whatever enormous explosion tears through our digital world next will come from exactly that: an individual recognizing the potential of the small, where others see only scale.

Print Citations

CMS: Ford, Paul. "Reboot the World." In *The Reference Shelf: Internet Abuses and Privacy Rights*, edited by Betsy Maury, 198-203. Ipswich, MA: H.W. Wilson, 2017.

MLA: Ford, Paul. "Reboot the World." *The Reference Shelf: Internet Abuses and Privacy Rights*. Ed. Betsy Maury. Ipswich: H.W. Wilson, 2017. 198-203. Print.

APA: Ford, P. (2017). Reboot the world. In Betsy Maury (Ed.), *The Reference Shelf: Internet Abuses and Privacy Rights* (pp. 198-203). Ipswich, MA: H.W. Wilson. (Original work published 2016)

Bibliography

"2016 Presidential Campaign Hacking Fast Facts." *CNN*, Cable News Network. Feb 26 2017. Web. 3 Mar 2017.

Bolton, Alexander. "Schiff: Trump's Attacks on the Intelligence Community Are 'Deeply Counterproductive.'" *The Hill*, Capitol Hill Publishing Corp. Feb 19 2017. Web. 27 Feb 2017.

Borchers, Callum. "Donald Trump Wonders Why the *National Enquirer* Didn't Win a Pulitzer Prize: Here's Why." *The Washington Post*. Jul 22 2016. Web. 27 Feb 2017.

"Bots and Botnets—A Growing Threat." *Norton*, Symantec Inc. 2016. Web. 27 Feb 2017.

Burrus, Daniel. "The Internet of Things Is Far Bigger Than Anyone Realizes." *Wired*, Condé Nast. Nov 2014. Web. 26 Feb 2017.

Calderone, Michael. "Donald Trump Boosts the *National Enquirer* as Likely Showdown with Hillary Clinton Looms." *The Huffington Post*, Huffington Post Co.. May 4 2016. Web. 27 Feb 2017.

Chavez, Danette. "New FCC Chairman Is Making Good on Threats to Dismantle Net Neutrality." *A.V. Club*, Onion Inc. Feb 24, 2017. Web. 25 Feb 2017.

Ciluffo, Frank J. "Emerging Cyber Threats to the United States." *George Washington University*. Center for Cyber and Homeland Security. Feb 25 2016. Pdf. 27 Feb 2017.

"Cyber Crime Costs Global Economy $445 Billion a Year: Report." *Reuters*, Reuters. Jun 9 2014. Web. 3 Mar 2017.

"Cybersecurity Spotlight: The Ransomware Battle." *Tech Pro*, ZD Net. Aug 2016. Web. 27 Feb 2017.

Dewan, Angela and Kara Fox. "Trump and Russia: What the Fallout Could Be." *CNN*, Cable News Network. Mar 5 2017. Web 5 Mar 2017.

Eddy, Max. "The Best VPN Services of 2017." *PC Mag*, Ziff Davis, LLC. Jan 31, 2017.

Ehrenfreund, Max. "New Poll: Republicans and Democrats Both Overwhelmingly Support Net Neutrality." *The Washington Post*, Nash Holdings. Nov 12 2014. Web. 25 Feb 2017.

Elgin, Ben, Riley, Michael, Kocieniewski, David, and Joshua Brustein. "How Much of Your Audience Is Fake?" *Bloomberg*, Bloomberg, L.P. Sep 24, 2015. Web. 25 Feb 2017.

Finn, Jeff. "Why Aren't IoT Manufacturers Doing More to Prevent Botnet Attacks?" *IoT Evolution*, IOT Evolution World. Feb 23, 2017. Web. 27 Feb 2017.

Franceschi-Bicchierai, Lorenzo. "Police Have Arrested a Suspect in a Massive 'Internet of Things' Attack." *Motherboard*, Vice Media. Feb 23 2017. Web. 27 Feb 2017.

Gao, George. "What Americans Think about NSA Surveillance, National Security and Privacy." *Pew Research*, Pew Research Center. May 29 2015. Web. 25 Feb 2017.

Gordon, Whitson. "Here's Everywhere You Should Enable Two-Factor Authentication Right Now." *Lifehacker*, Gizmodo Media Group. Dec 10, 2013.

Graves, Allison. "Fact-Check: Did 3 Million Undocumented Immigrants Vote in This Year's Eection?" *Politifact*, Politifact. Nov 18 2016. Web. 3 Mar 2017.

Gross, Grant. "What to Expect from the Trump Administration on Cybersecurity." *CSO*, IDG News Service. Feb 22, 2017. Web. 25 Feb 2017.

"Hanging Out with the Script Kiddies." *BBC News*, BBC. Feb 17 2016. Web. 3 Mar 2017.

Holt, Thomas. "Here's How Hackers Make Millions Selling Your Stolen Passwords." *Slate*. Slate Group. Jun 29, 2016.

Hu, Elise. "3.7 Million Comments Later, Here's Where Net Neutrality Stands." *NPR*, National Public Radio. Sep 17 2014. Web. 25 Feb 2017.

Khazan, Olga. "Why Fake News Targeted Trump Supporters." *The Atlantic*, Atlantic Monthly Group. Feb 2 2017. Web. 27 Feb 2017.

Lafrance, Adrienne. "The Internet Is Mostly Bots." *The Atlantic*, Atlantic Monthly Group. Jan 31, 2017. Web. 26 Feb 2017.

———. "Trump's Incoherent Ideas about 'the Cyber.'" *The Atlantic*, Atlantic Monthly Group. Sep 27, 2016. Web. 25 Feb 2017.

Lohr, Steve and Katie Benner. "Targets of C.I.A. Hacking Revealed by Wikileaks: Smartphones and Smart TVs." *The New York Times*, The New York Times Co. Mar 7 2017. Web. 7 Mar 2017.

Madrigal, Alexis C. and Adrienne Lafrance. "Net Neutrality: A Guide to (and History of) a Contested Idea." *The Atlantic*, Atlantic Monthly Group. Apr 25, 2014. Web. 25 Feb 2017.

Magid, Larry. "Why Cyber Security Matters to Everyone." *Forbes*. Forbes Inc. Oct 1, 2014.

Maheshwari, Sapna. "10 Times Trump Spread Fake News." *The New York Times*, The New York Times Co. Jan 18 2017. Web. 27 Feb 2017.

Mitchell, Amy, Gottfried, Jeffrey, Barthel, Michael, and Elisa Shearer. "The Modern News Consumer." *Pew Research*, Pew Research Center. Jul 7 2016. Web. 27 Feb 2017.

Morgan, Steve. "Cybersecurity Market Reaches $75 Billion in 2015; Expected to Reach $170 Billion by 2020." *Forbes*. Forbes, Inc. Dec 20, 2015.

"Net Neutrality." *EFF*, Electronic Frontier Foundation. 2015. Web. 25 Feb 2017.

"Network Neutrality, Explained." *Vox*, Vox Media. May 21 2015. Web. 25 Feb 2017.

Newman, Lily Hay. "Apple's Finally Offering Bug Bounties—With the Highest Rewards Ever." *Wired*, Condé Nast. Aug 4 2016. Web. 3 Mar 2017.

———. "What We Know about Friday's Massive East Coast Internet Outage." *Wired*, Condé Nast. Oct 21, 2016. Web. 25 Feb 2017.

Nine Elements. "Nine Elements." *Digital Citizenship,* Mike Ribble. 2017. Web. 3 Mar 2017.

Parkinson, Robert G. "Fake News? That's a Very Old Story." *The Washington Post*, Nash Holdings. Nov 25 2016. Web. 27 Feb 2017.

Patterson, Thomas E. "News Coverage of the 2016 Presidential Primaries: Horse Race Reporting Has Consequences." *Shorentein Center*, Harvard Kennedy School. Jul 11 2016. Web. 27 Feb 2017.

Pogue, David. "The Bright Side of Internet Shaming." *Scientific American*. Oct 1 2016. Web. 25 Feb 2017.

Powers, Shawn M. and Michael Jablonski. *The Real Cyber War: The Political Economy of Internet Freedom*. Chicago: University of Chicago Press, 2015.

Quackenbush, Daniel. "Public Perceptions of Media Bias: A Meta-Analysis of American Media Outlets during the 2012 Presidential Election." *The Elon Journal of Undergraduate Research in Communications*. Vol. 4, No. 2, 2013.

Rainie, Lee. "The State of Privacy in Post-Snowden America." *Pew Research*, Pew Research Center. Sep 21 2016. Web. 27 Feb 2017.

Reardon, Marguerite. "Net Neutrality: How We Got from There to Here." *CNET*, CBS Interactive, Inc. Feb 24, 2015. Web. 25 Feb 2017.

Rubenking, Neil J. "The Best Password Managers of 2017." *PC Mag*, Ziff Davis LLC. Feb 15 2017. Web. 26 Feb 2017.

Rubin, Jennifer. "Commentary: Why Did Russia Want Trump to Win?" *Chicago Tribune*, Tribune Media. Dec 12 2016. Web. 3 Mar 2017.

Sadowski, Jathan. "Why Does Privacy Matter? One Scholar's Answer." *The Atlantic*, Atlantic Monthly Group. Feb 26 2013. Web. 3 Mar 2017.

Sagar, Rahul. "Trump Says That Classified Leaks Are Devastating America: Here's the Real Issue with Secrets and Leaks." *The Washington Post*. Feb 27 2017. Web. 27 Feb 2017.

Sammons, John and Michael Cross. *The Basics of Cyber Safety: Computer and Mobile Device Safety Made Easy*. New York: Syngress, 2017.

Samuelson, Robert J. "Robert Samuelson: Media Bias Explained in Two Studies." *The Washington Post*. Apr 23 2014. Web. 27 Feb 2017.

Shane, Scott. "From Headline to Photograph, a Fake News Masterpiece." *The New York Times*, The New York Times Co. Jan 18 2017. Web. 27 Feb 2017.

Shane, Scott, Mazzetti, Mark, and Matthew Rosenberg. "WikiLeaks Releases Trove of Alleged C.I.A. Hacking Documents." *The New York Times, The* New York Times Co. Mar 7 2017. Web. 7 Mar 2017.

Sherman, Erik. "The Reason Companies Don't Fix Cybersecurity." *CBS News*, CBS. Mar 12 2015. Web. 3 Mar 2017.

Siddiqui, Faiz and Susan Svrluga. "N.C. Man Told Police He Went to D.C. Pizzeria with Gun to Investigate Conspiracy Theory." *The Washington Post*. Dec 5, 2016. Web. 27 Feb 2017.

Simonite, Tom. "First Detailed Public Map of U.S. Internet Backbone Could Make It Stronger." *MIT Technology Review*, MIT Press. Sep 15 2015. Web. 25 Feb 2017.

Sottek, T.C. and Joshua Kopstein. "Everything You Need to Know about PRISM." *The Verge*, VOX Media. Jul 17, 2013. Web. 25 Feb 2017.

Stelter, Brian. "How Leaks and Investigative Journalists Led to Flynn's Resignation." *CNN*, Cable News Network. Feb 14 2017. Web. 26 Feb 2017.

"The Last Lap." *Pew Research*, Pew Research Center. Oct 31 2000. Web. 27 Feb 2017.

"The Right to Privacy." *UMKC*, University of Missouri Kansas City. 2015. Web. 25 Feb 2017.

Thompson, Derek. "Trump's 3 a.m. Phone Call." *The Atlantic*, Atlantic Monthly Group. Feb 8 2017. Web. 25 Feb 2017.

Timberg, Craig. "A Disaster Foretold – And Ignored." *The Washington Post*, Nash Holdings. Jun 22 2015. Web. 3 Mar 2017.

Valeriano, Brandon, Maness, Ryan C. and Benjamin Jensen. "5 Things We Can Learn from the Russian Hacking Scandal." *The Washington Post*, Nash Holdings. Jan 9 2017. Web. 3 Mar 2017.

Wakabayashi, Daisuke and Mike Isaac. "In Race against Fake News, Google and Facebook Stroll to the Starting Line." *The New York Times*, The New York Times Co. Jan 25 2017. Web. 27 Feb 2017.

Wallace, Tim and Alicia Parlapiano. "Crowd Scientists Say Women's March in Washington Had 3 Times as Many People as Trump's Inauguration." *The New York Times*, The New York Times Media Co. Jan 22 2017. Web. 27 Feb 2017.

Wang, Jie and Zachary A. Kissel. *Introduction to Network Security: Theory and Practice*. Hoboken, NJ: Wiley Press, 2015.

Ward, Mark. "Exposing the Hidden History of Computer Hacking." *BBC News*, BBC. Oct 27 2014. Web. 3 Mar 2017.

"What You Know Depends on What You Watch: Current Events Knowledge across Popular News Sources." *Public Mind*, Fairleigh Dickinson University. May 3 2012. Web. 27 Feb 2017.

Wing, Nick. "Final Popular Vote Total Shows Hillary Clinton Won Almost 3 Million More Ballots Than Donald Trump." *The Huffington Post*, Huffington Post Co. Dec 20 2016. Web. 3 Mar 2017.

Yagoda, Ben. "A Short History of 'Hack.'" *The New Yorker*, Condé Nast. Mar 6 2014. Web. 2 Mar 2017.

Zetter, Kim. "Hacker Lexicon: What Are White Hat, Gray Hat, and Black Hat Hackers?" *Wired*, Condé Nast. Apr 13 2014. Web. 3 Mar 2017.

Zimmerman, Carlota. "6 Ways to Spring Clean Your Social Media Presence." *The Huffington Post*, Post Co. Apr 8 2015. Web. 25 Feb 2017.Dislike Trump." The Washington Post. Nash Holdings. Jun 20 2016. Web. 17 Aug 2016.

Winter, Tom. "Trump Bankruptcy Math Doesn't Add Up." *NBC News*. National Broadcasting Company. Jun 24 2016. Web. 18 Aug 2016.

Wolf, Richard and Gregory Korte. "Supreme Court Strikes Blow Against Gerryman-dering." *USA Today*. Gannett Company. Jun 29 2015. Web. 15 Aug 2016

Wolf, Richard. "Supreme Court Upholds Virginia Redistricting." *USA Today*. May 23 2016. Web. 15 Aug 2016.

"Women and Leadership." *Pew Research*. Pew Research Center. Jan 14 2015. Web. 19 Aug 2016.

Worstall, Tim. "$15 Minimum Wage Threatens 5.3 Million US Manufacturing Jobs." *Forbes*. Forbes, Inc. Sep 2 2015. Web. 16 Aug 2016.

Zong, Jie and Jeanne Batalova. "Frequently Requested Statistics on Immigrants and Immigration in the United States." *MPI*. Migration Policy Institute. Apr 14 2016. Web. Aug 17 2016.

Websites

Electronic Frontier Foundation

www.eff.org

The Electronic Frontier Foundation (EFF) is a nonprofit digital rights organization based in California. The EFF supports legislation to protect net neutrality and other digital rights initiatives, provides news and information about threats to digital privacy and government programs/legislative efforts that might affect personal privacy and digital security and provides visitors with an ongoing database of websites and other information on the digital rights debate.

Federal Communication Commission (FCC)

www.fcc.gov

The Federal Communications Commission (FCC), initiated in 1934 is a federal agency responsible for regulating communication by television, telephone, satellite, and cable. The FCC has been the primary governmental actor in the net neutrality debate and has adopted neutrality as one of the core principles of Internet freedom.

Free Press

www.freepress.net

Free Press is a nonprofit advocacy group that supports net neutrality and the principles of the open Web. Started in 2003, Free Press is the leading organization of the Web-activist organization Save the Internet, who gathers supporters of net neutrality and opposes government or corporate censorship of Internet traffic.

The Institute of Electrical and Electronic Engineers (IEEE)

www.ieee.org

The IEEE is a professional association of individuals involved in computer and electrical sciences, engineering, and related disciplines. The organization is one of the most influential in the United States in terms of establishing cybersecurity standards, through the IEEE Standards Association. The IEEE works closely with the US National Institute of Standards and Technology to develop cybersecurity standards for all utility systems.

The Information Systems Audit and Control Association (ISACA)

www.isaca.org

The ISACA is an independent international organization supporting professionals in information systems and technology. The organization provides news on cybersecurity issues, threats, and resources and maintains a resource page for individuals interested in the latest developments in cybersecurity technology and legislation.

National Institute of Standards and Technology (NIST)

www.nist.gov

The National Institute of Standards and Technology (NIST) is a nonregulatory branch of the US government responsible for analyzing US industry and creating/managing researcher programs in technology, Information technology, measurement, and physics. The NIST publishes studies and information on cybersecurity and information technology.

Wired

www.wired.com

Wired is a US magazine published by Condé Nast that specializes in news and information about the impact, economics, and politics of technology in the United States and international culture. The magazine, headquartered in San Francisco, publishes a print edition of its monthly publication and also publishes electronic versions of print articles through *Wired News*.

CNET

www.cnet.com

CNET is a technology publication produced by CBS Interactive since 2008, but founded in 1994. Articles on *CNET* cover emerging consumer technology, technology industry politics and developments, and is one of the most globally popular technology sites. *CNET* covers cyberthreats, viruses, and cybersecurity news and provides useful information for consumers on how to avoid invasions of digital privacy and other threats.

Pew Research Center

www.pewresearch.org

The Pew Research Center is one of the world's most respected social science research and polling organizations. Pew regularly publishes studies on the press, public interaction with news media and related topics. In addition, Pew Research conducts polling that measures public opinion on Internet use, social media, government surveillance, and a variety of other cyber threats.

American Civil Liberties Union (ACLU)

www.aclu.org

The American Civil Liberties Union (ACLU) is a nonprofit, nonpartisan organization that lobbies on behalf of citizens to protect the US Bill of Rights. The ACLU lobbies and creates litigation regarding freedom of speech and expression and freedom of the press. The ACLU supports net neutrality and lobbies for open Internet protections.

Index